306.38
KLA

Taking Retirement

Other Nonfiction Books by Carl H. Klaus

My Vegetable Love: A Journal of a Growing Season

Weathering Winter: A Gardener's Daybook

CARL H. KLAUS

Taking Retirement
A Beginner's Diary

BEACON PRESS

BOSTON

BEACON PRESS
25 Beacon Street
Boston, Massachusetts 02108-2892
www.beacon.org

Beacon Press books are published under the auspices of
the Unitarian Universalist Association of Congregations.

05 04 03 02 01 00   8 7 6 5 4 3 2

This book is printed on recycled acid-free paper that contains at least 20 percent
postconsumer waste and meets the uncoated paper ANSI/NISO specifications for
permanence as revised in 1992.

Text design by Christopher Kuntze
Composition by Wilsted & Taylor Publishing Services

Library of Congress Cataloging-in-Publication Data

Klaus, Carl H.
    Taking retirement : a beginner's diary / Carl H. Klaus.
        p.   cm.
    ISBN 0-8070-7218-4 (cloth)
    ISBN 0-8070-7219-2 (pbk.)
    1. Retirement—Iowa—Iowa City.   2. Retirees—Iowa—Iowa City—
Psychology.   3. Retirees—Iowa—Iowa City—Attitudes.   I. Title.
HQ1064.U616487   1999
306.3'8—dc21   99-21651

In Memory of Aunt Ada

Taking Retirement

Friday / February 21, 1997

Retirement. I've been phasing into it slowly, gently (three years at three-quarter time, two years at half-time), so I figured it would be an easy transition when the no-time time begins a few months from now. I'd step into my new life so well prepared for it that I'd hardly miss my old one. Just a simple matter of putting one foot in front of another on my way to the brave new world of AARP—the American Association of Retired Persons. As a retired person—a retiree—I'd no longer feel the old compulsions to go into the office, check the mail, chat with my colleagues, confer with my students, or do any of the other things I've been doing the past forty years. I'd hang out instead in my attic study, overlooking the backyard, and watch the seasons unfold. But just to make sure I didn't go to seed, I'd keep a hand in by teaching one of my favorite courses in the non-fiction writing program that I used to direct—a course in prose style, or the personal essay, or the art of the journal. One course a year—enough to keep in touch with the students, keep myself stimulated, and keep my office too. But without any of the hassle.

No more department meetings, no more committees, no more salary reviews. Free at last! Free to tend my garden for the rest of my days. Free to read what I want, write when I want, teach when I want, go fishing, visit the children and grandchildren. And travel with Kate to all those alluring places in the glossy brochures that clutter our mailbox every spring and fall. Hike Machu Picchu, explore the Galápagos, take a villa in Tuscany, tour the Holy Land, visit the Forbidden City, and behold the Great Barrier Reef. No wonder I chose to retire at sixty-five rather than seventy. Especially with more to spend than if I were working full time—thanks to Social Security and forty years of investment in TIAA-CREF, otherwise known as Teachers Insurance Annuity Association and College Retirement Equities Fund. My pot of gold at the end of the rainbow.

The only problem is that some of my plans began to change, and not by choice, when I stopped in a few weeks ago to visit my colleague Paul, who now directs the nonfiction program. The minute I sat down and started to discuss my teaching plans for next year, I could see the smile on Paul's face beginning to droop. When I asked him what was wrong, he told me that our department chair, Dee, had been fretting about low enrollments in some of our nonfiction courses, especially given the recent additions to our nonfiction staff. So, as he explained it, there'll probably be no chance for me to teach a course next year or any other time in the near future. No room for me, no need for me. No fault of Paul's or of Dee's, but those words reverberated in my head as I listened to him reviewing the numbers, just the way I'd advised him to do when I passed him the baton a few years ago. As he leaned back in his office chair, ticking things off with his fingers, it dawned on me that I'd not been keeping track as closely as I used to. It also dawned on me that I'd soon have fewer professional options than I'd imagined. I too was ticking things off.

Then I found out from Dee that the department will be short of office space for several more years. So I'll probably have to give up the office I've had the past twenty-five years—my office overlooking the river—and take up residence in "the emeritus suite," a three-room ghetto for retired professors overlooking the parking lot. A place so crammed with metal lockers and similar amenities that only one or two of my retired colleagues have ever used it. Once upon a time, retired faculty kept their offices as long as they wished, so the department was like an extended family, and retirement was not an eviction notice. But now I might be evicted altogether, for the emeritus suite, as I discovered just a few days ago, has been converted into office space to house our visiting professors and the department's honors program. Talk about being out of touch! You'd think I was already retired, given how little I know about what's been going on around the building while I've been phasing in. Or phasing out, to put it more accurately. And not just out of my office, but also out of the community of my colleagues.

Out of it, just at the moment when a new person's coming into the nonfiction program who's sure to be a wonderful colleague—a person who'll fill the vacancy created by my departure and so in a sense will be my replacement. Though I met Sara just a few days ago during her campus interview, I've been hearing about her from members of the search committee, also from my longtime friend and former colleague Bob, who's directing her doctoral work at Brown and sang her praises in a recommendation that's exuberantly over the top—"She can charm bees from flowers and words from dictionaries." Last summer, I exchanged a few e-mails with Sara about her thesis on the essay—the subject of my own study the past twenty years—and just from that exchange I was buzzing about her too. Then a few weeks ago, I looked at her teaching materials and noticed that she's offered courses not only on the essay but also on prose style, covering some of the same material that I've been dealing with the past forty years. And doing it with more pizzazz, though she's only been teaching a few years. A lot more pizzazz, as I could see from watching her run a two-hour workshop a few days ago. The room was abuzz when she finished. So when the department met yesterday afternoon to consider our two job candidates,

I could hardly contain myself as I waited to make a strong closing statement for Sara—even though she hasn't yet finished her doctoral thesis and several people are worried about bringing in someone without a degree in hand. I don't think I've given such an impassioned talk since my heart attack twelve years ago—I could feel the pulse throbbing in my temples.

Only then, in the flush of my excitement about Sara, did I realize that I'd delivered my valedictory—that I'd probably never have another occasion to address the whole department. And only then did I realize that I was far less ready for retirement than I'd supposed—that I have, in fact, such mixed feelings about giving up the classroom, my office, and the community of my colleagues and students that I thought I'd better start keeping a dairy. A diary where I can deal with the bittersweet feelings I'm experiencing even now as I sit up here in the attic writing this piece. A diary that might help me through this suddenly dismaying phase-in-phase-out—and beyond. For I don't want my final day of teaching, just a few months from now, to be a day of mourning. I want to take retirement rather than feel as if it's taking me unawares. Maybe even seize it joyously. But at least behold it without looking back so longingly that I turn into a pillar of regret.

Saturday / February 22

Last night I e-mailed Sara a one-word letter of congratulations, and this morning she replied: "Thank you. THANK YOU. You have been enormously helpful. As you know, this job wouldn't even exist without you. I am fitting both my shoes into one of your footprints, and very grateful to have discovered their impression in the sand." Such a gracious and flattering note that I responded in kind—"Your feet are bigger than you think." And I meant it, meant it so much that it made me keenly aware just then of how easily replaceable I've turned out to be. No one, of course, is replaceable. "One mind less, one world less," as Orwell says in "The Hanging." Still, it's hard to ignore the contrary truth that resonates through the halls of every place I've ever worked whenever someone decides to change jobs or move elsewhere or retire—"No one is irreplaceable." I've sometimes uttered that line myself, especially when a big name has decided to leave. But then again, I'd have to admit that I've sometimes heard a little voice within me saying, "It'll be different with you. It won't be so easy for them to replace you." Come to think of it, though, I've rarely heard that voice the past two years since Paul's taken over the nonfiction program and done such a fine job of it. And now with the coming of Sara, I don't expect I'll ever hear it again. So the most haunting thing about her lovely message is the image of my footprints in the sand, likely to last no longer than the next incoming tide.

Sunday / February 23

Tides be damned, there's a life to be lived, and that means it's time to get started on the vegetable garden. This morning I planned the spring garden and planted a few tomato seeds, keeping myself focused on the task at hand, on the dry seeds in the wet germinating mix, on the prospect of fruits to come. No matter what happens at the building, I'll have homegrown tomatoes in June or early July. Fresh produce just a few weeks after I retire. Maybe Kate's right when she tells me, "Just get on with your life, and retirement will take care of itself."

On days like this, in fact, I wonder why I'm worrying about it at all, especially when I think about my parents, neither of whom lived long enough to retire. Even if they had lived to be sixty-five or seventy, they'd probably have kept on working until they dropped dead in their tracks. Like most people of their generation, who were born long before the time of ample pension plans and Social Security— my father in 1879, my mother in 1903—they couldn't have afforded to retire, particularly after my father, a doctor, lost everything he owned, including his home, in the stock market crash of 1929, and my mother returned to schoolteaching after he died in 1934. When I think of how hard it was for some of the relatives who raised me during the Depression era in Cleveland, and harder still for the immigrant parents of my childhood friends, I feel as if I've been richly spoiled by the retirement funds I've accumulated during my years of working at Iowa. A far cry from the way it used to be for college professors. A far cry from the way it still is for many clerical, factory, and service workers, given the recent wave of downsizing and cost-cutting programs. No wonder so many people have to work two part-time jobs just to make ends meet, without any chance of a comfortable retirement. No wonder McDonald's has been running want ads for elderly employees. They make me feel like the beneficiary of such a rare windfall that I should keep my mouth shut and get on with my life—gardening, reading, and puttering around the house, as I did today. But no sooner do I vow to shut up than something happens that starts me fretting again. And then I understand the embarrassing truth of E. B. White's acknowledgment that "Only a person who is congenitally self-centered has the effrontery and the stamina to write essays." Or to keep a retirement journal.

Monday / February 24

Today I was back in the pre-retirement world, getting ready for tomorrow's workshop in the art of the journal, a course I created this year as an outgrowth of *My Vegetable Love*, the journal I wrote two years ago. It's the last course I'll ever teach here, and happily (or sadly) it seems like one of the best I've ever taught. Eight gifted women and I, turning our days into daybooks, our lives into journals. I wonder if it's exciting just because it's a new kind of venture for all of us. I'm teaching something I've never taught before, and they're writing journals in a much more artistically conscious way than they've ever done before. I also wonder if it's so special for me because it's the last course of my career. Perhaps I shouldn't even be worrying about such questions and simply be thankful that it's been so satisfying, especially when I remember how it was with my colleague Jix, who retired last year after teaching a course that according to him was one of the most disappointing of his career. Maybe, after all, there's a truth to the cliché of quitting while one's ahead, particularly considering the recent growth of my retirement funds. But then again, what a pleasure it would be to have another go at this course. But then again, what a pleasure it would be to stop going back and forth like this. I wonder if everyone goes through such mood swings on the verge of retirement, or if it's just me and this day. But one thing's for sure—I can't ever remember myself having such ups and downs, such highs and lows, as if I were on drugs or had somehow lost control of myself.

Tuesday / February 25

At breakfast this morning, I devoured a two-page feature in the *Des Moines Register,* called "New Beat for the Old Reporter." A piece about a recently retired columnist, whose stuff I've been reading the past thirty-five years, without ever realizing we're almost the same age—just five months apart. He's always looked so much older than me, especially in this morning's article, balding at the front, gray around the edges, that I was doubly surprised after mentioning it to Kate, who smiled at me across the breakfast table and said, "Have you looked in the mirror lately and seen what's going on—the thinning hair, the sagging cheeks, the growing waistline?" Only your best friends will tell you! I was also touched by the discovery that his decision to retire "came as a surprise to everyone, even himself," because he "suddenly realized it was time to go. 'I was so tired of it.'"

Though I've never been tired of the students, or the give-and-take of classroom discussion, or the office hours, or the mentoring, I'm so burnt out from forty years of reading and commenting on student writing—a lifetime with the editorial pencil in hand—that

I sometimes feel as if I can hardly bring myself to look at another set of student essays. And it's not just the tediousness of making the comments again and again. It's the emotional and intellectual exhaustion that comes from repeatedly making the effort to produce comments that are evaluative but constructive, probing but encouraging. Now I'm beginning to wonder what makes other people decide that it's time to go. Boredom? Burnout? Buyout? Illness? Wanderlust? New ventures? Old hungers? Or the sand running swiftly down from top to bottom? And I wonder how they feel about it once they've decided to go.

A few more classes like the one I had this afternoon, and I'll be ready to retire—without any qualms at all. Discussion got off to a slow start, everyone sitting silent around the big seminar table as if they'd all lost their voices at once. And it didn't get any better the rest of the session, so I had to offer a more pointed critique of both manuscripts than I care to make in class, especially when I'm concerned about the confidence of the students, as I was this afternoon. By the end of the two-hour workshop, I felt much more drained than usual—also more in touch with the burnout I was feeling five years ago when I decided to go on phased-in retirement. And now after dinner, as I sit up here in our attic study finishing this entry, I'm also feeling in touch with another post-workshop evening twelve years ago today, another February 25, when I first started feeling uncomfortable spasms in my neck that turned out to be the signs of a heart attack. A heart attack, followed by a triple bypass, that changed the course of my life as much as I now feel it's being changed by my forthcoming retirement. But in this case, there's no kind of bypass available.

Wednesday / February 26

Kate's birthday, and once again I was elated to give her some better gifts than the heart attack I had twelve years ago. Especially an illustrated book about trees from around the world—my contribution to the library she's building for herself and for Heritage Trees of Iowa City, the long-term preservation project she's been spearheading the past several years. That book is also an emblem of the traveling we hope to do in the years to come, a leafy reminder of why I should be looking forward to retirement. Skimming its pages after she opened it at lunch, I gazed at seductive photographs of trees and places I've never seen before—the grass trees of Australasia, the fever trees of South Africa, the araucaria trees of Chile.

But this afternoon I was back at the office for conferences with Angela, who's working on an M.F.A. thesis about her Chicano heritage, and Jean, who's keeping a journal about coping with her mother's rapidly failing memory. Both compelling projects that I hope can be turned into publishable manuscripts. So the thought of abandoning the know-how I've developed during forty years of teaching is difficult to accept, particularly when students ask if I can serve on their theses after I've retired. I wonder if it might be possible for me to stay on as an unpaid consultant to the program. As an adjunct professor rather than a professor emeritus. As someone who can help colleagues and students develop their manuscripts and get them placed with agents and publishers.

Or am I just looking for excuses to avoid the unavoidable? And if that's the case, why can't I just let go of it all without trying to hang on in one way or the other? Retirement, after all, is a time for new ventures, yet for some reason I seem wedded to my same old job. What a strange thing—to know better, yet not be able to let go. As if it were an addiction rather than a profession.

Thursday / February 27

In the midst of such fretting, there's nothing like the spectacle of a tomato seedling just beginning to emerge, its neck arching out of the soil. Only four days after being planted, thanks to the warmth of the living room radiator directly under the seed tray. I christen it with a little mist from Kate's spray bottle and think of the months ahead. I imagine myself taking up watercolors, so I can do detailed studies of emergent seedlings. I'm inspired by the ethereally beautiful, larger-than-life watercolor of leeks by our dear friend Jo Ann— a lovely pair, suspended in midair—that arrived late yesterday afternoon as the climactic present in Kate's birthday bounty. Better to look forward rather than back. Better to focus on the joy rather than the sadness of my coming retirement. Better to stop spouting such platitudes lest I turn into a latter-day Polonius and not come to terms with the fact that it's time for me to leave even though I'm not yet ready to let go of what I've been doing for almost two-thirds of my life. And I don't know if I'll ever be ready. Now I'm beginning to understand why some of my older colleagues seemed prickly or distant when they were facing retirement.

Friday / February 28

"Looking forward to your retirement party?" My colleague, Jon, clearly meant well by the question he asked me when our paths crossed in the office corridor this afternoon. But in my current mood, a retirement party is the last thing I want to hear about. So my response to Jon was a bit crusty—a response that left him looking a little less bright-eyed than usual, especially since I didn't feel like going into a long-winded explanation just then.

How could I tactfully explain that such parties usually give me the creeps? They seem like a thinly veiled expulsion, complete with going-away gifts and celebratory farewells. A few years ago I wrote a note to Dee, asking her not to plan any such thing for me. No luggage, thank you, or emotional baggage, or anything else to send me on my way. I should have known that she'd urge me to reconsider and I wouldn't have the gumption to refuse, especially given Dee's irrepressibly genial and earnest manner. Now I'll have to write her another note, asking once again to be spared the ceremonies and the remembrances and all the other stuff that sometimes make me feel as if I'm at a memorial service rather than a retirement party. For I don't want to be buried alive, don't want my story to be told until my story is complete, and certainly don't want to hear it being told. Especially when I'd much rather stay on as an unpaid editorial consultant to the nonfiction program. Maybe I should propose that idea to Dee as something I'd much rather have than a party or a going-away present.

Saturday / March 1

Though I've been writing about retirement for a week or so, I woke up early this morning with the sudden realization that I—the so-called English professor—don't really know what the word itself means. Oh yes, I know that it usually refers to the act of giving up a longtime job or business, career or profession, usually because of advancing age. But a quick check in the dictionary reminded me of its derivation from the Old French verb *retirer* (literally, to draw back). So, in its root sense, retirement denotes the act of withdrawing to a private or secluded place, as in going to bed. Or to giving ground, as in retreating or withdrawing from battle. Retirement, in other words, is deeply connected with the act of giving up, giving in, retreating, as it were, from life itself. And that's not what I'm ready for at all, which is probably why I was put out by Jon's well-meaning remark yesterday and by the whole idea of retirement ceremonies. Perhaps I just need to get it through my head that I'm not retiring in the root sense of the word, not retreating, not giving up anything but my classroom teaching, my tenured job, and probably my office. Even if I'm up here in the seclusion of the attic, I'm still going to be writing new books and essays, revising my textbooks, keeping in touch with colleagues, collaborators, and students. And when I'm not up here, I'll be gardening, traveling, cooking, and so on.

But Jon's remark reminds me that others might be inclined to perceive me as retreating into a world of inactive graybeards (even though I don't have a beard at all). In fact, the mail these days has been bringing me so many cards and letters and flyers and advertisements, most of them trying to sell me retirement housing, retirement planning, retirement counseling, retirement insurance, that it's sometimes very hard to see myself as anything but a retiree. Or a big old cash cow that everyone wants to get a piece of.

Sunday / March 2

Though I'm not a cash cow, this whole retirement process has been making me wonder who I am, especially this afternoon when I was staring at the blank screen of my computer, confronting the question more directly than usual, because I had to write a note about myself for the jacket flap of my forthcoming daybook, *Weathering Winter*. Just a few sentences, a short paragraph, that would put me in a nutshell, the catchy sort of prose I've written so often in years past that it usually takes no more than an hour. But today I fussed over the thing for several hours, because today for the first time in twenty-five years I couldn't refer to myself as a professor of English, since the book will be published several months after I retire. The minute I realized I'd be losing that title, I suddenly began to experience something like an identity crisis, the sort of thing I can't remember since my sophomore slump, when I switched from being a premed student to being an English major. Who am I, I wondered this afternoon, if not a professor of English? And a faint voice whispered in my ear, "You're about to become a professor emeritus of English." My first promotion in twenty-five years. The only problem is that I've never craved that venerable title, whose Latin word for retired makes it sound "ever so much more lofty," according to Kate. Nor have I ever thought it fit me, since I've always been too rambunctious to be addressed in such a high-flown way. Besides, who would want to buy a book by a professor emeritus, except another professor emeritus? So I decided to avoid any mention of professorial titles and referred to myself instead as the "founder and former director of Iowa's nonfiction writing program." I was pleased at first with how adroitly I implied my retirement without calling myself a professor emeritus. But now I can't help wondering why I wasn't willing to identify myself openly as a retired professor. Am I embarrassed, perhaps, at being known as someone who's retired? And why should I be, given that someone who's getting on in years might know a few things about weathering winter. Besides, now that I think of it, why do I feel compelled to refer to any of the titles that I once held? I mean, what's the good of retirement if it doesn't free you from the titles and other claptrap that pervade the world of corporations, governments, and academic institutions? Come to think of it, who am I anyway? A retiring professor? A cynical author? A gardener? Or a person who's lost his bearings?

Monday / March 3

The painters and wallpaperers arrived this morning to begin putting the house in order "for our golden years," as Kate says, wryly reminding me that she's ten years younger than I and not all that happy about being lumped in with the golden oldies. "I'm not retiring," she said a few days ago, and "I'm sick of hearing all this talk about it, as if that's all you think about anymore." But she's evidently not averse to planning our golden years projects, which started last summer when we had the second-floor bathroom deconstructed all the way down to the bricks and an elegant room designed by Kate constructed in its place. A room fitted out with handmade oak cupboards, handcut tiles and decorative tile borders, brass fittings, a ruby red granite counter, and an old-fashioned door key with a braided silk tassel. A monument to self-indulgence after twenty-seven years of bathing at the far edge of comfort and respectability.

Retirement, it seems, is the final fling. The love boat, the trip-around-the-world, the Jeep Grand Cherokee Limited, the bathroom-of-our-dreams. Now I'm beginning to understand why my retired colleague Jix and his wife, Jean, just finished building a spacious two-story, glassed-in addition to their house, including an elevator. "Whatever turns you on," as Kate says. The only question is whether I have enough gold to gussy up this nineteenth-century brick house for the fling of our desires, without having to look for a new job in a new profession. I was thinking along those lines a few days ago, when I got another e-mail from Sara, thanking me for some advice I'd given her about rental housing in Iowa City. "You sound just like a realtor," she said, playfully picking up on all the housing suggestions I'd offered her, and for a moment I wondered how I might do in that arena. The old competitive instincts feel almost as sharp as ever, especially after some forty years of honing them to a fine edge.

Tuesday / March 4

This afternoon's workshop was so lively, and I felt so energized by the discussion, that it made me wonder why I decided not to continue teaching beyond this semester—as if I didn't already know the answer. I was listening to the discussion of some richly detailed journal installments by Priscilla and Vanessa, but I found myself looking back five years to the time when I was still directing the nonfiction program, also teaching a full load of courses, advising some forty students in the program, sitting on a dozen M.A. and Ph.D. thesis committees, chairing a special reading group on the essay for six doctoral students in nonfiction, and grousing about the fact that I had virtually no time for my writing, or for traveling with Kate, or for anything beyond the press of my academic commitments. No wonder I wanted out.

But now I wonder why I couldn't foresee how much more appealing my lot might be on a drastically reduced workload—so appealing that I sometimes wish I could keep this comfortable berth forever. The only problem is that I would never have discovered this happy arrangement without taking part in the university's phased-in early retirement plan, the financial inducements of which I accepted in exchange for agreeing to retire completely at the age of sixty-five. And without agreeing to retire, I couldn't have afforded to work part-time, so I'd certainly not have had enough spare time to keep the journal that led to both of my daybooks, and I'd probably never have hit upon the idea of teaching a workshop in journal writing. Now that I'm thinking about the matter like this, taking everything into account, it looks like this phase-in-phase-out plan has turned out far better than I could have imagined, even though it includes my upcoming retirement and the end of my teaching career. And that charming rationalization suddenly puts me in mind of a haunting couplet by Richard Wilbur from the end of "New Year's Eve":

> *We fray into the future, rarely wrought*
> *Save in the tapestries of afterthought.*

No wonder I'm keeping this journal.

Wednesday / March 5

Sometimes, though, this journal makes me feel as if I'm becoming obsessed with retirement, writing about it every day, worrying about every twist and turn in the road, rather than enjoying the scenery—and the surprises—along the way. But at breakfast this morning, when I mentioned the possibility of giving up this journal and working on other things, like the garden and my book on the personal essay, Kate stopped scanning the newspaper and told me in her sternest, no-nonsense tone of voice, "You can't keep starting these journals and then dropping them, like you did with that other one last fall." I never thought she'd bring up my journal about the journal-writing course, especially after I explained how it was getting in the way of the course itself.

But I couldn't make a similar case against this one. And even if I had decided to stop keeping it this morning, the rest of the day would have convinced me that it isn't the journal that keeps me thinking about retirement but all the other reminders of it that come welling in on me every day. Like the flyer that arrived today from Blue Cross/Blue Shield, inviting me to think about my upcoming sixty-fifth birthday this May and the need to supplement my forthcoming Medicare insurance with a "wraparound" policy (of which there are ten kinds to choose from). Or the recently gyrating stock market that makes me wonder whether I should reallocate some of my retirement funds. Or my upcoming trip to Cleveland this weekend, to visit my ninety-five-year-old Aunt Ada and help her adjust to the move she recently made from her longtime apartment into a retirement home. Or the well-meaning question that my hairdresser Chris put to me this afternoon when I sat down in the chair and took off my glasses: "So tell me—what are you and Kate planning to do once you're retired?"

Thursday / March 6

Henceforth, perhaps, I'll be known not as a retired professor of English but as an active winterologist, thanks to an hour-long radio program about winter, for which I was interviewed last month by Wisconsin Public Radio. The nationally syndicated program aired in Wisconsin last Sunday, and since then I've received several calls and e-mails, all telling me how "thoughtful" and "informative" I sounded. At first, I assumed it was just the affection of my daughter Amelia, who lives in Wisconsin, and the eagerness of Sarah, marketing director at the university press, whose mother also heard the program in Wisconsin. But a few other favorable reports led me to imagine that I sounded more knowledgeable and articulate than the thick-tongued fellow I felt like during most of the interview. The past few days, in fact, I began to think about doing some radio essays on gardening or winter or retirement or writing, or anything else that might come to mind. A new venture and a way to continue teaching as well. For a moment or two, I even imagined myself being invited to do a weekly or biweekly essay on one of the PBS radio programs. Something with an evocative title, like "Tending My Garden: A Letter from the Heartland." So beguiling a series that I'd become the darling of millions. An E. B. White of the airwaves. But then I remembered the nasally, slow-talking pontificator I used to hear when I still listened to myself being interviewed on the radio, and soon enough I decided, after all, that I'd rather not listen to the program when it airs next week in Iowa. Still, there's nothing like a good daydream, especially on the eve of retirement.

Friday / March 7

On a cool March day, there's also nothing like the promise of an early summer tomato, so it was a pleasure to transplant the seedlings that germinated last week, now that their first true leaves have fully unfurled. And then without further ado, Kate transported me to the Cedar Rapids airport for my flight to Cleveland to visit Aunt Ada. Actually, she's my mother's first cousin, but she's always been like an aunt or a fairy godmother, especially during my childhood when I sometimes spent weekends with her and her husband, Bernie, after my father and mother died. The last time I visited Aunt Ada, some five years ago, Kate and I and a host of other relatives gathered in Cleveland to celebrate her ninetieth birthday. And she was still the most effervescent relative in my life, still up to a few comic vaudeville routines with her younger brother, Jerry, in the gracious apartment they shared, and then to decking herself out in an elegant lavender dress for a celebratory dinner, where she played the belle of the ball, with toasts and good memories all around. But this time I knew would be different, for Jerry passed away just a few months ago, leaving Aunt Ada in grief at the loss of her last close relative and friend, leaving her too with no choice but to move into a retirement home last week, a move that she and Jerry had been resisting for several years. From my recent phone conversations with Aunt Ada, I've also realized that she's in a bad way over her loss of hearing, her diminishing eyesight, her failing health, and everything else in her immediate world. It's no wonder I've been getting SOS calls and letters from Lois, my former sister-in-law, who tends Aunt Ada's many needs as if Ada were her own aunt or mother.

But nothing I'd heard from Lois or from my brother, Marshall, could have prepared me for what happened when I first saw Aunt Ada again this afternoon. Oh yes, she was still carefully dressed, and she still cared intensely about her favorite art objects, as I could tell from the suggestions she kept making to my cousin Joanne and her husband, Marvin, who were hanging her pictures when I walked into her room at the retirement home. But this time, the first I can ever remember, she didn't greet me as "little Carly," with the familiar twinkle in her eye and the playful use of the double diminutive that she knew I detested from years of having been greeted that way by most of my other relatives. No, this time instead, it was "my dear, dear Carl, how good of you to come." And then I knew for sure that things were in a bad way, especially a moment later when she said, "Come give me a hug," a request I'd never heard from her before. So fragile that I worried about holding her too tight lest I crush her in my arms. Her eyes tearing, her voice crackling, all she could say to me just then was, "The quality of life. The quality of life." And then I knew her anguish was so profound that nothing could relieve it but death itself. Aunt Ada, it seemed, had reached the point of no return, a place that I can only imagine right now by remembering how delicate she felt, how frail her bones, when I took her in my arms.

Yet just a while later, when I was about to go out to dinner with Joanne, Marvin, and Lois, Aunt Ada wanted me to meet her "dear friend, Alice," a diminutive lady who appeared at her door, smiling, and without a word took Aunt Ada's hand and started walking down the hall, arm in arm, hand in hand, as if the quality of life could never have been better. And I could never have been more uncertain about what it means to retire or when one has passed the point of no return.

Saturday / March 8

At dinner last night, Marvin, a retired elementary school principal, could not have been more certain about retirement. "You should keep on working as long as you believe in what you're doing and it gives you satisfaction. Which means that it's time to quit, time to retire, when the work doesn't satisfy you any longer, or you can't bring yourself to do it any longer." It sounded as if Marvin was talking about boredom and burnout. But when I asked him about his own situation, it turned out that he retired a few years ago, in his early sixties, earlier than he had planned, when the superintendent of his school system demanded that he cut the budget by firing some of the young elementary school teachers whom he had hired. "They were excellent teachers, who didn't deserve to be fired, so I didn't feel I could continue to work in that kind of a situation."

Given the intensity of Marvin's feelings about leaving a career that had given him so much satisfaction, I was fascinated this morning as I listened to Lois talk casually about retiring "sometime next year" from her job as a research assistant at Case-Western Reserve University. She's always seemed so knowledgeable and serious about the projects in which she's involved that I've assumed her work to be as central in her life as mine or Marvin's has been in ours. But when I pressed the matter a bit, inviting her to talk about her work as a research assistant, she devalued her job so quickly that I could see how she might not feel the anguish of retiring from a cherished career: "Oh no, I don't usually do any of the scientific analysis. I just make myself useful to the project, do whatever needs to be done, which means that I often put myself in a position of being used. It's a habit of mine."

For someone whose life has followed such a pattern—and I suppose there must be millions of such people, especially women—retirement might well be a nonevent. Or better still a liberating experience. How else to account for the congratulatory remarks I've been getting recently from secretaries in the department and elsewhere around town? At first I was puzzled, wondering if there was something wrong with me for being so troubled by retirement, or something wrong with them for taking it so joyously. But now I'm beginning to see that retirement, like everything else in the world, is so deeply differentiated by gender, culture, profession, and everything else in human experience that my story of it—and my feelings about it—are probably as quirky as all the others.

Which reminds me of my conversation this afternoon with Aunt Ada. I was trying to find out about her life during the 1920s, in the years before I was born. I was curious about how she met Bernie and what she'd been doing before they were married. And she didn't hold anything back. "I was teaching elementary school. I received my teaching license, you see, in the mid-'20s, the same time as your mother. But no sooner did I meet Bernie and begin dating him than he started to meet me every day on my way to school, telling me that he wanted to marry me—wanted to marry me so much that he threatened to jump off a bridge if I didn't agree. Can you believe it? Jump off a bridge for me? So what could I do? But back then, you couldn't continue to teach if you were married." At that point, she pulled out her old teaching license from the Cleveland Board of Education just to show me the restriction against marriage. "Besides, Bernie and his family would have been embarrassed if I continued to work after we were married. So that's when I retired."

Sunday / March 9

This morning after breakfast, Lois and I went over to visit Jack and Barbara, longtime friends of hers and Marshall's—friends whom I also knew from my earlier days in Cleveland. I was eager to visit, just to thank Jack in person for his generous medical advice during Kate's recent bouts with cancer. But I was also curious to see Jack and Barbara for the first time in forty-five years, just to find out if he's actually as vigorous in person as he sounds over the phone—still carrying on a full-time medical practice in his early seventies—and to see if Barbara's still as calm and composed as I remember. I was snooping in a way, though I also thought I might get another perspective on retirement, as indeed I did. For there were Jack and Barbara, looking almost as shiny and put-together as they had almost fifty years ago—he so animated about his ongoing practice, despite a cast on his leg from a recent accident, that he made me feel as if I was the one hobbling around. Especially when he said, "The only reason I might give up my practice would be all the trouble of dealing with the insurance companies."

But Barbara didn't say much about her career as a social worker or about retirement, even when I questioned her closely about it, which made me notice again how differently men and women have been acculturated to think about working and retirement. Or so it seems they were in the past, in my generation and earlier. Nowadays, with women employed in the full range of jobs and professions available to men, I wonder if women's attitudes toward retirement will be so different from those of men, so comparatively subdued, for example, as they seem to be in the case of Lois and Barbara. I wonder how my younger women colleagues will respond to retirement when they start approaching it some ten or twenty years from now.

Ten or twenty years from now, if I'm still around to ponder such matters, I probably won't be thinking about retirement from work but from life itself—a thought that came welling in upon me this afternoon when Aunt Ada and I were taking a walk outside. I was showing her the bright green tips and shoots of crocus, daffodils, hyacinths, and tulips breaking through the soil, pointing out each of the different kinds, as if I were an elementary school teacher and she one of my students, learning about the growth cycle of spring bulbs. Then back into the building, where we went to a lounge and reading area, sat down close to each other on a couch, and I paged slowly through a large photographic guide to historic sites in Boston, reading her the captions below each of the pictures, repeating myself once or twice with each caption, to make sure that she heard me. Occasionally, we talked about the need for her to get a new pair of hearing aids, so she can get on more easily with people in the home and enjoy more of the cultural and social activities that take place there. And she told me about planning to take part in some studio art sessions at the retirement home, so she can try her hand again at making some things of her own. Like the puppets she created to entertain her students some seventy years ago. Yet nothing she said sticks so clearly in my mind as her parting words when I was still holding her hand in mine—"You and all the others have lives of your own. I know that. I know you can't stay here. I just wish you didn't have to leave me alone in this place. But that's how it has to be, and there's nothing I can do about it." Nor was there anything I could do just then that might ease the pain for either of us. I was leaving and so was she, both of us heading for places that would put us further apart than ever before.

Monday / March 10

Home by noon, and none too soon, given the e-mail I found waiting for me from Barbara, associate chair of the department:

> Dear Carl,
>   April 24th is the date of the honors ceremony. I am hoping that you will allow us to include in the event a short speech honoring your work here, as you honored Jix last year. We would invite Kate to the event, as Jean was invited last year.
>   If you have specific, additional ideas of what would be

pleasing to you, I hope that you will tell me. I would like to arrange what would be most meaningful for you and for the community.

Barbara

Just the kind of ceremonial event I'd been hoping to avoid and probably could have, if I'd written a note to Dee as I intended to do after my run-in with Jon. But now the planning is so far along that just after I finished reading Barbara's e-mail and went running out of my office to see if I could head off the ceremony, I bumped into my colleague Jim, who showed me a handout he'd just received, soliciting contributions for a gift to me and my colleague David, who's also retiring this May. The minute I saw that request, I felt trapped, and the old fight-or-flight reaction took hold of me. How else to account for the e-mail I sent to Barbara:

> Dear Barbara,
>
> Thanks for contacting me about the honors ceremony, for the truth of the matter is that I don't want any kind of speech about me delivered at the forthcoming honors ceremony, or anywhere else for that matter. Nor do I want a party or gifts or remembrances or anything else of the sort. Not now or any other time while I'm still alive and doing my thing.
>
> I've been meaning to write a note to Dee, explaining my reasons for wanting things this way, but I've been so busy of late that I just haven't gotten around to it.
>
> Sometime in the next week or two, I expect to send her an explanatory note, and I'll send a copy to you, so perhaps you will understand my very strong feelings on this score (even if you don't necessarily agree with them).
>
> So, you needn't worry about planning anything for me.
>
> Yours,
>
> Carl

Now, several hours later, as I sit here in the attic contemplating my response, the opening paragraph of it seems much more intense and harshly worded than need be; the last sentence seems abrupt and insulting; and the note as a whole makes me cringe at my incredible failure to thank Barbara for the time and effort she's given to making arrangements that most people would be grateful for. What is it, I wonder, that caused me to react so badly to her generous and thoughtful note? Maybe it was the brief visit I made to my parents' grave site this morning before flying home from Cleveland—the capstone to a weekend so burdened with a sense of aging and mortality that the mere thought of a retirement ceremony made me feel as if I were being buried myself. Maybe it's the uneasiness I've often noticed among my colleagues at other retirement parties, as if they were taking part in a ritual they didn't believe in and that I don't want to subject them to once again. Maybe it was the fact that Barbara's e-mail reminded me that my teaching days are definitely coming to an end just a couple of months from now. Maybe it's that I don't want to hear someone telling my story before my story is done. Whatever the case, it looks like the only thing I can do right now is to get in touch with Dee as soon as possible, to see if I can stop the retirement train from taking its usual course. And get in touch with Barbara, to apologize as soon as possible.

Tuesday / March 11

"But won't you just let us give you a present, if it's an oak tree, planted in Reno Street Neighborhood Park, so you can see it every day when you're out walking the dog?" The minute that Dee spoke, I could feel my skin tingling, for I was touched by the thoughtfulness of such a gift and the earnestness of her question. I was also touched by memories of other department chairs I've known during my career at Iowa, especially John, who hired me thirty-five years ago and now inspires me by soldiering on some twenty years after he retired, still writing, still smiling, despite his infirmities. So how could I refuse an oak tree, planted in the neighborhood park just a stone's throw from our house—the park that Kate labored to create some twenty-five years ago, and that both of us have devoted ourselves to maintaining ever since? How, indeed, could I refuse it, especially after Dee had agreed to forego the retirement ceremony? For a moment, it felt as if I was getting exactly what I wanted—not a suitcase, nor a watch, but an oak tree, free of any ceremonial encumbrances. It also seemed that Dee understood my desire to forego the ritual ending of things that can't be so easily ended. A few minutes later, though, when I turned to the matters that I'd been hoping to arrange—like the continuance of my office in exchange for my service as an editorial consultant to the nonfiction program—Dee was more circumspect. Oh yes, she was gracious as always, thanking me for "such a generous offer to the department." She also conceded that "for some people" my idea of retirement might make more sense than the abrupt professional parting of the ways that usually takes place. But the smile suddenly disappeared from her face when she told me, "The office situation is still so cloudy and complex that I won't know anything for several more weeks."

My feelings were mixed as I left her office. I was pleased at the prospect of an oak tree in the park and a retirement without any ceremony, but troubled at the thought of having to give up my office and give up my involvement in a program that I worked so hard to create and direct. I was also troubled by my continuing inability to let go, by my craven desire to hang on, as if my life depended on it. And maybe in some ways it does. How else to explain this irrepressible and almost irrational desire of mine to have it both ways, to retire without completely retiring? As if I couldn't take a hint from this afternoon's workshop discussion of journal installments by Judith and Jean—both about the decline of an aging parent.

Wednesday / March 12

This morning with Kate, I lapsed into a few mournful remarks about the end of my teaching career, now only seven weeks away, as

I noticed before breakfast when I checked the calendar hanging on the side of the refrigerator. And that must have been the thing—my counting the weeks, like a prisoner on death row—that riled her, for no sooner had I announced the fateful number than she reminded me, "That's what you bargained for, and now it's time to bite the bullet."

I was surprised by Kate's stern reproof, given her gentle urgings the past few years to keep my hand in by teaching a class now and then, as if she'd been worried about my going to seed or hanging around the house with nothing worthwhile to do. But this morning, I guess she was probably just fed up with my continued fretting and grieving. I wonder what she'd think if she were reading these entries day by day, as she did when I was writing my gardening journal. I wonder what my students would think if they were privy to these maudlin musings. So much for my professorial air of composure!

Thursday / March 13

Though I'm ending my career with the university, I'm beginning to make my presence known on the World Wide Web, thanks to the artistry of my Webmaster, Joe, who just finished creating and launching a site where anyone can find a virtual version of me. Actually, the site is devoted primarily to *My Vegetable Love* but also includes links to a biographical sketch and snapshot, an article about the nonfiction program, and a preview of the winter book, which will be added to the site when it's published next fall.

Last night, when I first visited my site, to check the layout, the links, and the typographical accuracy, I was delighted by Joe's colorful, tasteful, and user-friendly design. And pleased at the prospect of having a long-lived existence on the Web, especially in view of Joe's promise to get the site indexed on all the major search engines. But this afternoon when I beheld the finished thing illuminating my screen—all my suggestions incorporated, all the errors corrected, all the links taking me swiftly to samples of my work or reviews of it or notes about my life and professional career—I began to feel like a postmodern Narcissus, staring at his virtual image in an electronic pool, especially with the snapshot of me in the garden, tending my snow peas. And then I was beset once again by those nagging questions that came to me a few weeks ago when I finished my biographical note for the winter book. Who am I anyway? A retiring professor? A cynical author? A gardener? Or a person who's lost his bearings?

Friday / March 14

Those questions are still on my mind, especially after my entrepreneurial venture of this morning. Actually, it started a week or so ago, when I received an e-mail from Sarah at the press, telling me about "a new gardening Web site that may interest you . . . as a way to promote your book." Included in her message was a copy of the site's want ad, a hyped-up little come-on that left me less than interested in cultivating that particular garden, especially because its postmodern name—"VerdeStyle"—made me feel that it wasn't the place for a pre-postmodern fellow like me. During the past several days, though, I had begun to think about VerdeStyle again, probably because of being in touch with Joe about my own Web site, also because of several e-mails I received from Sarah and from Linzee, the press advertising director, about their marketing and promotional plans for the new book. Their efforts made me feel that I ought to be doing something too—something that might prod me to do more garden writing and essay writing in the months and years to come. So I got up early this morning and wrote an e-mail offering my services to VerdeStyle in the form of a weekly column called "Tending My Garden: A Letter from the Heartland."

A letter of application—something I haven't tried my hand at for the past twenty years. I warmed to the task and set out to produce an engaging little piece in a plain but lively style, a letter exemplifying the kind of essays I would write for VerdeStyle. Pieces about gardening and living, with a homespun turn of mind, suggested by my proposed title for the column. The same title that I had imagined for my radio pieces a week or so ago, a title that I actually cooked up several months ago when my nephew David, a lawyer in Washington, D.C., suggested that I try to do a syndicated column in the spirit of my daybooks. Though David and I exchanged a heady bunch of e-mails exploring the possibility, I never did get beyond a call to my former student Jon, a feature writer at the *Chicago Tribune,* inquiring about the routine for launching a syndicated column. But this time, I finished the letter and mailed it this afternoon, as if it were meant to be. Maybe VerdeStyle will turn out to be my style, and I'll get to tend my garden for thousands of websters —assuming, of course, that they're not put off by someone "approaching retirement."

Saturday / March 15

Just before dinner last night, Lynda and Ron, our friends from Chicago, arrived for a weekend visit. Lynda is a sometime actress, now teaching English at a suburban community college, and Ron is a former college play director, now working as a theater design consultant with a nationwide record of successful projects. Lynda enters carrying a shopping bag full of goodies, which she places in the center of the kitchen table—"an embarrassment of gifts," as Kate says—a large bag of shelled pecans, several pounds of prosciutto, and three clay pigs with tails wide enough and flat enough to support a clay pot in the garden. And most touching of all, an illustrated ceramic bowl, with a haunting message around the bottom of its rim, "TIME BEGAN IN A GARDEN TIME BEGAN IN A GARDEN TIME BEGAN IN A GARDEN ..." Ron, as usual, enters carrying nothing but his theatrically compelling self.

They've come to see the Bill T. Jones Dance Company, performing at the university tomorrow night—an avant-garde group that's billed as challenging the conventional expectations of what dancers, dance roles, and dance itself might be. But no matter what Bill T. Jones and his dancers might do, I know that the performance of Lynda and Ron will also command my attention. It's not that I think of Lynda and Ron as being stagy. It's just that they fill the room with such a striking presence they sometimes make me feel as if they're on stage and I'm in the audience, transfixed by their dramatically different ways of being—also by the fact that they're ten years apart, just like Kate and me. Lynda moves gracefully around the room, amusing us with quirky tales of life at home, at school, on the road, in Puerto Rico. Ron slowly carries his large torso on top of his bowed legs, a balancing act it seems, as he tells us nonchalantly about the vacation-retirement home he's planning to build in Puerto Rico. Lynda talks quickly, vivaciously, her voice resonant with the idiom and inflections of her Tennessee childhood. Ron speaks so softly that I sometimes have trouble hearing him, even with my hearing aids set at full volume. Ron is a former high school and college football player from inner-city Chicago, whose years on the field have left their marks on his body, especially on his legs. So I wonder how he continues his worldwide consulting and traveling, especially given the fact that he's only a year or two younger than I. When does he plan to retire? "Not anytime soon." How does he keep himself in shape? "Jogging every morning I'm home, or working out at the local basketball court." He's a man of few words, but they speak volumes about how to survive.

Sunday / March 16

Backstage after the performance last night also had me thinking about survival. It all started when Lynda and Ron took Kate and me in hand to see the dancers "up close," thanks to Ron's middle-aged partner, who's involved with a beautiful young member of the troupe. Both of us hung back a bit, uneasy about going behind the curtain, intruding upon the private world of the dancers. "We don't belong here" is the way that Kate put it, and I felt the same. And it wasn't any better when I first saw a few of them dashing in and out of their dressing rooms—some in street clothes, others still in costume, wiping off their makeup, combing their hair, making telephone calls, sauntering back and forth, as if to vent the remnants of energy and movement they'd stored up for the performance. Lynda and Ron were drawn to them like moths to a flame, their eyes brighter than at any other time this weekend—illuminated, it seemed, by the fire of the dancers. Such intensity, and so evanescent, that I couldn't help thinking just then about the brevity of a dancer's career, wondering how they deal with their enforced early retirement, how they survive without the lifts and elevations, the twists and turns and leaps on which they thrive. But no one backstage seemed to be pondering such a gloomy prospect just then—not Lynda and Ron, and certainly not the dancers, so I kept my thoughts to myself. This morning after Lynda and Ron headed back to Chicago, I spent a few hours at the kitchen sink, planting several flats of lettuce seed and other salad greens for the spring garden. A fresh start. No one could see me dancing just then, but it sure did give me a lift.

Monday / March 17

The stock markets have been so bullish again this year, but also so unstable that I decided to move everything I have in the CREF growth fund into TIAA's conservative real estate fund and wait for the market to calm down a bit before going back into the growth fund. Ever fretful, I don't want to risk the remarkable gains of the past few years just to accumulate more, especially now that our retirement kitty is big enough that we'll be able to live quite comfortably, come what may. Still, the impulse to accumulate more—to live better or just to hedge against inflation—is almost irrepressible, as I discovered this afternoon just a few minutes after making the transfer, when my conservative sense of well-being suddenly gave way to an uneasy feeling that I might have transferred things a bit too soon. But then just as quickly, the other voice inside my head reminded me that I'm only a few months from retirement and shouldn't be taking risks in such an unstable market. A market that some people are expecting to drop 10, 15, or 20 percent when correction time rolls around, but that others are predicting will continue to rise, given the vast amounts of money that baby boomers need to invest for retirement. Who do I want to bet on—the contrarian bears or the bullish baby boomers? Or some other factor, like foreign investors, interest rates, price/earnings ratios, unemployment levels, or market psychology itself?

So many things to consider that I know so little about that I sometimes wish I had no choice in the investment of my retirement funds, that everything were already as irrevocable as my impending retirement. But when I think about all the money I've tied up in my conservative TIAA annuity, I'm grateful for the choice I have in the CREF mutual funds. The only problem is that the market's now so unstable, I don't know what to do. A few months ago, my long-range plan of having 60 percent invested in the conservative TIAA annuity, and 40 percent in CREF's venturesome growth fund seemed to make perfect sense. A balanced set of investments, combining a substantial percentage of stability with the opportunity to capitalize on future increases in the stock market. But now, it seems, I'm beginning to feel the legacy of my Depression-era childhood. Now, too, I'm beginning to understand why there are so many books about investing for retirement and so few about coping with retirement itself. Right now, in fact, retirement seems like it might be just what I need to recover from all the uncertainty I've been going through the past few weeks. But then again, it will probably have its own peculiar uncertainties, so perhaps the best thing to do is to follow Kate's advice—"stop fussing around and get on with your life."

Tuesday / March 18

Getting on with your life. Sometimes I have trouble with Kate's mantra. Like this morning—I spent an hour or so planting several flats of broccoli, cabbage, and cauliflower seeds for the spring garden. But no sooner did I start planting the seeds than I began looking forward to stir-fried broccoli and pork tenderloin strips, homemade sauerkraut and garlic bologna, steamed cauliflower dressed with olive oil, lemon, and crushed garlic. And so on. My mind's taste buds tingling with fresh vegetables and other good things to come during the first month of my retirement. I wondered whether Kate would consider my anticipatory pleasure to be a means of getting on with my life or dwelling so far in the future as to be out of touch with my life. And how about the conversation we had over lunch, trying to decide where to go this coming September—the Canadian Maritimes or the Canadian Rockies?—to be far, far away from here when school begins, as well as to celebrate my retirement, our thirtieth anniversary, and the publication of the winter book. Getting on with my life or running away from it? And the same question came to mind when I was in the workshop this afternoon, thinking about how much of my life has been spent around a seminar table, listening to students discuss each other's writing.

I guess what I'm feeling right now is that my whole life is so much in transition, torn between the past and the future, that it's difficult to live primarily in the present, which I assume is what Kate means when she talks about getting on with my life. Sometimes, in fact, my situation makes me as panicky as I felt some forty years ago in Ithaca, New York, when I found myself one afternoon in the middle of a narrow bridge, swaying in the wind over a deep gorge. As if my life were suspended between two cliffs, both in view, both alluring, yet both precariously out of reach.

Wednesday / March 19

Actually, the journey to retirement is less like a swaying bridge than a twisting path, littered with forms to be completed and papers to be filed in time to keep the money flowing in and the health insurance paying out without a hitch. Today, for example, I called our Staff Benefits office, as suggested at an informational meeting last fall, to schedule an appointment for putting all my papers in order at least one month prior to May 16, the legal date of my retirement from the university. In my conversation with Nancy, associate director of Staff Benefits, I discovered that she will assist me in filing papers for the Blue Cross/Blue Shield supplemental health insurance policy, as well as for my TIAA-CREF retirement income. But before she can file the papers with TIAA-CREF, I have to procure the appropriate forms from TIAA-CREF. As for Social Security and Medicare, I will have to confer with a staff member at the Social Security office here in town. There's a place for everything, and everything's in its place. A bureaucrat's delight, a compulsive's turn-on, a paranoid's panic. Yet millions of Americans go through this process every year without any public outcries of complaint, so perhaps it's much easier than I imagine. Or maybe it's so complicated and time-consuming that it doesn't leave one any time for the emotional upheavals I've been going through the past month. Maybe that's what's so good about all the books on retirement housing, health insurance, and financial planning—you don't have to think about the psychological anxieties. As if to confirm these suppositions, my brother called this evening from California, wondering what I'm doing with my retirement funds, given the rocky state of the stock market, but he never asked me how I feel about my impending retirement. Come to think of it, I didn't ask him how he was feeling a few years ago when he went through it, but I did ask him what he was doing with his CREF funds. Is money, after all, the only thing we have in common these days? Or is it, perhaps, just a convenient measure of how we feel about retirement and the accomplishments of our working life? If so, I should be elated at the thought of being financially more secure than ever before—especially when I remember how I had to take out a bank loan some thirty years ago just to get up enough money for my wedding suit, which prompted my banker to suggest that rather than getting married, I ought to think of declaring bankruptcy.

Thursday / March 20

This afternoon at the funeral of Tillie, the ninety-one-year-old widow of a former colleague, I couldn't help thinking about the things that survive us when we shuffle off this mortal coil and retire altogether. Tillie, for her part, inspired enough good memories, enough "Tillie Tales," to keep a church full of people in stitches for almost an hour and a half. Stories told by her children that reminded other folks of their own memorable encounters with Tillie. Stories of Tillie in her late eighties still driving her boatlike Buick, still appearing at cocktail parties dressed in one of her fanciful costumes (once, according to my friends Jean and Jix, got up in scarves and bangles as "the seventh daughter of the Nile"), still telling fortunes (as she once did in a reading of Kate's palm), still matchmaking, still reading voraciously, still serving high tea (as she did to my daughter Hannah and her friend Carol when they were art students here at the university), still cooking gourmet dinners, still taking in young roomers, still redecorating the rooms in her rambling nineteenth-century home, and still in touch with her husband, Joe, though he had died some twelve years ago. A few stories about Tillie and Joe are so well known that no one even needed to tell them, but they surely must have been on the minds of everyone this afternoon. Tillie and Joe reading Victorian novels to each other every evening after dinner, as if the high Victorian era were still alive in the late twentieth century. Tillie and Joe staunchly opposing the local Presbyterian minister's plan to build a new church and tear down "Old Brick"—a mid-nineteenth-century pile in Romanesque style—until their irrepressible and "divisive" opposition brought them nationwide attention when they were excommunicated from the church by the Synod of Iowa. Tillie and Joe never really retired until the very end, and probably not even then. So they left behind a churchful of good memories and an old brick church.

Friday / March 21

The first day of spring and my thoughts are greening up a bit, thanks to seeding up a few six-packs of peppers this morning. Also thanks to Dee's playful headline in her weekly departmental newsletter that "THE UI IS RUMORED TO HAVE A LITTLE MONEY"—for salary increases. Probably no more than 2 or 3 percent, given the reports I've heard. Dee, as usual, has requested that each department member submit an updated résumé and a statement of no more than two pages in length summarizing one's teaching, awards, publications, and service during the past year, in order to provide the departmental salary review committee with sufficient information to advise the chair in her determination of salaries for next year. So much paperwork and so much deliberation by so many people for so little money! I'm delighted to think that for the first time in thirty-five years, I don't have to take part in this charade. But I'm also a bit depressed by the thought that my résumé, my life, is no longer of any interest here—assuming, of course, that it ever was. On the other hand, I'm delighted by the possibility that my take-home pay next year might be 10 percent higher than it is this year.

Without having to submit a résumé or do a lick of work to earn it! Maybe retirement's not such a bad thing after all. Maybe that's why I've seen so many Gray Panthers roaming around the national parks and other vacation spots the past few years. Maybe that's why all the travel groups have been courting me. I'm a valuable commodity—more valuable now than I ever was during my working life!

Saturday / March 22

Come to think of it, there's no telling how valuable I might be, especially after reading and thinking about the message inside my fortune cookie this evening:

When winter comes, the heavens will rain success on you.

On first reading it, I was charmed by the wry oriental wit and the deadpan irony of predicting rain in the middle of winter. A promised deluge of success that turns out, after all, to be a verbal illusion. But it also occurred to me that winter might be a metaphor for advanced age and retirement—a season of life rather than a time of year. In which case, the message could be construed as a genuine promise of success for someone my age, approaching retirement. Then I couldn't help wondering when the rain might fall, or what it might fall upon. Certainly not on my academic career, which is almost over. But it could have something to do with the letter I wrote to VerdeStyle and the weekly column I proposed, which I might be invited to produce for their Web site or for some other place. Maybe I'll become a successful columnist after all. (So far, though, I haven't heard anything from VerdeStyle.) Or it could have something to do with my winter book, which might turn out to be a much bigger success than I've imagined, given the thousands of people who have a natural interest in reading about winter. Or the rain of success could mean that after thirty years of entering the Publisher's Clearing House contests, Kate and I are on the verge of winning the big giveaway. But then again, there's that unmistakable sense of irony, of paradox, in the promise of a winter rain. So, at last, I don't know what to make of my apparent good fortune, except perhaps to use it as an epigraph for my forthcoming winter book, where readers galore can make of it what they want.

Sunday / March 23

Actually, I'm much less interested in a rain of success than a little peace of mind, so I walked up the backyard this afternoon to visit my neighbor Jim, who's always seemed so laid back and at home with things that I figured his experience might shed some light on my own. Jim retired about seven years ago, when he was sixty-two, after twenty years of owning a local trophy shop, which he managed with the help of his wife, Carol, and two of his sons. Before that, he was a short-range trucker, driving the routes between here and Chicago. I remember when he retired, because I started seeing him in his yard during the weekdays, fussing over his duck boat and his decoys, a sure sign that he wasn't at work. But I never asked him what happened until today.

"Well, it was a weekend in the fall, and I was out deer hunting. With a bow and arrow. And when I came back with a buck and went out to the shop, my boys said I didn't need to come in any longer. They could keep it going on their own with Carol." A puzzling reply, which raised more questions than it answered, but I didn't feel like probing the matter, since it wasn't any of my business. Yet I wondered how he felt about being told he wasn't needed, especially given my own situation. "Well, it hurt some at first. You can see why. I bought the business when it was nothing. Made it what it was. But I wasn't the only one there. So I decided to take a week off, go hunting, and think about it, 'cause it was my decision. I was owner and president back then and I still am. But I decided if that's how it was, I'd go through with it. Besides I was old enough to begin drawing Social Security."

I was also curious about how it was for him at first, since he stopped abruptly, whereas I've been phasing in for five years. "Well, just think of it, I'd been getting up every morning for twenty years, every morning, ever since we bought the shop, and going in to work, so you can imagine how it was at first. Back then, I could've cared less about a flower or a vegetable. And it was that way for about five or six months. Now it's a different thing, now that I've got all the bulbs and flowers and vegetables. Now I get up in the morning and can't wait to get out in the yard and take care of things. Now there's not enough time in a day for everything. And sometimes they call, wanting me to come and help out for a few hours. Now they need me from time to time. Isn't that something?" We had a good laugh over that one, though I don't think I'll ever get such a call myself.

We also talked about his financial plans, given that Carol's planning to retire a few years from now, and they intend to leave the shop to the boys, but want to make sure they'll have enough income to keep them going comfortably for the rest of their lives. And I couldn't help thinking how different (and often difficult) it is for people in business, especially a small family business, compared to the way it is for those of us whose futures have been carefully arranged for by the university or some other institution. So I came away feeling that I've had a remarkably good deal with such a long, phased-in retirement, such a well-planned retirement fund, and no hassle. No wonder Kate was a bit prickly the other day, when I was being maudlin about things. Yet the knowledge of my good fortune still doesn't make me feel any better about what I'll be losing this May. And I don't yet know what to do about it. But it sure would be nice to go at things as comfortably as Jim.

Monday / March 24

I'm beginning to think that one of the reasons I'm uneasy about retirement is that it seems to be pushing me more and more into a world populated largely by older people—folks over sixty or sixty-five. I first noticed it a couple of weeks ago when I went to visit Aunt Ada in Cleveland. Partly, of course, it was the result of her being in a retirement home, where everybody's in their late sixties and over—and on Aunt Ada's wing, in their eighties and over. But even outside her place I was consorting only with people in their mid-sixties and over, like Joanne, Marvin, Lois, Jack, and Marcia. In fact, the only younger person I spent any appreciable time with that weekend was my niece, Susan, who drove me to the cemetery and helped find my parents' graves the morning of my flight home, and she's almost fifty. No wonder I enjoyed the Greek restaurant the night before, where all the waiters were in their late teens or early twenties, as vibrant as the students here on campus.

I don't feel very comfortable writing about this problem, because it makes me sound as if I'm guilty of ageism, of being prejudiced against my own kind, as if the flaming fried goat cheese and other Greek food wouldn't have tasted just as good if my waiter had been in his sixties. But there's no denying the fact that when I give up the classroom and my involvement in the nonfiction program, I'll be losing my daily contact with people in their twenties to forties, losing the special challenge of being confronted by viewpoints so different from my own that they compel me to keep an open mind. It's not that I don't wish to spend time with people of my generation. In fact, I find myself most at home, most comfortable with people my age, as I noticed yesterday when I was talking to Jim.

It's just that I don't want to be ghettoized in a world of the aged, any more than I want to be confined to the world of any particular age group—old or young, Sun City or Fun City. For I know all too well from a couple of unpleasant incidents a few years ago that some of my younger colleagues harbor some disturbing prejudices against their older colleagues. And just to set the record straight, I can also remember my own exasperation some thirty years ago with the crotchety ways of "the old men," as I used to call them. The tensions between youth and age are inescapable, especially given the contemporary exploitation and commercialization of those cultural divisions. But I'd much rather live with those bracing and stimulating tensions, with the full range of human experience, than wall myself off in a world of the aged. Now I'm beginning to understand why Kate doesn't want to be isolated or lumped in with all of us retirees.

Tuesday / March 25

Spring break this week and most of the students have headed south or headed home. So I decided to stay home and start the main crop of tomatoes in time to have a sturdy set of plants ready to set out in May. I also wanted to see if I could strike up a conversation with our painter, Mr. Hesse, about work and retirement. Though he told me once just to call him Erich, I've never gotten over the habit of addressing my elders in a formal and respectful way, especially someone so precise in his ways as Mr. Hesse. He and his daughter, Karen, who does the wallpapering, have been working in our house the past three weeks, steadily making their way through the laborious job of removing all the old paper, priming the walls, painting the ceilings, and hanging new paper in the living room, the dining room, and the hallway up to the second floor. An embossed regency stripe that requires the utmost attention to detail, especially in a nineteenth-century house like ours where none of the walls or ceilings is plumb. Though we haven't exchanged many words beyond the usual pleasantries about the weather and the garden, I've observed Mr. Hesse long enough to admire his old-fashioned dedication to his craft, and to passing it on as carefully as possible to Karen. In his white overalls, with his neatly trimmed mustache and his taciturn ways, he reminds me of the lean old painter and wallpaperer who did the high-ceilinged rooms in my Uncle Manny's apartment sixty years ago. Also dressed in white overalls and sporting a neatly trimmed mustache, he arrived each day with a brass spittoon that he placed at the foot of his tall ladder, and he never missed the mark. Mr. Hesse doesn't bring a spittoon, but he does go outside to his truck every hour or two for a short cigarette break. And then he's back in again, silently working to prep the walls, paint the ceiling, or clean up the paper trimmings after Karen's finished hanging a section. The only time he says much of anything is when she's eyeballing a difficult stretch of wall, trying to figure out exactly where to start and how to make the cuts in order to have the fewest joints and the most uninterrupted runs of paper. Then he's right at her elbow, pointing out this and that—the master wallpaperer now unable to continue his craft except by being a master teacher for his solitary disciple. So I wondered how long he's been working as a painter and wallpaperer. "My whole life. I learned it growing up." Then I could sense how proud he must be of having passed his craft on to Karen. And then I wondered how long he plans to keep working, and that's when his body suddenly stiffened, and he spoke up more loudly than I've ever heard him speak before. "As long as I can. You quit, you die." He spit out the last sentence so fiercely that I was momentarily taken aback, as was Karen, who quickly intervened. "Oh Dad, you don't really mean that." But he did, even though he spluttered something like a retraction a few seconds later, "Well, well, I guess not. But . . ." Though he didn't finish the sentence, it was clear from what he said that for Mr. Hesse retirement is out of the question.

I've never heard such a blunt equation between retirement and quitting, nor have I ever heard such a blunt connection between retirement and death, so at first I considered his remark to be quite extreme, as I suppose Karen did too. But the more I've thought about the matter the past several hours, the more I'm beginning to think that perhaps I've been troubled by my impending retirement because teaching for me has been part of my existence for so many years that to give it up now is like putting an end to my life. Or like forsaking such a major part of it—"that one talent which is death to hide"—that everything else sometimes seems trivial by comparison. No wonder I've been clinging to it, bargaining with Dee to continue a while longer, like Everyman bargaining with Death. The more I think about it, the more I wish I'd stuck with my tomatoes and let Mr. Hesse get on with his work.

Wednesday / March 26

At the Staff Benefits office this morning, I expected just a cut-and-dried signing of forms to activate my TIAA-CREF income and set up a supplemental health insurance policy. But I should have known better from my previous encounters with Nancy, who's a financial whiz and willing to offer her perspective on TIAA-CREF's various retirement accounts and the different options for receiving income from each of them. Faced with so many appetizing choices, which she explained in detail, it was good to hear her sensible advice: "Once you've settled on a balanced long-range plan like yours, it's best to stick with it, otherwise you're at the whims of a market that you can't really predict one way or the other."

Though I was grateful for her financial wisdom, I also felt compelled to tell Nancy about some of the transitional problems I've been experiencing and my hunch that some people might appreciate the chance to talk with counselors about the problems of adjusting to retirement. She agreed with me on that score and with my impression that there seem to be very few books on the subject: "We used to have someone from our office do a short segment on it, but since she left for Arizona we don't have anyone who talks about the lifestyle changes and adjustment problems that people usually go through when they're facing retirement. And I've not seen much about it in the pamphlets and books that come my way."

But the university will take care of my medigap insurance for the rest of my life, and for a relatively small monthly payment it will continue to provide health insurance for Kate. Like the good provider who plans for every contingency, it will also give me a $4,000 paid-up life insurance policy (otherwise known as "the burial policy"), a hangover from the days when faculty were so ill-paid that the university didn't want to suffer the embarrassment of having its employees disposed of in a pauper's grave.

Thursday / March 27

The past several days I've been working on revisions for the fifth edition of *Fields of Writing,* a textbook anthology I've long had a hand in with four other collaborators. Many hands make light work, so none of us has a great deal to do whenever it needs to be revised. This time, for example, I only had to write biographical headnotes and questions for seven new selections in my part of the text. Yet I've never had such a hard time bringing myself to do the work. Four years ago, when we did the previous edition, I finished my share of the revisions in two or three weekends, in time to meet the publisher's deadline with no problem at all. This time it's been so bad that I didn't even want to mention it in this diary. I'm a month late and I've been getting calls from Kristin, our project editor, offering to help in any way that she can.

Sometimes I think the project has gone stale for me, as it has to some extent for my collaborators. Fifteen years and five editions is a long distance run for any textbook, even one with the widespread following of *Fields,* given its collection of material from the humanities, social sciences, and sciences. But I also think that my impending retirement has begun to affect the way I feel about everything I do, especially outside professional work that takes me away from Kate or the garden or writing projects of my own. Yet there was a little stretch of time this week when I was reading an excerpt from Anne Frank's diary and writing a headnote for it that I felt so totally involved in the project I could have kept working on it for hours and days on end. Then again, the brevity of her life, a vibrant young woman of my own generation, made me all the more conscious of how little time I have to spare.

Friday / March 28

Spare time. It all depends on how you spend it and what you get in return. Today, for example, while Mr. Hesse and Karen were finishing up in the dining room, Kate and I spent the morning clearing things off the counter and walls of the kitchen in time for Mr. Hesse to start stripping wallpaper this afternoon. Then we moved on to the half-bath, which doubles as a cooking-gardening library and pantry. Boxing up all the surface cookware and found objects, all the books and pictures, put me in mind of how barren it looked when we first moved in some twenty-seven years ago. It also made me wonder about the time when we'll have to move out of this place for good. So many possessions—I felt burdened by the mere thought of them all, and overburdened by the memories attached to everything I was carrying from one room to another. Like the color print of a woodchuck standing on its hind legs, a leaf in its paws, reminding me not only of all the groundhogs that have beset the vegetable garden in years past, but also what will come of my plot after I'm gone. I also remember the spring morning in 1983, when I bought that print at the gift shop of the Air Force Academy, where I was chairing an editorial conference to plan a book-length collection of writing programs designed at the Institute on Writing, which I directed in the late '70s and early '80s. A million-dollar collaborative project of the University of Iowa and the National Endowment for the Humanities that would radically change the teaching of writing at colleges and universities throughout the country —now a distant memory, less durable in its influence, I suppose, than the offspring of all the groundhogs living in the wilderness park behind our backyard. In the midst of those gloomy thoughts,

Kate turned up an old wood-burned block with the message "No Winter Lasts Forever"—an anonymous gift that appeared in my office mailbox several years ago, the donor of which still remains anonymous. Maybe I should use that maxim as an epigraph in my winter book. Live long enough, it seems, and everything comes together—from an old woodblock to a new fortune cookie to an early spring day, so warm and sunny that in late afternoon I retreated to the garden and planted my first outdoor seeds of the season—a twenty-foot row of spinach. Speaking of time well spent—it was the first time all day that I felt relaxed and rewarded for my labors.

Saturday / March 29

Today, I decided to sketch out an annual retirement budget—the first time I've tried to construct a budget of any kind the past thirty years. And it was a pleasure to discover that we'll have about $450 more a month for living expenses than we now have. A 10 percent increase, just as I'd projected last fall. To which Kate responded at lunch, "Is that all?" I thought 10 percent more was a big deal, especially given the fact that most people would be elated just to have as much spending money in retirement as when they were working full time. Yet I felt a bit defensive, so I reminded her that we might have a lot more if we weren't involved in our golden years project of repainting and repapering the house, which I figured would be followed by more such projects: refinishing all the wood floors, reupholstering all the furniture, replacing all the major kitchen appliances, and so on. But in the midst of this explanation, I realized we'd actually have more than I projected, because the retirement payouts will come to us every month, twelve months a year, rather than only ten months each year as they now do on my university salary. So, when everything is taken into account, we'll probably have about 20 percent more a year to live on than in the past. Enough to pay for the month-long trips that Kate and I have been dreaming of.

The only problem is that I didn't take into account the need to replace our fourteen-year-old Mazda, now on its last legs, as I discovered early this afternoon when it died on me a mile from home. I had to have it towed to the gas station, and then I walked home, trying to figure out how the payments on a new car would affect our budget. The more I thought about those payments, the more I wondered whether we really needed to replace the old Mazda, given the new Jeep Grand Cherokee we bought last year. Before the Jeep, we only had one car, and I walked back and forth to work most days, in order to leave the car at home for Kate's errands around town. But ever since we've had two cars, I've been driving to work most days, with the result that I've gained more than fifteen pounds the past year. So by the time I got back home from the gas station, I had not only vowed to start walking to work every day, but also to start on a diet, eating somewhat less each meal—"getting up from the table a bit hungry," as my cardiologist has often advised—so I can keep coming back for more. But I won't begin my diet until tomorrow, for late this afternoon Kate and I had a date to decorate Easter eggs with our neighbors Marybeth and Ken, and how could I refuse any of the cakes and cookies and candies and wine and cheeses they laid before us? Ken and I talked briefly about how soon he might retire from the university, given the size of his TIAA-CREF accounts. But mostly we savored the wine and the sweets and the colorful eggs and didn't let ourselves be too distracted by dollars or pounds or any other calculable things.

Sunday / March 30

Easter Sunday. Hardly a good day to begin a diet, especially with the basket of dark chocolates and assorted truffles (champagne, raspberry, and Grand Marnier) that the bunny left by Kate's bedside early this morning. She thought the critter had forgotten her, but that's because he doesn't arrive until just before dawn on Easter

Sunday. Not to be outdone by the rabbit, I put together a festive breakfast of lox and eggs and onions with fresh bagels, just to get a little of my Jewish heritage into the ceremonies.

But Easter dinner was the big show, featuring a leg of lamb that I larded with garlic and basted with a marinade of olive oil, crushed rosemary, grated black pepper, and pulverized green peppercorns. Accompanied by steamed red potatoes, asparagus, and a fat-free, wine-rich gravy that I stirred up from the skimmed lamb drippings, it was just what the doctor ordered for Kate, me, and her mother, Lib. Especially given the fresh fruit salad that followed—a concoction of dark grapes, green grapes, cantaloupe, and minced celery lightly tossed with Kate's homemade lemon mayonnaise and a bit of lime juice. I'm not sure what my cardiologist would think of Kate's dessert—a frozen mousse of fat-free yogurt, egg whites, and grated lemon, covered with fresh strawberries steeped in creme de cassis, and topped with fresh whipped cream from the nearby Guernsey dairy. But so far as I could determine only the whipped cream was sinful, so I only took a second helping of the mousse and the fruit covering.

Lib also did justice to everything on the menu—a meal so true to the spirit of all the Easter dinners she once served us that it made me painfully aware of how much she herself has changed during the past thirty years. Once a robust and vigorous woman, almost as tall as Kate's five-foot-eight, Lib's osteoporosis and emphysema have now shrunken her frame, sapped her strength, and left her dependent upon a cane and a wheelchair. As if she were a cautionary tale about the limits of aging and the bounds of retirement. A tale so completely at odds with the Easter story that I can hardly bear to think of the two at once, lest the cognitive dissonance drive me crazy with despair. Better to think of the ride we took on the way over, Lib sitting high in the front seat of the Jeep, exclaiming upon the beauty of the day, the mild air, the blue sky, and the lamb to come.

Monday / March 31

Today marks a breakthrough of sorts in this transitional trauma of mine. A breakthrough that I probably wouldn't have noticed— that probably wouldn't even have taken place—had I not been writing a thank-you note to my friend Patti for the fan letter she sent me a few days ago telling me how much she enjoyed the vegetable book. I was pleased and surprised, as I always am, by notes and letters about the book. But this one also included an unusual request:

> I am curious if you will be teaching your class on the journal again? I'll be 50 next year and it's been a long time since I went to school but I do enjoy writing.

After reading Patti's letter, I intended to tell her that I'm retiring from the university this spring, so I won't be teaching the journal course or any other writing courses again. But when I told my colleague Mary about Patti's request, she suggested that I offer a course at home, or at one of the local watering holes, meeting with a few folks who want to study with me but can't do it under university auspices. How strange that I never thought of that possibility myself. Suddenly, the range of my professional options seemed more spacious than I'd imagined. So I answered Patti's question with Mary's suggestion in mind:

> If I find myself hankering to offer the course again, as I might in a year or two, and I can find a handful of people as eager and talented as you, I might just look for a convenient log, or picnic table, or gazebo, or other agreeable site, and offer the course gratis under my own auspices.

But no sooner had I sent off that bouncy reply than I began to think about what I'd written, and it occurred to me that my answer was hedged in with so many contingencies, so many ifs and mights, that I was tacitly telling Patti (and myself!) that I'm not very interested in offering the journal course again, at least not right away. A surprising turn of events, given the opportunity to work with people as talented as Patti. Something, it seems, has been going on in my head that I didn't even know about until I answered Patti and then started to ponder the implications of my answer. I seem to be pulling back, to be withdrawing from my earlier hunger to keep teaching, and now I wonder what else has been going on in my head without my knowing it as yet. "How do I know what I think," so the saying goes, "until I see what I've said."

Speaking of which, I also don't want to forget what I said to my graduate student Dan, when we were walking home today, about the art of teaching being something that develops gradually over years of experience. So it may not be an illusion when I sometimes feel as if I'm giving up something I now do much better than ever before—at the top of my form—because it's the product of ripeness. But judging from my letter to Patti, it looks like I'd just as soon quit while I'm still ripe rather than rot on the vine.

Tuesday / April 1

"Why didn't you just tell him you're not a freelancer?" Kate was reproving me for beating around the bush with the editor who called this morning from a glossy gardening magazine, wanting me to do a piece about growing corn, or pole beans, or watermelons for one of their upcoming summer issues. I didn't mean to be evasive or string him along. I told him right off that I didn't know enough about the different varieties to produce an informative article, but I didn't want to hang up without making a pitch for the gardening column I've been thinking about, especially since I still haven't gotten any response from VerdeStyle. He, in turn, wanted to know if I could give him the names of other people in the Midwest who could do a piece for the magazine. Each of us was trying to use the other, but neither of us got what we wanted. I couldn't think of any names beyond my friend Mary, who writes and gardens in Kalona, fifteen miles from here. And he already had someone doing a monthly gardening essay for the magazine. Oh yes, he flattered me with some nice remarks about the vegetable book. But I could tell right off from some of his questions—"Is your garden beautiful?" "Are your friends' gardens beautiful?"—that he was more interested in glossy photographs than reflective essays. So, after all, I couldn't disagree with the gist of Kate's question—that the magazine and I were not meant for each other.

Though I'm not a freelance journalist, though I don't write articles for newspapers and magazines, I couldn't help thinking that in just a few weeks I'll be free to carry my lance for anyone I wish. Including myself. A thought that was especially appealing when I stepped outside after breakfast and beheld a morning so bright and mild that I would gladly have spent it seeding in an early crop of shell peas and snow peas had I not been obliged to prepare comments on some of my students' journal installments for this afternoon's workshop.

But the workshop itself produced such a lively discussion of the challenging and unusual entries by Elizabeth and Shanti that at dinnertime with Kate, I felt a bit wistful when I noticed that I only have five more classes to teach. And this time she took a different approach to my counting—"You sound as if you're in the process of mourning something that you might well be celebrating." Though she's probably right, the liveliness of the students and the vibrancy of their writing still make it a bit difficult for me to imagine a future without them.

Wednesday / April 2

At our neighborhood park this morning, Kate and I had a brief meeting with Bob, the city's park superintendent, to choose a site for my retirement tree. He was pointing out the property line nearest our house, Kate was choosing a site within the lot line, and I was standing by, wondering what would be the best time to plant the tree. Bob's a man of few words, so his answer was quite brief—"Sometime before the end of this month or in the fall." I in turn said we'd contact him again in September if we couldn't arrange to have it planted this month. But after a brief pause, he looked down and said, "I won't be here after August." Such a surprising and mysterious announcement that I immediately asked him why, and he answered, "I'm retiring too." It turns out he's just a couple of months younger than I. A coincidence that made me wonder why he decided to retire now rather than continuing on until seventy. "Burnout" was his immediate answer, another surprising response from so taciturn and seemingly calm a person. But when I pressed him a bit more, he also said, "I have some other things I want to do. I think it's time to move on. And I want to spend more time with my grandchildren." And before I knew it, he was talking about his children and other relatives, talking about travel, talking more than I'd ever heard him talk before, when he wasn't being distracted by calls coming in over his portable telephone, or by questions from the supervisor of a crew that was installing a new set of swings and play equipment in the park. All of which helped me to see how frazzled I'd be in such a position, and why he had a slight smile on his face—the first time I've ever seen him smile—when he told me, "Let's get together for coffee after we've done it."

After talking with Bob, I could also feel a little smile creeping over my gloomy, heavyset features, not only because I'd found a compatriot where I least expected to find one, but also because his enthusiasm for retirement was so infectious that it made me feel better about my decision than I have in weeks. So this afternoon when I saw a note in Dee's weekly newsletter, reminding us of the opportunity to march in graduation with one of our doctoral students and give them their academic hood, I immediately thought of

Dan, who's studied with me in the classroom and in the garden for the past five or six years. And my smile returned as I thought about the two of us marching together, he to receive his doctorate, I to receive my release from school, my walking papers, for the first time in sixty years. Dan was also planning to ask me just before I called him this afternoon. So I'll mark my retirement in my own fashion, wearing my carnelian doctoral robe from Cornell, the robe that Kate and Lib gave me for my fiftieth birthday. Maybe Kate and I will even throw a little party after I've graduated.

Thursday / April 3

Though I'm beginning to feel more comfortable about leaving the classroom, I'm still uneasy about losing touch with my colleagues and students in the nonfiction program. Especially my colleague Carol, whose office is next door to mine and who shares my intense interest in the personal essay. We've chatted so often the past thirty years about so many aspects of the profession that I know where she stands on a wide range of academic and professional questions, including the merits of the university's various retirement options. I also know that she's planning to retire in a few years when she's sixty-five. But it occurred to me this morning that I don't really know why she doesn't intend to keep on teaching, though I had a hunch that she might be as burnt-out as I am from the burdens of responding to student writing. I also thought she might want more time to travel, for she's an inveterate traveler—and not just to France, where her late husband, Pierre, was born and raised, but also to Africa, Southeast Asia, Central America, and elsewhere in Europe. So I was surprised when she told me, "I want to make room for the younger people." Though I've occasionally said the same thing to some of my colleagues, it's never been uppermost in my mind, probably because I'm not as unselfish as Carol. When I asked her if she had any other reasons, she also spoke of wanting "more time to work on my own writing." But then she was off on another tangent that made me sit up and pay special attention: "I also think we have to be careful about not teaching any longer than we're fit to be in the classroom, particularly now that we have the choice to work beyond seventy if we wish to. Given that choice, I think it's a matter of being morally responsible in deciding when to retire."

Carol's perspective on things made me all the more eager to retain my office at least for the few more years that she might be next door. So this afternoon I spoke with Dee again, since I thought there might be more space available now that the Writers' Workshop is moving out of the building to a restored house elsewhere on campus. But according to Dee, "There's a space fight in the offing and no telling how it might work out. We'll just have to wait and see." How strange to contemplate the fate of my office, the place that's always seemed to be my own, suddenly contingent upon a squabble among several departments over a piece of the corridor once occupied by the workshop. Then again, I realize that no matter who wins the fight, everyone will have to vacate the building from mid-May to late August, so the university can remove all the asbestos and revamp the wiring for computers and telephones. Maybe all that time away from the place will enable me to wean myself from the office and the building once and for all.

How strange to feel so tied to an office that one has to envision a three- or four-month period of getting over one's dependency upon it. And why, I wonder, do I need to keep an office in the building if I have a faculty study in the university library? And an oak tree in Reno Street Neighborhood Park. If I didn't know any better, I'd say that the office is essential to staying in touch with colleagues and students, as in a sense it is. But I also have a hunch that the office is a psychological necessity, a tangible bit of evidence that I still have a place, still command a valuable piece of space, in the university. A thought that makes me realize I'm still trying to have it both ways, still bargaining to avoid the inevitable, as if it were a life and death matter.

Friday / April 4

Last night my youngest daughter, a nurse in Madison, Wisconsin, blew into town for an overnight visit before an all-day pediatrics conference today at our university medical school. Amelia came, as usual, bearing several large heads of garlic from her garden—she knows how to arouse my fatherly affection and my gardener's envy over something I can't grow very well in my clayey soil. But this time she was less interested in talking about the spring garden than in telling me how she and her husband, Joe, a schoolteacher in Madison, have been trying to figure out how much they need to save each year to have a comfortable retirement thirty years from now. Last night I gave her a few words of advice based on my own experience, this morning we talked about it again at breakfast, and then I did a financial projection for her based on an annual investment of $5,000 in a growth stock fund, with an average annual increase of 10 percent, which turned out to yield about $1,200,000. A figure that brought a big smile to her face and a "Wow!" to her lips, until I reminded her that thirty years from now given an annual inflation rate of 4 percent, her investment might actually be worth only $360,000 in current dollars. Like a disciple of Nancy, my Staff Benefits adviser, I was using my desktop calculator, a computer investment program, and a few cautious monetary principles, all of which provoked Amelia to exclaim, as she has before, "Gee, Dad, you'd make a great retirement counselor." And then she was off to her conference, while I sat around mulling over her suggestion a few minutes longer than usual.

At lunch today with Kate, I was also mulling over some trips we might take in the years to come, especially because we were dining at the Mekong, where we each had a bowl of hot and sour soup and some spring rolls, which made me feel as if we could be in Vietnam rather than Iowa City. Yesterday, we lunched at La Perlita, a nearby Mexican family restaurant, where the refried beans, the lightweight rice, and the corn tortilla stuffed with guacamole and vegetables had me thinking about a trip south of the border. All week long, in fact, we've been lunching out, while Mr. Hesse and Karen have been working in the kitchen, so during the past few days I've also been to southern France, northern Italy, and north Africa without doing too much damage to my diet. But the place that's really been on our minds these days is Canada, for we're still trying to decide between a cabin in the Rockies or an inn by the ocean, between mountain game and Atlantic salmon. On the way home from work, I stopped at Prairie Lights Bookstore and picked up a few travel guides to help us make the decision. Such a delicious choice that I'm sure Kate's right about retirement. It is a cause for celebration. I just wish the academic ties weren't so hard to unbind, or that at least I could understand why I sometimes feel them so strongly.

Saturday / April 5

Sometimes I think that my difficulty in breaking free from this place is the result of having worked here for thirty-five years, almost my entire professional career, more than half of my entire lifetime. Surely the ties wouldn't bind so strongly had I been teaching here only ten or fifteen or even twenty years. But when I consider my recently retired colleagues, it seems to me that most of them have moved on much more easily, without any of the reluctance I've felt about giving up my office and moving out of the building.

Though I don't expect to shed any tears this May, it does seem as if I'm going through something that the self-help folks and counselors would call separation anxiety and grief—the trauma of transition. Parting, after all, is not such sweet sorrow. Still, my reaction seems more than a bit misplaced, especially because most of my present colleagues are so much younger than I and their scholarly interests so different from my own that I feel as if we have nothing to share, except the coincidence of being in the same academic department. And they evidently feel the same about me. Thirty years ago, the department was a much more collegial place, where people of all ages and interests visited with each other almost every day in the lounge, in the main office, and in offices throughout the building. So I can see how retirement back then might have been much more painful, except for the fact that people back then didn't have to leave their offices and the extended family of the department.

As the department has changed, I've mourned its changing, but now it's so different, so at odds with the community I once cherished, that I should be ready to move on. Besides, if I'm having this much trouble moving out of my office and the department, I wonder what it will be like when the time comes to move out of this beloved home that Kate and I have been living in the past twenty-seven years. A forbidding prospect that came to mind when I was talking on the phone this morning with Aunt Ada, and she was still fretting about having left her longtime apartment. And what will it be like when the time comes to leave this world altogether? Retirement, after all, is a preparation for other journeys to come, and if I can't adjust to this move, I'll never be able to accept the one that all of us at last are compelled to make.

Sunday / April 6

This morning at the supermarket I noticed my former colleague and fellow gardener Fred coming in the automatic entryway, so shrunken by age that I almost didn't recognize him. Hardly the dapper person I remember from his lavish retirement party some twelve years ago at the Memorial Union, overlooking the Iowa River. I can still see him back then, dressed in a suit and colorful tie, his face aglow with the warmth of the occasion—and deservedly, since he was there to receive the accolades not only of his colleagues but also of his former graduate students, who honored him by creating and funding a special academic award in his name. I also remember Fred's party, because it was my first public outing after my heart attack and bypass, an event so heady for me too that I was almost dizzy by the time Kate pulled me away just an hour after we arrived. And I hadn't even had a single glass of wine. Though Fred was seventy back then and I just fifty-three, I was still so weak from my month-long ordeal in the hospital that I felt as if our ages were reversed and I should be retiring rather than he. Just a couple of months later, Fred suffered a heart attack, which I thought he might not survive, given the reports of his condition that I heard from a nurse and former neighbor who was tending him in the intensive care unit. Ever since, I've felt a special connection to Fred, even though we've never had much to do with each other beyond our heart attacks and our gardens. But Fred's spectacular daylily garden alone would be enough to claim my admiration, with the hundreds of colorful hybrids it contains, some of them developed by Fred himself. Still, when I first saw him this morning I didn't want to catch his attention, because I didn't want to hear a voice or mind as diminished as his body seemed to be. But then he noticed me, quickly walked over to greet me, and without a moment's hesitation spoke up in the same lively voice I remember from years back—"I noticed in Dee's newsletter that you're retiring this spring." After confirming her announcement, I was about to ask Fred how he feels about retirement, but before I could get my question into words, he gave me his answer—"It's easy to get into that groove"—and just as quickly he was off to do his morning's shopping. Which left me thinking that if I can keep going as well as Fred, I might be just as groovy some twelve years from now.

But it was hard to be groovy today, given the extraordinary wind that blew in from the north, blowing out the power for three hours, and ravaging trees all over town, including our sixty-foot mulberry tree, which split down the center of its trunk, one-half standing, the other half lying on the grass in the corner of the backyard. Though it's always been a messy tree, whose fruit has never tasted quite as vivid as it looked, I've become so accustomed to its high arching branches, lightly shading the red raspberries below, that I'll miss it as I'd miss anyone who's lived on the borders of my life for almost thirty years. Kate says I should think about what kind of tree I'd like to plant in its place, except that I probably won't live long enough to see anything arching its branches high over the raspberry canes. Especially if I don't get myself into a better groove than I'm in right now—now that I'm just beginning to start work on our federal income taxes.

Monday / April 7

This afternoon I had a surprise visit from Dale, a former graduate student, as bright-eyed as when I first met him some fifteen years ago, especially when he discovered that I'm working on this journal and then scanned a few of the beginning entries. "That's just the way it was with my father. He wanted to keep his hand in too, wanted to keep his office at the university, wanted all the things you've been talking about." And his father managed to get everything he wanted without any trouble. Everything! So now I'm wondering why I can't work things out as favorably for myself. Is it something in me, this department, this building, or just an unfortunate combination of circumstances? It certainly wasn't this way when Fred retired. I can still remember his book-lined office overlooking the river just a floor below mine. But then again, I can also remember that Fred didn't use his office that much, so it was often occupied by a graduate teaching assistant or visiting faculty member. Which makes me wonder if I'll use an office enough to justify my having one, or whether like Lear I just want to retain as many of the trappings as possible. Kate says it's all tied up with my childhood, with my not wanting to let go of things after losing both of my parents and then moving around so often from one relative to the next. And I suppose she's right, given my pack-rat mentality and my compulsion to keep everything carefully controlled in my perfectly rectangular garden beds. It sure would be nice to get free of those childhood compulsions, especially after sixty years of inhabiting such a walled-in place. So maybe I should call up Dee and tell her to forget about the office—that I'll be moving out this May as scheduled. The only problem is that I can't imagine what I'll do with all the books and other stuff I've collected there, nor where I'll arrange to meet with colleagues and students. The old ways do indeed die hard.

Tuesday / April 8

Kate found an article this morning on the front page of the *Des Moines Register* announcing a contest for people in their sixties to write a short inspirational piece about some kind of adversity they've overcome. After reading the article and its sample list of adversities—crippling disease, loss of a loved one, loss of one's home—I could see that my upcoming retirement wouldn't be an appropriate subject. But I was less interested in the contest than in Kate's question about it: "I wonder why they're sponsoring it? This is the fourth year in a row. What do you suppose they want to get out of it?" I was wondering the same thing myself, until I noticed that the best submissions will be collected in a book and the proceeds from the sale of it go back to a foundation to support more of the same. A self-perpetuating enterprise devoted to the greater glory of the person in whose name the foundation exists. Maybe that's what I should do—work out a self-perpetuating enterprise to the greater glory of myself. Or is that what I'm already doing in this diary of mine?

The only problem at the moment is that I can't see anything glorious about the fact that it took me almost four hours today to write a page of comments on each of the two journal installments for this afternoon's workshop. Time was that I could have produced those commentaries in a couple of hours at most, but nowadays I find myself so weary from years of forcing myself to be attentive and tactful and constructive in my comments that I can hardly bring myself to write them any longer. Even on work as well written as Mitra's and Vanessa's stuff was today. By the time I was done with my comments and all my convenient distractions from working on them—like watering the seedlings, making fresh coffee, checking the stock market, touching up a few of my own journal entries—I could see that I'd clearly come to the end of the line and couldn't bring myself to do it anymore, not after this semester's over. Nor ever again. And then I knew with a certainty I've never felt before that however much I enjoy the liveliness and stimulation of classroom teaching, I'm no longer willing to make the detailed written comments that go hand in hand with this kind of teaching. Having reached that sad—and somewhat selfish—conclusion, I announced it bluntly to Kate, who didn't even try to weaken my resolve, for I think she could see there was no budging me this time.

So today will go down in the tablets of my memory as the day when I decided that I no longer had the wherewithal to be a teacher of writing. And as if to confirm that resolution, the workshop itself was an exhausting affair, largely because I felt obliged to point out some important but overlooked motifs in each of the manuscripts that were painful for Mitra and Vanessa to think about, though they were clearly grateful for my having done so. After the workshop, I stopped in to visit my colleague Hamilton, who's in his late fifties, to tell him about my resolution for the day, and he told me he's been coming to the same conclusion about himself. And no wonder, given his additional duties as editor of the *Iowa Review*.

The only good part of this day was the dinner we had of grilled sirloin, baked potatoes, spinach salad, and red wine. Diet be damned, I needed that meal. And the dark chocolate Easter egg to finish it off.

Wednesday / April 9

An afternoon at the office to follow up on yesterday's workshop, but Mitra and Vanessa called in to postpone their conferences, and no one else from the course stopped by, nor did Angela, Julia, or Mary, whose M.F.A. theses I'm directing. A quiet afternoon, exactly what I once longed for when I was still teaching full time and also directing the writing program. But the longer I sat there pecking away at my correspondence, the more I began to feel a bit uneasy with the solitude. It put me in mind of how the students drifted away after I stepped down as director of the program and Paul had taken over. Besieged one semester, abandoned the next. "They flee from me that sometime did me seek!" Only this time they're drifting away even before I've retired, so I wonder what it might be like six months or a year or two from now, when I'm not offering any courses or directing any dissertations or sitting on any thesis committees. What then? What if I have an office and no one comes to visit? And the telephone never rings? And the mail dwindles down to textbook ads, departmental memos, institutional newsletters, and the like? If a professor is in his office and no one comes to see him, does he shed any light? To be needed, to be sought after, to be of help, like a doctor on call, is a special pleasure, I now see, just when I'm on the verge of no longer being needed or wanted and therefore being helpless to offer my help to those who can use it. How strange that I now seem to crave the attention of students seeking my response to their work when I can hardly bear to produce any written comments on their work. Perhaps I shouldn't want to keep my office, since it will only serve to remind me that I have no reason for keeping it.

Thursday / April 10

How strange it is to be so preoccupied with something that you hardly notice anything else going on around you, even if it's happening in your own backyard. Like today, I was so hung up over the end of my teaching career, I didn't even pay homage to the end of the mulberry, which our tree man came to cut down right after lunch. When he showed up Kate said, "Don't you want to go out and say hello?" To which I responded, "Wouldn't it be more appropriate to go out and say goodbye?" Though I did go out, I didn't feel anything as I stood there, looking at it in neatly sawed-up sections. I thought instead about a prose piece by W. S. Merwin called "Unchopping a Tree," a sardonic set of directions for putting a tree together again after it's been chopped down. I also thought about writing a sardonic piece of my own, called "Unending a Career," but I couldn't imagine how to begin, so I turned my attention to finishing the taxes, a sure way to keep myself distracted for several hours.

I've always preferred to do the taxes myself, not only for the satisfaction of keeping my own books in order, but also to have a specific idea of what I've been doing each year and how things compare from one year to the next. The big news for last year is that I made more than ever before, thanks to my part-time salary, the interest on my TIAA account, royalties from textbooks, and the remaining part of the advance for the vegetable book. Given the extraordinary combination of circumstances, it's probably the first and last time that I'll ever feel rich enough to refinance the house for a new Jeep Grand Cherokee and a completely remodeled bathroom. It's also, I hope, the first and last time I ever have to pay Uncle Sam almost four thousand dollars in additional taxes. All of which had me thinking about another sardonic piece called "Unspending a Windfall."

Friday / April 11

On my way home from school this afternoon, I ran into my friend Wendy at the co-op, and she asked me how I was feeling about my upcoming retirement. I told her it was a mixed bag—one day up, the next day down, and sometimes a roller coaster from one hour or minute to the next. I think she must have been waiting for me to say something like that, for no sooner was I done with my manic-depressive account than she launched into a story about a friend of hers who's retiring this semester and speaks of it as "A kind of death," but then went to see a therapist who told her that "It's also an opportunity." Though Wendy didn't say exactly what the "opportunity" involved, she kept repeating those two completely different views of it, almost like a mantra—"It's a kind of death, but it's also an opportunity, a death but also an opportunity"—as if it were an archetypal story of death and rebirth, like the Phoenix riddle or the cycle of the seasons. I was thinking the same thing about the four inches of snow that fell today. It'll probably do in the aconites, crocus, squills, and other early spring flowering bulbs, but it'll also be a boon for anything that survives it, like the spinach I seeded outside a couple of weeks ago and the radishes I planted last week. So it'll be a trade-off of sorts. A death but also an opportunity.

Saturday / April 12

At Barbie's dinner party last night, I was still thinking about Wendy's mantra, for the fields were still covered with snow, all the way out to Barbie's hilltop retreat in the rolling countryside outside of Iowa City. So much snow, in fact, that Kate parked the Jeep out by the barn and we walked the rest of the way to her house. I didn't spot any of Barbie's horses, but I did see a corner of the pond she designed where the wild geese stop over on their way north and south, the pond that's ringed in summer with tall prairie grass and staked all year 'round with wood duck boxes. Just outside her doorway, I peeked in the window at the roomful of thirty-five homeless cats she's taken in during the past ten years or so that she's been living in the country since her husband passed away. All those sleek and well-fed creatures, each on its own chair or table or bookshelf, the whole group almost motionless, as in a diorama or an ancient

Egyptian tableau. And then in the house itself, I was surprised, as I always am, by the pack of well-groomed dogs that eagerly greeted me—outcasts like the cats until they found their way into the care of Barbie. Oh yes, there were other guests for dinner, a genial gathering of artists, writers, and academicians, riding our hobbyhorses back and forth across the evening. But it was Barbie's world, a haven for abused and abandoned animals, a wildlife refuge of sorts, complete with bluebird and kestrel boxes, that held me in thrall. And Barbie herself—a diminutive seventy-year-old once quite active in the life of Iowa City and the Democratic Party and the League of Women Voters but now retired to the countryside, fiercely standing her ground against all hunters, conserving a place for herself, her creatures, and all the other wild things that thrive on her land. A death but also an opportunity.

Sunday / April 13

"Lifestyles in Retirement," an illustrated booklet from TIAA-CREF, arrived in the mail a few days ago, together with the forms I have to fill out in order to start receiving my annuity payments. Just the thing I needed this morning to distract me a bit from the troubles of transition, also from the hassle of figuring out my state income taxes. Given the collage on the cover, I could see that it would sweeten my imagination: a gothic-style brick and stone building in the upper right-hand corner, with a casually dressed, gray-haired, suntanned couple hand in hand on the well-manicured grounds in front, their lower limbs overlaid with an antique globe in the lower right-hand corner, focused on England and the European continent; a white frame colonial house pictured to the left of the globe; a few pieces of foreign currency in the lower left-hand corner, the one on top from Japan; a library with a grand piano directly above the currency, the upper portion of the bookshelves merging with the image of a serene lake in the upper left-hand corner, a dock jutting out from shore on the left and oak trees turning red on the right. A rising graph in the center of the collage is superimposed on the lake, the library, the house, and the gothic edifice, as if to suggest the availability of all lifestyles in the world of TIAA-CREF. Though our campus isn't gothic, Kate's hair isn't gray, our house isn't colonial, and it doesn't contain a grand piano or a globe, I could still connect with the collage, having always wished for a serene little lake of my own, where I might dangle my legs over a dock, waiting for the fish to rise at sunset.

Inside the booklet, I could also connect with some of the ways that a recently surveyed group of TIAA retirees have been spending their free time on travel, hobbies, physical recreation, volunteer work, new careers, consulting, part-time or even full-time jobs. For a few minutes, it made me feel much better about retirement, as if it weren't a stage in the journey toward death but a world of opportunities for life. A time of "refirement," according to the brochure, rather than retirement, of a "second middle age" rather than aging and decline. And in one sense, I could hardly disagree, given all the writing, gardening, and traveling I've been able to do just on phased-in retirement. But the excerpted testimony was so uniformly glowing that it seemed as if almost all the dark edges and unpleasant sides of golden pond had been carefully whited out, except where they crept in around the edges, with vague references to how "some people may find that the adjustments require inner strength and are occasions for personal growth." It must be that I'm one of those people—I've always been one of the uncomfortable minority. I just hope the personal growth takes place sooner rather than later. In the meantime, I turned to Doris Grumbach's *Coming into the End Zone*, a compelling work that I taught in the journal course last fall, a yearlong memoir occasioned by her seventieth birthday, and there in the introduction I found a more bracing spiritual companion:

Seventy seems disastrous, so without redeeming moments that, in despair, I am taking notes, hoping to find in the recording process a positive value to living so long, some glory to survival, even vainglory if true glory is impossible.

Monday / April 14

A few months before my heart attack, my family practice doctor told me that "the secret of aging is to stay flexible." Though her specialty was gerontology, I can't remember why she gave me that bit of advice back then, since I was only fifty-three, nor can I even remember what had taken me to her office—a stiff knee, an aching back, or a bad case of the jitters. But her advice sounded like a bromide that might come in handy someday, though I never imagined I'd have occasion to use it just a few months later, when my cardiologist presented me with the life and death options of whether or not to have a triple bypass. My preference was to be back in the classroom, teaching the course in prose style that seemed so important I could hardly imagine myself entrusting it to someone else. But a little voice inside me said, "Stay flexible, stay flexible," and before I knew it I was repeating that command as if it were a mantra that would save my life. The only problem was that my family practice doctor came to visit me a few days before the operation and told me that she "couldn't possibly imagine having to go through such a dreadful procedure." I wanted just then to remind her of the advice she'd given me a few months back, but I kept my mouth shut and kept repeating my mantra all the time she was sitting at the foot of my bed in her long blue overcoat with a compassionate look on her face, as if she had come to visit me for the last time.

I never did see her again, since I decided that she was probably not to be trusted if she couldn't follow her own advice. But her words have come back to me every now and then, as they did this noon, when I walked out into the backyard and noticed that the spring flowers had survived the snowstorm by staying flexible, by the natural expedience of bending rather than breaking, by arching their necks rather than losing their heads. The spectacle of all those flowers still in bloom excited me so much that I wanted to tell everyone the good news of how they'd survived. I wanted to spread my mantra far and wide, or share it at least with the people who were on my mind today. Like my colleague Miriam, who e-mailed me this morning from England, all adither about the conflicting suggestions of the reviewers for the fourth edition of our collaborative drama anthology. And my colleague Carol, who told me this morning that "writing commentaries on student papers is like giving blood" and that she feels "anemic" from having done it for so long. And Kate with whom I've been debating the pros and cons of a side trip to Vancouver during our vacation in the Canadian Rockies. I wanted to tell all of them and Doris Grumbach too. And all the pepper seedlings that I transplanted this morning. "Stay flexible." But then it occurred to me that the peppers didn't need to hear it, and that none of those women would care to hear such advice from me. So I kept my mouth shut and repeated my mantra to myself, seeing as how I'm more in need of such wisdom than any of them are.

Tuesday / April 15

The only trouble with my mantra is that it doesn't give me the peace of mind I'd like to have, especially when I feel moved to give someone a piece of my mind. Like this morning, when I sent an e-mail to Paul, answering his e-mail question of whether I'd be willing to have a prospective graduate student visit the workshop next week:

> Dear Paul—
> Of course she's welcome to sit in, but then again it seems passing strange to visit the class of someone who's not going to be teaching in the program anymore, and who's offering a

course on a kind of nonfiction writing that will probably not be taught in the near future (or perhaps ever again). Not a very reliable exposure to the program, but I'm happy as ever to be observed, especially as I go through my final gyrations. It will, at least, make good copy for TAKING RETIREMENT: A BEGINNER'S DIARY.

Paul evidently didn't sympathize with my sarcastic note, given his curtly dismissive reply:

> It was her request (and she knows the details), Carl, however passing strange. A good experience is a good experience, period. And I imagine she also wants a sense of our students in action.
>
> Thanks for the quick response.

That little note made me feel even more out of sorts, wondering why Paul hadn't excluded me from the request that he sent to others in the program, for he surely knew that I might be sensitive about the situation. But no sooner did I feel put out by his note than I began to feel embarrassed by my hypersensitive behavior. Probably I'd not have been so tetchy about Paul's reply had today's journal class not been so depleted by a few absences—justifiable absences that I knew about in advance, but enough to reduce the group to a mere handful of people. An unfortunate shrinkage, given the fact that we were discussing a substantially revised manuscript for the first time this semester—a manuscript in which Priscilla had evolved a powerful story of the complications in her new marriage as a way of bearing witness to the even more complicated circumstances of her blindness. Though the group was small, the discussion was so fruitful that at the end of class Mitra pulled me aside and told me, "This course and your comments are more valuable to me than anything else I've done here." Such lavish praise from the most demanding critic in the group made me think that at least a few students might regret my departure the next year or two. But my self-pitying reaction also made me realize that I haven't been making as much progress as I thought in this therapeutic journal of mine, especially when I remember my sarcastic e-mail to Paul. But perhaps my self-pity is just a result of today being the deadline for payment of the $3,900 that I owe the Internal Revenue Service.

Wednesday / April 16

Only one month before my contractual retirement date of May 16, and five weeks before everyone has to be out of the building for the summer remodeling and rewiring project, but I still haven't heard anything about the status of my office. So I decided to visit Dee's administrative assistant, Gayle, on the chance that she might know what's going on. Gayle was agreeable as usual, but she didn't have any idea of when the office question would be resolved. But she did have a memorandum from Staff Benefits, indicating that my "termination papers" need to be filed by the department "approximately three weeks prior to termination date," in order "to make sure" that I start receiving my "retirement income on time." It never occurred to me that I would be "terminated," so at first it seemed a bit chilling, as if I were looking at the papers to be filed prior to a legal execution. And I wasn't comforted by Staff Benefits' bureaucratic announcement, "It is our goal that this employee retire with the least amount of problems," as if to suggest that "problems" of some kind are almost certain to arise. Though I didn't want to sound unduly anxious, I couldn't resist the most obvious question of whether my termination papers had been filed. And Gayle assured me with a comforting smile that everything would be taken care of on time. "Not to worry." Not to worry, I told myself, though I couldn't help wondering what other papers might be passing back and forth between one office and another to assure that I "retire with the least amount of problems." I wonder what they'd think if they knew about all the problems I've been going through in my head and this diary.

But my problems seemed small-time a few minutes later when I walked down the hall to meet with Priscilla about the journal of her recent marriage to a person she met on the Internet. Priscilla as usual took me by surprise, telling me how excited she was by yesterday's discussion of her work, a discussion that yielded her ten pages of notes. I'm still amazed at her ability to take such detailed notes, even though I know how adept she is with her portable computer and how speedy she evidently was as a secretary before the onset of her blindness. But then again, I'm still amazed at the vividly detailed descriptions she's able to produce of her day-to-day experience—so specific, so richly envisioned that I can always follow her activities in my mind's eye, as if I were living through them myself. Most of all, I'm impressed by her prickly and irrepressible good humor, as if self-pity were no longer part of her vocabulary, as it had been when I first encountered her a few years ago in an undergraduate honors seminar on the essay. Not to worry, I thought, after meeting with Priscilla. The only thing you have to fear is fear itself. And self-pity.

Thursday / April 17

Some days are so filled with good vibes that I don't need a mantra, a maxim, an epigram, or any other kind of pithy saying to buoy me up or point me on my way, nor do I need a diary to make sense of where I've been. On days such as this, it seems as if all my problems are in the past, or at least that the present is so trouble-free that the future looks as promising as the yellow brick road to Oz. I felt such a day might lie ahead when I checked the garden this morning and discovered that the radishes I seeded in a couple of weeks ago had begun to break ground. A harbinger of good things to come. And the rest of the morning kept their promise, thanks to a productive meeting with Donna, my new textbook editor at St. Martin's, come visiting from New York. So buoyant and eager and unabashedly proud of her promotion from traveler to editor that I momentarily wished I were as youthful as she, just setting forth on my own journey. But the minute she asked me to tell her "the story of *Fields* and how this new edition might be marketed," my wish gave way to gratitude for being exactly where I am, especially when I realized how intimidating it must be to work for St. Martin's now that it's been bought out by a publishing conglomerate. I'd hate to be in Donna's shoes if her book list doesn't meet the corporate expectations. No wonder she seemed a bit frantic around the edges. Still, it was a pleasure to tell her the story of *Fields,* all the way back to its first edition in the early 1980s, and to imagine ways of promoting the new edition that just a few weeks ago had seemed so tedious I could hardly bring myself to work on it. Donna was so eager to promote it that she proposed to stimulate the interest of the marketing staff by giving all of them—all seventy-five of them!—copies of *My Vegetable Love.* In the world of publishing, it seems, linkage is all, even if it involves a gardening journal and a college textbook.

This afternoon with Kate, when we were mapping our jaunt to the Canadian Rockies, I didn't have to do any promotional routines to rouse her interest in a few side trips. "This is it," she tells me whenever I fret about the costs of travel. I think she's never gotten over her father's death when he was only fifty-six (just a year older than Kate is right now), before her parents had a chance to enjoy the future they'd planned for themselves. Given the plans that Kate and I discussed this afternoon, it looks like we'll not only be driving to the Canadian Rockies in our Jeep Grand Cherokee and then taking the Rocky Mountain Railtour to Vancouver for a three- or four-day visit, but we'll also be hopping a ferry to Victoria Island for another side visit of three or four days. And why not, since we don't have to worry about being back for the fall semester? At this rate, before the week is out we might add a boat trip to Alaska, a bobsled to the Yukon, and an icebreaker to the North Pole. And why not? This is it. Isn't it?

Friday / April 18

If yesterday was a pleasurable day, then why not this one too? After all, how could I complain about a leisurely morning at the computer, writing a few e-mails, followed by Kate's refreshing lunch of lox, sliced tomatoes, sliced sweet onions, goat cheese, capers, fresh baked rye bread, marinated artichokes, and calamata olives? A meal made all the more piquant by a chilled Pilsner Urquel and a report from Kate that the nursery intends to plant my swamp white oak before the end of April. And how could I complain about an even more pleasant afternoon checking over a few corrected pages for the winter book and then delivering them to the press, where I finally saw the finished artwork for the cover. An evocative woodcut of an indoor/outdoor scene, depicting a writer's desk cluttered with flowering plants, seed catalogs, and a journal in the foreground, with a window in the background, looking out upon a bare-branched tree, a solitary bird, and a snow-flaked sky. A wintry scene perfectly suited to the book, for Claudia, the artist, based it on a view of our yard from the attic study where I wrote most of the journal. All things considered, I should have been even more buoyant today than yesterday.

Yet something about the day left me feeling a bit depressed. At first I thought it might be a result of all the sweet things that have come my way the past two days. A sugary high followed by an all too sugary low. But the more I thought about it, the more troubled I was by how little I've done the past two days. Nothing but a couple of journal entries and a few e-mails to show for myself. And it wasn't any better in the garden, where I couldn't bring myself to do much more in late afternoon than trim the onion plants and heel them into the compost heap, rather than go to the trouble of working up a few rows of soil and planting them. Such a wasted day, it made me wonder if I'll be frittering things away like this when retirement comes around. No wonder Kate has sometimes been worried about me going to seed. I was worrying about the same thing earlier this morning, when I couldn't find my wristwatch and then realized that I haven't been wearing it the past few weeks, though I used to wear it every day. Maybe I've been giving in to retirement far more than I'd realized, far more than is good for me, or Kate, or any of the books I hope to finish over the next few years. But then again, I wonder why I should feel driven to keep working on a book or garden project or anything else for that matter, when it's just that kind of compulsive behavior that got me into heart trouble in the first place. Why can't I just get up in the morning and travel calmly through the day without a care in the world—without my temples pounding, without a single moment of self-induced stress—as if I'd gone fishing. And not to catch any fish but just to get my line wet. I mean, what's retirement for, if it doesn't allow one the leisure to retire, to withdraw to the lake of one's dreams? Come to think of it, what *is* retirement for? How strange that I've been keeping this diary for two months, and I've never considered what retirement is for, or what I really want to do with the time that is left. I've been so hung up about keeping my hand in and keeping my office that I haven't kept my eye on the object. This is it, and I don't even know what to do with it.

Saturday / April 19

Sometimes I think that if I knew what to do with my life, I wouldn't be spending most of my Saturday mornings with a feather duster and a vacuum cleaner in hand. I'd be off instead at a nearby lake with a rod and reel in my hands. My Saturday housecleaning routine started some twenty years ago, when Kate was heavily involved in playwriting, and I was heavily involved in feeling guilty about how much of her time she'd given to housework in the years when we were first married and I was trying to make a go of my career. Nowadays, I sometimes feel that I've balanced the score, but she still does most of the laundry, all of the ironing, much of the shopping, and most of the meal planning, so there's no chance of my catching up—even though I do the dishes and most of the dinnertime cooking—for she prepares most of the special holiday meals and dinner parties. Sometimes I think we should just hire someone to do the weekly housecleaning, until Kate reminds me of how much trouble it is just to get the place ready for a housecleaner. So I've just kept on doing it myself, sometimes feeling like a martyr, sometimes like a liberated male, especially after I've been on my hands and knees, washing and waxing the kitchen floor. But always feeling delighted at how much better the place looks when I'm done with my Saturday housework. Preserve the surface and you preserve everything, as they used to say Down East, when it was time to repaint the lobster boats. I just wish that someone had come up with as simple and reassuring a maxim for retirement.

When I was dusting the living room furniture this morning, I pondered some of the Preacher's words from Ecclesiastes, thinking that I probably couldn't find a better maxim for retirement than his declaration, "To everything there is a season, and a time to every purpose under the heaven." A time to work and a time to retire, I thought to myself. The only problem is that I couldn't possibly imagine how his words might apply to my housecleaning, given my discomfort with it at all times and seasons of the year. Especially on a day so beguiling as this one—the air so mild, the sky so picturesque with puff clouds, that it seemed like a time to be outside rather than a time to be inside. So this afternoon I retired to the garden where it was a blessing to be on my hands and knees, harvesting some of the perennial Egyptian onions and transplanting some of the red hamburger onions. "There's a time to plant and a time to pluck up that which is planted," but today, in defiance of the Preacher, those times converged for me on a single afternoon. Which made me wonder if the same might be true of other things in my life, especially when people tell me that I seem to be working as much in semi-retirement as I did when I was fully employed. Which made me think that perhaps the times and seasons of my life are less distinct and separate than I once thought they were. So whatever comes of my life will only be revealed in the fullness of time, preferably when I'm on my knees in the garden.

Sunday / April 20

Last night in bed I started reading the final draft of Dan's doctoral thesis—a full-length memoir of his first marriage and divorce that I finished reading this afternoon. An artful and lively narrative, filled with resonant reflections, that left me with a sense of wonder at Dan's ability to keep living with a failed marriage five or six years after it ended—reliving it daily in his writing—even after he'd married Maura, whom he met here in Iowa City. How different from my own situation after being divorced some thirty-three years ago, when my friends and a therapist told me that the best thing I could do for my sanity was to put my former marriage behind me. So I studied forgetfulness, while Dan has striven to remember. There's a time and a place for everything under the heaven, but who can say which of us has found the answer to such a conundrum. Perhaps I should be forgetting and remembering, looking forward and looking back, as Janus-faced as the sign of Gemini that marks my birth. So it seems altogether fitting that this afternoon, Kate and I spent some time looking forward to our Canadian trip. The only problem is that the more time we spent pondering our travel plans, the more apparent it became that we couldn't include a side trip to Victoria Island without dropping or reducing some other portion of the trip, given the time we'd allotted to all the other places along the way. There's a time and place for everything, and Victoria Island seemed to fit some other trip, like a journey along the western coast of Canada. Whereas a three-day visit to our friend Trudy, who lives in Dubois, Wyoming and who called this afternoon to confirm our arrangements, seems exactly right for a venture in the Rocky Mountains.

Then as if to put a period to all these ventures in time and space,

Kate came home from the supermarket late this afternoon with a dent in the fender of the new Jeep, thanks to an errant grocery cart—misplaced in the parking lot rather than in the store. The damage was evidently done by a hit-and-run cart-pusher, though neither Kate nor the manager of the store could figure out whether the culprit was on foot or in a car. But one thing is clear—something was definitely in the wrong place at the wrong time.

Monday / April 21

This morning I stopped at the supermarket, where Gary, the manager, took a snapshot of the damaged fender for his insurance company, apologized profusely for the accident, though it was certainly no fault of his, and assured me that his company would pay the repair costs. Then I went to the auto–body shop for an estimate and discovered it would be $335 just to fix a little dimple in the fender. Then back to Gary with a copy of the estimate and profuse apologies from him once again, this time because of the message from headquarters that I'll have to get another estimate and wait for company approval before I can get the fender repaired. At this rate, I'll probably be retired and packing for our Canadian trip before the dent is removed.

By comparison to this morning's runaround, this afternoon's visit to the Social Security office—my first ever to Franklin Delano Roosevelt's fabled creation—was a straight shot from beginning to end. And not just because my Social Security agent, Fran, was quite helpful in walking me through the rules and regulations of Social Security and Medicare, but also because she was very efficient in compiling my case history and in making sure that I get everything I'm entitled to—even to the point of informing me that the agency will make payments to my former wife, Meredith, if she is unemployed and not receiving payments from her own Social Security account. I must have looked somewhat concerned when Fran made that surprising announcement, for she quickly assured me that "payments to your former wife won't diminish anything that you're entitled to receive." I wasn't worried, just pleasantly surprised at the agency's spacious commitment to social security and Fran's eagerness to locate Meredith's file, even after my assurance that Meredith had retired last year and is probably receiving payments from her own account. The only puzzler was the necessity for me to prove my American citizenship at this late date by providing Fran with a copy of my birth certificate.

I also wondered when Fran intends to retire, and she told me without hesitation, "In a couple of years, when I'm fifty-five, but not before, otherwise I lose a bunch of attractive benefits." It didn't sound as if Fran would be shedding any tears over retirement. Yet it also seemed that she still enjoys the various parts of her job, from counseling retirees like me to tracking down former spouses like Meredith, whose file she managed to procure by the end of our visit, when she asked me, "Is her middle name Helen?" As I nodded yes, she looked up at me from her computer screen with the satisfied smile of a masterful government worker, capable of finding any file in the entire population of Americans, living or dead, employed or retired, at home or abroad—and finding it while carrying on a detailed interview. I thanked her for explaining everything so clearly and told her how impressed I was by the striking difference between her agency and the Internal Revenue Service, to which she quickly replied with a twinkle in her eye, "They do leave something to be desired, don't they?" And then I was on my way, pleasantly surprised at how much I'll be getting each month, each year for the rest of my life—so much compared to what I put in that it's no wonder the well is in danger of running dry.

Tuesday / April 22

The cherry tomato plants I started in February are now so big that I transplanted them into larger containers this morning and gave them a few hours of fresh air on the terrace, to help them get ready for the big clay pots where they'll spend the rest of the spring and summer. If only my pre-retirement routine were as simple as transplanting and acclimating a tomato plant, I'd be more than ready to spend the rest of my life in the backyard, given the five years I've had to phase out of life in the academy. But "phasing out," I've come to realize, is a more complicated process than that easygoing verb makes it sound, particularly for a sensitive plant like me. So responsive to everything that my leaves fold up at the slightest touch. Like this morning, when I was reading Jean's daybook about her mother's memory loss, I couldn't help wondering whether such a grim prospect might be in store for me, especially when I thought of how many people I've known or heard about who've been done in by it. The loss of one's memory, the repository of one's existence, one's sense of self, seems like a living death, a more dreadful demise than death itself.

No wonder I wasn't looking forward to this afternoon's workshop. One of the last three classes I'll probably ever teach here or anywhere else, and I'm confronted with an unsettling batch of entries about time and change in the life of an aging woman and her daughter. So disturbing that I was able to comment on them in detail without having Jean's manuscript in front of me, since I'd loaned my copy of it to our visitor, Gina. For the occasion, at least, my memory was intact. And my analytical powers too, given Vanessa's generous comments on the way out of class. Hearing such lavish praise was enough to buoy me up, come what may, and also to remind me how much we all need affirmation, no matter how long we live or what we happen to be doing.

Speaking of affirmation and what it can do for one, this evening's annual meeting of the Johnson County Heritage Trust featured a surprise award to Kate, who was singled out for the Trust's annual "Conservation Award" in recognition of her work for the Heritage Trees project. An award that included not only a certificate of recognition, but also a beautifully framed color photograph of sumacs against maples, both turning color in late fall. A powerful emblem of change that moved Kate to write a poem about the dizzying transformations of fall. And my leaves folded up the minute I read it.

Wednesday / April 23

Last night at the Heritage Trust meeting, the first person I encountered was Jix, retired just a year ago, for whom I wrote and delivered a piece celebrating the generosity of his professional career. A career I felt had not been properly appreciated in recent years, in light of the harsh judgments that some people had made of his last term as department chair. And he in turn had evidently wanted to return the favor by writing a piece for my retirement, only to learn after having finished it that I'd refused the usual ceremonies. "They told me you didn't want to be buried yet, and I heartily agree with your decision, but I'd already written this piece, so you can read it at your leisure." A strange moment when he handed me the envelope—my colleague and friend of thirty-five years—a moment made even more strange when my colleague Alan, who was standing nearby, reproved me for my refusal of a retirement ceremony. "Do you realize that what you're doing will fragment the institutional history and the departmental community even more than they already are?" I couldn't deny Alan's point, so I didn't even try. But there was something about his remarks that made me want to give him a sharp retort, though I didn't know why until I was out in the garden planting shell peas this morning and remembered that Alan hadn't attended the ceremony last year when I delivered my piece in honor of Jix. Maybe he had some other professional obligation, or perhaps he'd just forgotten, but the small turnout of colleagues last year definitely influenced my own decision to refuse such an affair this year.

Such vanity! And worse still when I read Jix's piece today. Though I found it a very generous celebration of my teaching and professional service that only he is old enough to know about (and value), I couldn't help noticing that he almost completely ignored all the writing I've done the past ten years. A puzzling oversight, since for me this has been the most creative period of my career. I'm embarrassed to admit such self-serving thoughts, yet I'm also relieved that he didn't get to tell his version of my story. Most of all, I wish I were not given to such unpleasant thoughts and feelings. But perhaps they're just a byproduct of the retirement bug, whose venom sometimes fills me with such a swollen sense of myself that nothing can satisfy me, except to stop pondering it, if such a thing is possible.

Thursday / April 24

I've been spending an hour or two each day the past several days making final arrangements for our visiting nonfiction writer, Adam—putting notices in the mailboxes and posters in the hall, ordering refreshments to follow the reading, writing an introduction of Adam, and so on—all of which I agreed to do, since I invited him to come. So many little details to make sure his visit goes smoothly today and tomorrow that I'm remembering once again how time-consuming it was to direct the program without a secretary or graduate assistant. Sometimes, in fact, I feel like a chump for having done it so long without a reduced teaching load, such as Paul has gotten. "Nobody gives you nothing," as Sugar Ray once observed, especially not the administrative powers that be. Whenever I contemplate that truth, I don't have any qualms about retirement. In fact, I wonder why I waited so long to get out. Perhaps I should keep that thought in mind as a constant source of protection, a vaccine of sorts, against the onset of nostalgia about the end of my career at the university.

Come to think of it, maybe everyone who retires needs to harbor a grudge of some kind against their former employer, in order to cope with the severance of such a long-term relationship. A divorce of sorts. Maybe that's why my former medical school colleague Janusz was grousing at lunch today about how he'd been "forced to retire" when he turned seventy, "forced to give up everything I do." Seven years later, and Janusz is still chafing, though I couldn't understand why he spoke of his retirement as the relinquishment of "everything," especially when he was called away from the table for an international conference call, an emblem of his distinguished surgical career. But when Janusz was away from the table, Adam shed some light on the subject by telling me that retirement for Janusz meant the end of his active career as a surgeon, which was the most important activity in his life. I certainly can't say that teaching holds such a preeminent value for me. Indeed, when Janusz came back to the table and told me, "You still have your writing," he reminded me that I had chosen to retire not only because I had burned out on student writing, but also because I wanted to work on my own writing. An important reminder that I need to keep more prominently in mind than any grievance I might have against the university for the terms of my prior employment.

When I introduced Adam at his reading this evening, I didn't allow myself to indulge the faint sense of nostalgia that I was feeling just then at the thought that I had made the final introduction of my academic career. Instead I secretly took pleasure in the thought that I was on the verge of having the freedom to write that has sustained Adam throughout his entire career. This is it, and I definitely know one of the most important things that I want to do with it. Writing, after all, is a supreme way of being in the world, a way of coming to terms with experience, a way of engaging others by putting my thoughts and feelings on the line, no matter where I might be, in the office, at home, or on the road.

Friday / April 25

A busy but pleasurable day beginning with Adam's essay workshop, which I enjoyed not only because of his journalistic take on things, but also because I was free to witness the discussion of student essays, rather than lead it or even take part in it. Then an hour in the office catching up with three days of unanswered e-mail, in the midst of which Kate called to tell me, "The nursery is going to plant your retirement tree sometime today. Where do you want it planted—in the back of the park by the new play equipment or in the front corner where you can see it from the kitchen window?" How could I resist the satisfaction of seeing my retirement tree whenever I'm cooking or doing the dishes? Then a long, pleasant lunch with Adam, talking about the world of publishing and literary nonfiction and our future book projects. Followed by Adam's thoughtful talk about varieties of nonfiction writing, which led to such a provocative discussion that it drew me into the give-and-take, and helped me to see that what I crave, after all, is not the opportunity to keep teaching, so much as occasions like this, wherever I might find them, that will keep me mentally stimulated—on my toes. And then I walked home by way of the park, to see my newly planted retirement tree, standing at the corner, just where I hoped it would be, as erect and sprightly as I was feeling just then after the session with Adam.

Saturday / April 26

At Janusz's dinner party last night, several people asked me what I plan to do during retirement. A question that I've come to realize is occasioned not only by a natural curiosity about my life, but also perhaps by the anxiety of some people who are still working full-time that the end of employment may create a vacuum in their lives that they cannot easily fill—that time may lie heavy on their hands. God forbid that anyone should have time for contemplation! When I tell them about my plans for writing, gardening, traveling, and reading, I can sometimes see the worry lines disappearing from their faces as I fill up my future days with so many things to do that I'll be busier in retirement than when I was working full time. No time for swinging in a hammock or casting my line in a nearby lake. Or even for conferring with former colleagues and students.

But last night the conversation took a different turn when I was talking to Mike, a university administrator, telling him about this journal and how it arose out of my dismay at the prospect of losing my office, my teaching, my contact with colleagues and students, and so on. He claimed to be "intensely concerned" about my situation and the need of the university "to be more creative in making use of its retired faculty." But his intense concern sounded a bit like the pious sympathy I've sometimes heard from administrators when they talk about a problem for which they have no ready solutions. I certainly wasn't comforted much by Mike's concern with "the waste of professional talent," since it seemed to suggest a commodification of folks like me, rather than an interest in our needs and how such an interest might naturally serve the well-being of the entire university community. I was remembering how the elders were always nearby, or right next door, or just down the hall, when I was growing up in Cleveland—how they were always cared for and always eager to give a hand, a memory, or a bit of wisdom—often reaching back to another century and another country. A sentimental analogy, I realize, but an emblem of a time when universities were more like extended families than international corporations, and retired faculty could still be found in their offices, reading and writing—and ready as always to talk with colleagues and students. A time when no one needed to be "more creative" about how to deal with retired faculty, and when retiring faculty didn't need to keep diaries like this to envision the rest of their lives.

Actually, the rest of my life was less of a problem today than usual, since I was so exhausted from Adam's visit that it was all I could do just to water the onions I planted last week, pray for rain, call Aunt Ada to find out how she likes her new hearing aids, write this irritable little entry, and get myself ready for dining out with Kate's friend Glenda, who's visiting for a few days from California.

Sunday / April 27

Another day of rest, nothing more demanding than the breakfast omelets I whipped up for Glenda and Kate, with fresh chives from the herb bed and grated asiago cheese, while I had my usual bowl of shredded wheat, decked out with fresh strawberries, and an English muffin with Kate's homemade tangelo marmalade. Comfort food all around.

Also comforting was an e-mail that I received from Trish, an author and friend who lives in St. Paul and teaches at the University of Minnesota.

> I realize you are now very close to the end of your last official semester. I hope it's feeling good and not disorienting. The journal sounds like a wise way to make the transition. I, of course, spent my '20s and early '30s in a kind of strange hippie-pensioner mode. I had jobs, but not a career, the way a university job gives you that professional sense. I loved being a poor writer actually! And I still feel weird having all the tasks and commitments of a "real job." So I think I'll take to retirement—from academia, not from writing of course!— very easily when it's my turn.

In the process of reading her thoughtful note, it gradually occurred to me that many of my hang-ups about retiring are probably just the result of having been trained to be a professor, whereas Trish's first commitment has always been to her writing. The thought of her being scripted so differently, though we're both academicians and writers, also made me realize that I've obviously been shaped by the patterns of an earlier era, when professors stayed on not only because there was more office space to house them, but also because most of them could hardly afford to do anything else. Now, by contrast, most academicians have such ample retirement funds that their options are as richly varied as the images on the cover of TIAA-CREF's retirement brochure. Given the lucre to roam with, why should I want to maintain an office in the department? Indeed, if I were forced to choose between my office and my retirement annuity, I'd be on my way without a moment's hesitation. I realize, of course, that my hypothetical choice might at first seem outlandish, yet it does reflect the altered conditions that now prevail for many of my retired colleagues and me. A trade-off has been made. A sense of community and an attachment to place have been replaced by a sense of independence and an attraction to a world of different places. So in a very real sense, my nostalgic ruminations of yesterday are beside the point, as is Mike's concern with "the waste of professional talent."

My professional talent is now committed to this diary, and the tomato seedlings that I need to harden off by mid-May, and a villa in Tuscany that I thought about at dinner this evening when I was savoring Kate's marinated veal roast, her Tuscan beans, a salad of mixed greens, and a glass of Montepulciano.

Monday / April 28

This morning at the building, I encountered my colleague David, who's also retiring this spring. Though our offices have been side by side the past twenty-five years, I've rarely seen David on campus, since he only comes in to teach his courses, meet with a few students, and attend department meetings. Otherwise he works at home. So I was interested in catching up on his plans for the future, especially since I wondered whether he might retire to a place in Florida where he's been vacationing the past several years. "We're thinking about it. Also thinking about selling our present home and buying a smaller one near Iowa City. But of course you're not leaving. You love it here, don't you?" There was a smile on his face when he asked me that question, a smile so marked by his well-known air of condescension that I could hardly ignore it. David was reminding me of his eastern seaboard heritage on the coast of Massachusetts and my midwestern background in Cleveland—also his undergraduate education at Harvard compared to mine at Michigan. But this morning I was surprised by David's unvarnished assertion that I "love it here," for no sooner had he spoken than I realized that I could not deny the fact that I do love it here in Iowa City. More than any other place I've lived or worked—so I've come to think of it as home and think of myself as an Iowan rather than an Ohioan. No matter how much I may yearn for a villa in Tuscany or a beach house on Kauai, the place of my dreams is here where I found the home that I longed for during all the years of my childhood wanderings from one relative's house to another. Perhaps that's why I've been having such nostalgic feelings whenever I think about this being my last semester, my last course, my last this, or my last that. The university, it seems, has been a home of sorts that gave me the opportunity to find my one true home with Kate, here in this old brick house where we've been living together the past twenty-seven years.

What a load of emotional baggage to lay on the subject of retirement! But at least it helps me to understand some of the emotional ups and downs I've been going through the past few months. And for that I'm grateful to David for his patronizing remark and its reminder that knowledge sometimes arrives in the most unlikely ways.

Tuesday / April 29

Dan turned up early this morning to rake the lawn, while I swept up the terrace. A spring cleaning of sorts and a parting of sorts too, since today might be one of the last times he'll be helping me in the

backyard as he has during the past five or six years he's been studying here at Iowa. So while putting the yard in order, we also tried to
put our lives in order, for we've come to know each other so well
over the past several years that Dan feels somewhat like another son
of mine (in fact, he's almost the same age as my son, Marshall). The
upcoming defense of his thesis, the memoir of his first marriage,
naturally led us to talk a bit about how differently each of us handled
our divorce, and then about retirement as another sort of divorce,
and the way his father handled retirement from the military by finding a similarly regimented life in community service groups, like
the Knights of Columbus and the Ancient Order of the Hiber-
nium. I wondered at that moment what my unregimented life at the
university might lead to in retirement—disorder and early chaos,
perhaps?

But Dan put an end to my musings when he asked me, "Have you
made any special plans for your last class?" I haven't made any such
plans, not wanting to lay a heavy trip on the students or on myself.
And this afternoon's meeting of the workshop, the next to the last
class I'll ever teach here, also had me thinking that it's probably a
good thing I haven't, since only four of the eight people in the course
were present when I first showed up in class. Even Vanessa, whose
journal was up for discussion, wasn't among the four on hand. Her
car had broken down on the way to class, and the others, as it turned
out, were absent for equally legitimate reasons. Family crises of one
sort or another. Still, I'm beginning to feel as if I'm living through
something like *Ten Little Indians,* and by next week's class, the last
of my career, there might be none of us around to take part in the
discussion.

Wednesday / April 30

As if yesterday's workshop weren't ominous enough, today was
fraught with bad omens from start to finish. It started with my real-

ization that the state taxes are due in the mail by midnight. So I spent the morning with my calculator in hand and discovered that I owe the state another $900. On top of the $3,900 extra that I recently paid to the feds, it's more incentive to keep working on my textbooks. At this rate, retirement will keep me busy just keeping up with the taxes.

On the other hand, Dan's thesis defense this afternoon led to such a stimulating discussion of all the ways it might be revised for publication that again I thought about the appeal of staying on as an editorial consultant. Yet the final episode of Dan's memoir, in which he takes his new wife to meet her predecessor, left me feeling so disturbed at his inability to let go of his former marriage that I suddenly came to feel quite upset by my own inability to make a clean break with the department. Then at last I decided that I should *not* try to stay on as a consultant to the nonfiction program. *Not* try to keep advising students about their M.F.A. theses and publishing opportunities. *Not* try to keep an office in the building. But start a new professional life, as a lone ranger, free of any prior obligations or encumbrances.

On my walk home, I realized that the weather had gradually turned so windy and rainy and cold it seemed as if we're heading back to March rather than being on the verge of May. But Kate had made such a tasty mango salsa to go with the fresh halibut steak that one bite of it was enough to make me feel as if I'd been transported to Hawaii and the mid-Pacific cuisine we both thrive on. An illusion that lasted until I got up to clear the table, looked outside, and noticed that the storm had ripped off the top half of our hundred-year-old pear tree and thrown its blossom-laden head on the wet ground. When Kate beheld the spectacle, her reaction was so disturbing that it left me shaking my own head—"That's it," she declared. "It'll have to come down. But there's no time to talk about it now." No time to talk, for we had to attend a meeting at the Civic Center, but I couldn't help feeling just then that the storm had brought me as powerful a message as I've ever received, that it's time to make a clean break with the past, as clean and sharp a break as the head of the pear tree from its former self.

Thursday / May 1

Our tree surgeon, Leon, cleared away the decapitated segment of the pear tree this morning, examined its trunk, and told us, "It's still got a few years left in it." I was so elated by his prognosis that I felt like bounding around the yard to celebrate its reprieve. Especially on so brisk and vivid a spring day as this. But no sooner did I bring Kate over to see Leon's clean slanting cut at the top of the tree than he pointed to its reddish-brown center and told me in his most somber voice, "It's all rotted out in there. The life is just in the cambium, around the edges. But I think it might keep going a few more years, and even if we have to take more of the trunk off, there's enough left on the rest to give you some more pears and to look good here in the center of the yard." For a moment, I imagined that Leon was giving a lecture upon aging and retirement, somewhat like a Shakespearean character, "finding sermons in trees and books in running brooks." But then again, I've known Leon for so many years that I realize he's as reluctant as I am to take down a tree, even one as deformed as our apple, which is almost as aged as the pear. Even after I offered to have Leon cut down the apple as a compromise to Kate for keeping the pear, Leon would have none of it. Instead, he sawed off the dead part of the apple's trunk that he's been removing bit by bit the past several years, and then told us, "It's also got a few years left in it."

Leon's words were still on my mind late this afternoon when Kate was putting together a French stew, especially after I told her about my resolution to make a clean break from everything in the department, and she gave me one of her booster-style outbursts—"Just keep your mind on the decision you made five years ago when you decided to phase out because you were burning yourself out. It was the right thing then, and it's the right thing now. Just keep thinking about what it leaves you free to do from now on. Just keep thinking about that." She dished up a few other things as well, like her father's early death and my coronary specialist's somber projection some twelve years ago that a bypass would probably give me five more years. But nothing hit home like the haunting question she asked me—"How many good years do you think we have left?"

Friday / May 2

This morning, shortly after the defense of her M.F.A. thesis, Marilyn surprised me by offering to mount a letter-writing campaign from students who would like me to keep on teaching or at least keep an office in the building. I was still so absorbed by her evocative collection of essays about the three years she spent abroad, teaching English as a foreign language to Japanese schoolchildren, that I barely took in the significance of her offer before I politely refused it. I was thinking, in fact, of how beautifully she writes about the experience of longing and loneliness, attachment and estrangement, without my realizing that the difficulties she experienced in pulling herself away from Japan and returning to America must have made her sensitive to my own situation. Now, as I sit up here in the attic, thinking about Marilyn's offer, I also remember her asking me how I felt about retirement several months ago when Sara was in town being interviewed, and I recall having said something of my mixed feelings about giving up my office, my teaching, and so on. But I never imagined it would stick so firmly in Marilyn's mind, though I probably should have, given the extraordinary sensitivity to people that she's always revealed in her essays. I also should have known better, given the fact that Marilyn is evidently having some trouble pulling herself away from Iowa City, and has decided to stay around for another year or two in order to turn her thesis into a full-length book. The desire to stay on, it seems, is so widespread that it can deeply influence any of us at any time in our lives.

The desire to be missed is also quite potent, as I discovered this afternoon when I started to think about Marilyn's offer. I thought that I'd gotten over that hang-up a few months ago when I was beginning this journal, but it's evidently a yearning that can be reawakened at any time, just by someone pushing the right button. Come to think of it, I suppose that most professors probably crave whatever kind of half-life they might have in the memory of their students, much as most authors probably relish whatever attachments they arouse in the feelings of their readers, much as most people facing their demise probably yearn to be affectionately remembered by their loved ones and their dearest friends. So, after all, I had a sweet hour or two this afternoon, musing upon how I might be missed by such splendid people as Marilyn and some of the others in the program. And I must be sure to thank her for the gift, then put it behind me lest I become addicted to it.

Saturday / May 3

Today I spent the whole day reading *A Different Kind of Monday*, a novel "for young adults" by my friend Bill, who teaches writing at the University of Pittsburgh. From six in the morning till eight at night I read, except for a half-hour walk with Kate and Pip. I've never read such a novel before—they didn't exist when I was growing up, or if they did exist they didn't make their way into my hands. Come to think of it, I can only remember a few times during the past forty-five years when I've spent a day or two reading any kind of novel nonstop just for the fun of it. Like the time I was in graduate school and someone gave me Ian Fleming's *Casino Royale*, or when I was in the hospital recovering from my heart attack and enjoyed the company of Don DeLillo's *White Noise*. Otherwise, most of my novel reading has been compelled by course assignments that I've given or received—the peculiar curse of being an English major and an English professor and therefore someone whose reading has always been dictated primarily by academic and professional obligation rather than pleasure. No wonder I was so envious of Kate the summer she was laid up with a wrenched neck and passed her days reading Dickens to distract herself from the pain, gleefully announcing from time to time how enjoyable it was to be free of all the academic flimflam from her years as an English major and graduate student. My plate has always been so full with student essays and theses that I've had little spare time for novels. But today was a different kind of Saturday for me. No housecleaning, no student essays, nothing but the story of Mark, a high school student whose life is forever changed when he borrows a copy of *Great Expectations* from the school library and finds within it three one-hundred dollar bills, together with a note inviting him to keep the money but also to undertake a quest.

Though I was initially curious just to see what Bill might do with his adolescent hero, no sooner did I start reading than I was drawn in by the mysterious Dickens-like premise of the story—also because I've always been a sucker for quests, riddles, treasure hunts, and portentous journeys of any kind, especially ones that are filled with literary allusions and echoes. And Bill's novel has all the trappings, with a mysterious sequence of nine assignments that lures Mark into a treasure hunt and ultimately yields him a fortune far greater than he at first imagined. Aspiration is at the heart of it all, as it's always been at the heart of Bill's widely known writing assignments. Ardor and struggle, too. But also a lingering sense of mystery that spoke to me just then about my own life and the unknown fortune that might come my way through the workings of my own imagination.

Sunday / May 4

I've been feeling so good the past few days about my decision to break free of the department that when Dan turned up this morning to finish raking the lawn, I felt obliged to thank him for the way that his memoir had provoked me to make such a decision. He in turn was equally frank, telling me right off that he considered my decision to be "wise, because it's based on a recognition of the way things are with the changing generations." I hadn't expected Dan to bring up the subject of generational gulfs and tensions, especially with the two of us facing each other over our rakes, almost thirty years dividing him from me—a gulf immediately visible in the difference between my thinning hair and his full head of it, not to mention his muscular physique and my bulging waistline. But as he continued to talk about the gulf, I could see that his thoughts were occasioned by an unusual—and illuminating—situation in the department where he's going to teach next year. "One of the things that's made me feel so excited about my new job is that I'm going to be in a department that consists almost entirely of people my own age or just several years older than me. There isn't an older generation at all, because the department is such a newly created thing. So it all feels extraordinarily vigorous and optimistic. And I think as we gradually age, another generation will come along, and another." His voice rose a bit and his eyes sparkled when he got to the point about almost everyone being his own age. And then as his voice trailed off, I quickly made a rough tally of the different age groups in our department—a handful of us in our sixties, a dozen or so in their fifties, and two or three dozen in their thirties and forties. Not quite as youthful a place as Dan's new department, but filled nonetheless with people whose ages, interests, and outlooks are so far apart from mine that it's no wonder we have little to share with each other. Come to think of it, I sometimes feel lucky that I'm still able to connect with folks like Dan, Marilyn, and my other students, although even that connection, I realize, is occasioned largely by the fact that we share the same interest in nonfiction writing. By the time that Dan had finished raking away the old thatch, I could see more clearly than ever before that I've been yearning to hang on in a place where I don't really belong. Now I just wish it hadn't taken me so long to reach such an obvious conclusion. But then as Dan was about to leave, I couldn't help wondering what I'll have left to write about in this diary, now that I've come to such a definitive resolution of the problems I've had about letting go of this place. And as usual, Dan had some more wisdom to impart: "Retirement is full of uncertainties, isn't it? So, don't worry, there'll probably be a whole series of problems—rises and falls and complications enough to keep you going for months or years to come."

Monday / May 5

"Rises and falls and complications"—those words kept coming back to me yesterday afternoon when Kate and I were at the opera, partly because the program consisted of two Puccini one-acts, *Gianni Schicchi* and *Fra Angelica*, both so melodically lush that the music kept rising and falling from start to finish; partly because both works are so dramatically complicated and different, one comic, the other tragic, though both are variations on the theme of mortality. I wondered what turn my own story might take, though I hoped it would at least be somewhere between the two, preferably seriocomic.

And this morning when I was telling Trish about the past few months, I thought about Dan's words again, especially when she said that "the more ups and downs, the better it is for your journal." Spoken like a devoted memoirist, I thought. I called Trish to talk about the possibility of our starting a nonfiction list for the University of Iowa Press, a project I first thought about last November when the winter book had just been accepted, but that I then put on the back burner until a few days ago when another university press invited me to consider starting such a list. I couldn't imagine doing such a thing alone, and I couldn't imagine anyone I'd rather do it with than Trish. So I was delighted by her immediate interest in the project, especially now because it seems like a natural way to keep my editorial hand in the world of nonfiction writing, without being in the classroom, the building, the department, or anything else of the sort.

I was also delighted by the opportunity to talk to Trish's husband, Terry, who retired several years ago from his position as head of the Family Program at the Hazelden Clinic. I knew that his retirement had been occasioned not only by a heart attack, but also by a sense that he'd worked himself out of a job as a result of having completely integrated his program into the overall treatment program of the clinic. "I really wasn't needed there," is the way he put it. Given such a dispassionate view of things, I was surprised to learn how difficult it had been for him to make the transition, especially because he "didn't want to give up the daily commute." I couldn't understand why anyone would want to make a hectic drive every day on the beltway, back and forth between St. Paul and Minneapolis, until Terry explained that "it was the sense of urgency" that made it seem so important to him. "I just didn't want to give it up, even though it was killing me, though I didn't know it until my heart attack. Isn't that stupid?" At this point in my own transition, nothing, I assured him, seemed stupid to me, especially when I discovered that he too had been "alarmed" at the thought of leaving his office, that it was a break he "didn't want to make." So his office was left open for a year, though he only went back to visit it once or twice. How fascinating (and comforting too) that even a sage therapist like Terry, who's written two books during his retirement while also enjoying the role of a "househusband," found it difficult to cope with the loss of his office. I wonder if anyone's ever written a book about the psychological significance of one's office. "You're writing it," is what Kate said when she finished reading this piece. But the book is about to be closed on that subject, when I start moving out next week.

Tuesday / May 6

"Do you have any last words?" I didn't expect anyone to ask me such a question at the end of today's workshop—the same question that's usually asked of prisoners about to be executed—so I didn't have any memorable advice to offer, except to say "Just keep writing." That's how I ended the workshop and my teaching career on this mild and sunny day in early May, when the crabapple was in full blossom and the narcissi were still hanging on. The session itself was a genial affair, thanks to a box of cookies from Judith sitting by my spot at the table, a lively discussion of Valicia's journal installment, a little applause, a few playful queries about whether I'd be willing to serve as a literary agent for people who want to get their journals published, and a lovely thank-you card from Jean. Then I went home to transplant a row of lettuce, followed by a bottle of champagne with Kate, who toasted me "for a job well done."

Several times during the day Kate asked me how I was feeling, but each time I had to admit that I didn't feel much of anything. No ups or downs. Just a flat emotional line from the beginning to the end of the day. Maybe because I've been writing about it so much in this journal I've already spent all my emotions, several times over. Maybe because I'm "in denial." Or because I'm finally seeing the payoff of my five-year phase-out, in the readiness I now feel just to walk away from it all, without any fanfare or any more reflections on my professional past.

At dinner, though, I couldn't help thinking of how I seem to have had three or four different careers during my thirty-five years here at Iowa—literary scholar, composition specialist, program director, and nonfiction writer—so many that I've recently come to feel as if I've been reinventing myself every nine or ten years. And perhaps that's how it will be in the years to come. But then again, I now feel as if the gardening and the traveling we want to do and the nonfiction books that I want to write and edit will probably keep me occupied in so many different ways that I won't have to look for any new occupations. And when I'm not tending to those affairs, I can serve as a financial guru for my brother, who called again from California this evening, wondering what I plan to do about getting back into the stock market, which has continued to rise while he and I have been sitting on the sidelines. Like Dan said, there'll be rises and falls and complications.

Wednesday / May 7

My first day of retirement. R/1. But it didn't feel any different from any other day of my working life. Probably because I spent the morning paying bills and most of the afternoon answering e-mail from yesterday and today. Like a couple of long-distance queries from Sara, wondering how to plan the two undergraduate essay courses she'll be teaching this fall. I offered to send her some of my course plans in the hope that she'll see her own stuff is so much better than mine that she needn't worry about what to do. I remember how uncertain I felt in the months before my first full-time teaching job at Bowdoin, but didn't have the nerve to ask anyone for help, lest they think I didn't know my way around a classroom. In the midst of that reverie, I received an e-mail from my friend Mary updating me on the June reading tour she's planned for her new collection of garden writing, *Bloom and Blossom*—a collection that includes several excerpts from the vegetable book—so I agreed to take part when she tours the bookstores in Iowa and Wisconsin. In midafternoon, I had an appointment with my graduate student Mary, whose M.F.A. thesis I've been directing the past year. And then as usual, I walked home from the office and prepared a dinner that Kate had carefully planned in advance—a breast of turkey, basted and roasted in a Mexican-style marinade of olive oil, white wine, chili powder, cayenne, cumin, garlic, grated pepper, and lime juice, accompanied by black beans and sautéed multicolored peppers.

All in all, the message of this day seems to be that life goes on during retirement pretty much as usual, except for the drenching, windblown rain that swept across the lot from early morning until late evening, when it let up enough for a walk with Pip. A brisk constitutional that nearly did me in when he lunged at something in the dark just as I was stepping on a muddy patch of sidewalk. Suddenly my feet were in midair, I was heading toward a sodden lawn, and the faint voice of a young woman was calling from across the street, "Are you alright, sir? Are you alright, sir?" Alright, except for my water-soaked, mud-laden pants and shoes and farm jacket and hands, all telling me that maybe retirement is fraught with more surprises than I'd imagined. Especially the surprise of someone calling me "sir."

Thursday / May 8

R/2, and it was hardly business as usual, considering the lavish dinner party that my colleague Carol surprised me with this evening. A retirement party without any of the rituals. Just a splendid six-course meal for a few of us from the nonfiction program and our spouses—an evening, actually—prepared and served in the elegant French style that Carol learned from her departed husband, Pierre, whose Gallic spirit hovered over the whole affair from the hors d'oeuvres to the dessert, from the smoked trout on crackers, the roasted and marinated pepper slices, and the stuffed, baked mushroom caps accompanied by Mumm's to the exquisite apple flan accompanied by sauterne. And it wasn't just Pierre whose presence I felt, but also my departed colleagues Bob and Curt, when the conversation led me into recollections of one and then the other. As if Carol's exquisite meal—and the excellent French wines provided by Dee—had called forth the spirits of others who fed us in the past and feed us still. All evening, we were so richly nourished by the food, the wine, the banter, the stories, and the shared memories that Kate and I walked home with a heady sense of the many ways a fine meal can nurture us. Now more clearly than before, I'm beginning to see why some bountiful meals have left me famished and others have fed me in ways beyond my ken.

Friday / May 9

At Paul's end-of-the-semester cocktail party this afternoon, a buoyant affair for faculty and students from the nonfiction program, I felt a distinct distance between myself and almost everyone else who was there. A puzzling distance that seemed to be emanating both from others and from me. It's the first time I've ever felt that way at a gathering of people from the program. Maybe it was just that I didn't have the same celebratory motives, not having been through the burdens of a full-time semester and therefore not feeling quite so fizzy as they. I was somewhere else in my thoughts and feelings, and perhaps that's what created the distance. Still, I'm struck by how different it felt today from the way it was at Paul's opening picnic this fall or his cocktail party after the reading I gave at the Prairie Lights Bookstore here in Iowa City. Then, of course, I was a momentary celebrity, having just launched the vegetable book, but then too on both occasions I felt like an important member of an academic and literary community, whereas today I felt like an outsider. I wish that Kate had also been at Paul's today, or that Carol had not been leaving just when I was arriving, for their social feelers are much more reliable than mine. But even without them to check my perceptions, I could hardly ignore the fact that no one sought me out, as in years past, to talk about their work or mine. And I in turn was drawn to Paul's intimate backyard, where I spent a few pleasurable minutes alone in his gazebo, contemplating my situation, before others started coming outside, which made me feel like going inside again. Everyone knows, of course, that I'm not returning to teach this fall, and I know it too, now that Kate and I have busily been mapping out the month-long trip to the Rockies that will put us far, far away from here when classes begin again in late

August. Still, I was surprised to see how quickly the gulf has emerged on both sides, the students evidently perceiving me as someone who's moving on, and I perceiving the students now as potential distractions from the writing and traveling that are uppermost in my mind. Oh yes, I'm still directing a few M.F.A. theses and sitting on a few others, but when those are finished sometime next year, I don't think I'll take on any more. How strange and fickle that I should feel this way, when just a few months ago I couldn't imagine the possibility of foregoing the opportunity to keep working with students on their theses and other manuscripts. At some point, I suppose, one has to draw the line and make the break without expecting the world to look or feel the same again, even a world that's been so much a part of one's life as this one has been of mine. And maybe that's what retirement ceremonies are really meant to do— to draw the line so clearly that no one can be misled about where they stand in the general scheme of things.

Saturday / May 10

Now if I can just get things squared away on the financial front, I'll feel much more secure about where I stand in the general scheme of things. Late yesterday afternoon, for example, the mailman brought me a letter from the Social Security Administration, telling me I had estimated my 1997 earnings to be $445,000! Not bad for a retiring English professor. The only problem is that the figure they reported is $400,000 more than the one I gave Fran a few weeks ago, and until it's corrected in the Chicago office I won't receive any of my Social Security benefits for this year. Maybe that's why I was feeling somewhat detached at Paul's cocktail party. I should have known things were going much too smoothly during my initial meeting with Fran, and now that there's an erroneous number in their computer bank, I wonder how long it will take to get things corrected.

I also wonder how long it will take before I get up the nerve to get back into the rising stock market, and accept the fact that I've lost the opportunity to make a quick gain of twenty-five thousand on my previous decision to withdraw my CREF funds from the market back in early March and wait for it to settle down again. Every time I've tried to second-guess the market—to move out of the growth fund during a relative high point in the market and reinvest during a low phase—I've timed things wrong one way or another. So I'm not going to play that game again. It's hard enough just to predict the vagaries of the weather, without trying to foretell the ups and downs of the stock market.

In keeping with that resolve, I spent most of the day transplanting all the broccoli, cabbage, and cauliflower seedlings, almost two weeks later than I've ever put them in the garden before, thanks to my foolish attempts to second-guess the weather. And then as a little reward for my labors, I cooked up a dinner that didn't require me to second-guess anything—just a couple of braised pork chops with a shallot-shitake mushroom gravy, accompanied by a wild rice–brown rice mix with sautéed red and orange peppers, and a leaf lettuce salad in a white wine vinaigrette.

Sunday / May 11

This afternoon at Hickory Hill, the wilderness park a few blocks from our house, some fifty friends and admirers of Nancy—Kate's Heritage Trees cohort—gathered to celebrate her eightieth birthday by dedicating a newly established grove in her name. A grove that will eventually include about sixty trees, typifying an upland oak savanna. Bur oaks, white oaks, shingle oaks, swamp white oaks, shagbark hickories, white pines, black maples, sugar maples, bitternuts, and so on. Kate spent the last month preparing site maps while Gert, her other Heritage Trees cohort, did some heavy-duty fundraising to pay for the first two specimen trees and a large boulder from a local quarry with a brass dedicatory plaque. And the two of them leaned on the city to donate a special area for the grove.

Only Nancy, I imagine, could have inspired such an exquisite botanical project, entirely in keeping with the other ecological projects she's launched during the past thirty years to preserve and enhance the well-being of the city and the county. And only Nancy could have inspired so many people to turn up on short notice on this cold windswept afternoon—including the mayor, the city council, the director of parks and recreation, and the city forester. I used to wonder how she could get so many people to follow her lead, until I noticed her favorite expression, "Wouldn't it be marvelous? Simply marvelous?" I first remember hearing her ask those buoyant questions some twenty-seven years ago, when she was boosting Kate's efforts to create our neighborhood park. So when I heard Nancy say those magic words again today at the end of the ceremonies—"This is marvelous, simply marvelous!"—I wanted to say the same thing myself. But after uttering the words to myself, sounding them inside my head a few times, I could tell that they didn't really belong to me. Still, it sure was a pleasure to behold Nancy, whose diminutive frame and curly white hair belie the force of her personality. So, come what may, I expect to keep hearing her mantra, even if I can't utter the words myself.

Monday / May 12

Today I spent so much time fussing over a thank-you letter for my retirement tree that I don't have anything to show for the day except the letter:

> Dear Colleagues,
> I wish you could behold the splendid retirement gift you've given me as easily as it was possible to view the illuminated page you gave to David—just by walking into Gayle's office, picking it up off her table, and turning it over in your hands. But as you may have surmised from Dee's newsletter a

couple of weeks ago, my gift is a bit too large for Gayle's place. Nine feet, seven inches tall, to be exact, not counting roots. A swamp white oak tree, with heady aspirations, though its head is a bit pointy as yet, given the careful way it's been pruned during its years in the nursery. Still, it's a sight worth seeing, even now before its leaves have begun to unfurl, standing like a sentinel, guyed to keep it steady, at the southeast corner of our neighborhood park, where it was planted on a sunny afternoon in late April. Thanks to the choice of its exact site by Kate, I can easily behold my swamp white oak just by looking north out our kitchen window, through a gap in the lower branches of our neighbor's apple tree, which I planted some twenty-five years ago. A tree within a tree. Or I can walk a couple of lots north, eyeball it up close from all angles, and check the soil to see if it needs watering. Also, of course, I can readily give it the annual feedings it will need during the next several years when it's putting down new roots and putting out new top growth. And if I want to see what my tree might look like in years to come, I can look directly across the park at the swamp white oak to the north, which was planted some twenty-five years ago (along with a number of other varieties throughout the park) in memory of Joan Scholes, the wife of our former colleague and my close friend Bob.

As you can see, I have high hopes for this tree—and for myself—so you can be sure I will tend it carefully until I shuffle off this mortal coil. Until then, you can also be sure I will continue to be grateful to you for having given it to me, as well as to Dee and Barbara for having chosen such a thoughtful gift and such a thoughtful place in which to plant it.

Sincerely,

Carl

It took me so long to write that letter just for my single tree, I wonder if Nancy will have world enough and time to do the courtesies for an entire grove. Unless, of course, she resorts to her marvelous mantra.

Tuesday / May 13

Tuesday. One of my regular teaching days in weeks past, in years past. And now that I'm free to spend it as I wish, I decided to do something completely unrelated to teaching—to have a different kind of Tuesday—by working on plans for our trip to the Rockies. It's turning out to be such a logistical challenge that not even the Preacher of Ecclesiastes could divine the time to see and do everything under the sun that Kate wants to cram into the schedule. It's at times like this that I wish we could just rent a lakeside cabin, kick off our shoes, and spend a few weeks reading, fishing, and lounging around without a care in the world. A relaxing vacation. A couch potato's paradise. To which she usually replies, "You can do that at home, if that's all you want. But I want to see as much of the earth as I can while I'm still able to see it." So, as things now stand, we'll be driving our Jeep Grand Cherokee for seven sightseeing days from here to Jasper at the top of the Canadian Rockies, then catch a train that takes two scenic days to wend its way through the mountains from Jasper to Vancouver, where we'll spend a few days at a turn-of-the-century hotel overlooking the bay, and then take an overnight train back to Jasper, where we'll start a six-day drive through the Canadian and American Rockies, spending a couple of nights on the Canadian side of Glacier before we head south to Yellowstone and the Tetons, then a few days at Trudy's log cabin in the mountains above Dubois, where I'll give the first reading of my winter book, and then home. Twenty-seven sight-filled days! No wonder it's turning out to be an elaborate planning project.

Kate's been plotting each day's drive in the opening stretch not only to be on time for the train, but also to see something worthwhile, and to wind up in an interesting hotel, motel, inn, or bed and breakfast with an appealing restaurant nearby; and I've been negotiating all the reservations with our travel agent, checking back and forth almost every day on this reservation and that. "Have you called Ruth back yet?" has been the standard line from Kate, and from me it's been, "Have you figured out where we're going to stay in Jasper?" And from Ruth it's usually been good news/bad news, like "I'm calling to tell you that I've heard from the Pollard in Red Lodge and they've confirmed your reservation, but the Inn at Jenny Lake is full. Which of your other options would you like me to try next?" So many guidebooks to be consulted, so many decisions to be made and revised along the way that it's like market research or scholarly investigation turned to the purposes of recreation. Sometimes, I think it would've been easier just to keep teaching.

Wednesday / May 14

Thanks to a prodding call from my textbook editor in New York, I spent all day finishing my share of the work for the revised edition of *Fields*, and then felt so relieved about being done that I found myself pondering the thought of being done with textbooks once and for all. What a reversal of my feelings just a month ago, when Donna's visit had me so energized about *Fields* that I imagined myself doing one or two more revisions of each before calling it quits. But now that I've decided to make a clean break with the English department and the nonfiction program, it seems to make sense that I should also make a clean break with St. Martin's. No more teaching, no more textbooks. After all, if this is it, I don't want to spend whatever is left of it revising a textbook that my collaborators can do without me. Better I should be working on my own books, or reading a good novel, or traveling, or gardening, or casting a line in one of the nearby lakes. Besides, if I'm no longer in the classroom, I can hardly claim to be in touch with the textbook needs of students and teachers, except by inference from my past experience.

But then again, I haven't taught a drama course the past ten or fifteen years, yet I haven't felt any compunctions about working on the drama anthology with Miriam, for what matters most is the quality of the plays we choose and the freshness of the production shots and theatrical reviews that Miriam compiles to go with the plays. Besides, I don't feel burnt out from working on textbooks. In fact, the collaborative experience of working with Miriam has usually been so stimulating (and financially rewarding) that I'm not sure I should throw it over just because I've decided to retire from teaching. (Especially given the projected costs of our upcoming trip to Canada and the other jaunts we're planning to take.) Maybe this is one of those issues that doesn't have to be resolved—until it's time to do another revision. "The secret to aging is to stay flexible." Especially if you know when to hold firm.

Thursday / May 15

Just when I was on my way to the post office this morning with the manuscript for St. Martin's, Dee called at home with the message I've been expecting the last few weeks: "It looks like you'll have to move out of your office by the end of next week, so we can make it available for one of the new professors we've appointed. You know how tight we are for office space. But I think we can get a student to help you with the packing and the moving." Dee sounded so uneasy that I should have interrupted her and told her not to worry about it, since I'd resolved to move out and move on like the rest of my retired colleagues. But she also seemed eager to be done with the conversation, and I was eager to get to the post office, so I decided to call her later today or tomorrow.

Then early this afternoon, just as I was on my way to a doctoral examination, I stopped to check my office mailbox and found a note in it from Dee—"Can I talk to you after Holly's exam?" It sounded as if she wanted to say something more about the decision. But no sooner did I walk into Dee's office than she was all smiles, telling me in her most cheerful voice about "the arrangement we've been able to work out so you won't have to leave the building right away." Given our conversation this morning, I was stunned by what she was telling me this afternoon. Especially when she went on to talk about her desire to have me move into one of the two offices in the erstwhile retirement suite, right next to the director of the honors program, and be there as a "source of wisdom" for any of our honors students who might be working in the area of nonfiction writing. How delicious!—that I, who took part in Michigan's honors program but didn't graduate with honors in English, would be invited to serve as a "special resource" for Iowa's honors students.

When Dee started to explain the arrangement she had worked out with the department's executive committee, I almost interrupted her right off to tell her that I'd made up my mind to move out and cut all my academic ties with the department. But I hesitated momentarily, because I didn't feel right about abruptly rejecting something I'd been pleading for almost the entire semester, especially before she had a chance to explain it in detail. When she spoke of the arrangement as lasting for two years and then being reviewed by both of us, I again heard the maxim of my old family doctor resonating in my head—"Stay flexible, stay flexible."

Before long I was thinking of how convenient a place it would be not only to visit with colleagues and to work with talented students, but also to keep a hand in without getting so entangled in the nonfiction program that I don't have time for my own writing. Also a place to house the six shelves of books in my current office, which I don't know what I'd have done with if I had to move out of the building right now. And when Dee took me over to look at the office and its outer sitting room, filled with upholstered furniture and side tables, it also occurred to me that I might hold forth there at late afternoon gatherings and assume the role of a grand old man, at least for a couple of years. Now I'm feeling more grateful to Dee than ever before. But now I'm also wondering what to think of myself. A lone ranger one week, a grand old man the next. But there's no time for thinking right now, because I have to move everything out of my old office into my new one in the next ten days, before the imminent shut-down of the building. Though Dan spoke of rises and falls and complications, I wonder if he imagined any last minute reprieves like this one.

Friday / May 16

The last day of my thirty-five years with the university—termination day—and it began with the breakdown of our aged Mazda in a supermarket parking lot, several miles from home. The battery fully charged, the engine spinning but refusing to kick in, as if it too was ready for retirement today. After waiting an hour for the AAA tow truck to arrive, I wished that I could also terminate the Mazda. All because I'd gone out to get a box of Milk Bones for Pip, when I should have stayed home and washed a summer dress shirt for Dan's graduation this afternoon.

Graduation. A colorful event, especially with all the faculty and students fluttering around on the balcony before the beginning of the ceremonies—preening their academic feathers, lining up in pairs, and checking the processional route, just before the stately march down the winding staircase to the main floor and then down the aisles of the spacious auditorium. I, it turns out, was the gaudiest of all the birds, in my bright carnelian robe with dark blue velvet trimming. Such vivid regalia that several of my colleagues fluttered nearby before the processional, eyeballing my Cornellian getup. For a moment or two just then, I wished that I'd attended the graduation ceremonies at Cornell after I completed my own doctorate some thirty years ago. But then I remembered how absurd it had felt when I trooped into the University of Michigan football stadium with thousands of other undergraduates and sat through a hot early summer morning, waving my program back and forth like a fan, only to receive a mimeographed form letter, telling me that my actual diploma would arrive several months later in the mail. By contrast, it seemed as if Iowa was doing something quite special for its graduates.

Once we were seated and the welcoming speeches had been made, it was a special challenge to keep my head up and my eyes open through the hooding of the several hundred doctoral recipients seated on stage. And I didn't always meet the challenge, especially after I had mounted the stage, placed the doctoral hood over Dan's shoulders, shaken his hand, given him a hug, smiled briefly for all the flashing cameras, and returned to my seat in the auditorium. After nodding off midway through the ceremonies, I was pleasantly awakened by the final burst of applause when all the new birds had been given their colorful tail feathers and it was time to fly the coop once and for all.

The only letdown was that I returned home to find a cliché-ridden form letter from the president of the university, expressing her "very best wishes and congratulations as you embark on the adventure of retirement." Given the fact that I've never met her personally, I suppose it's presumptuous to expect that such a letter would include any personal or specific references to "the contributions you have made to your students, your colleagues, and your profession during your years of devoted service." But then again, I couldn't help wishing that she had sent no letter rather than a form letter, especially since I hadn't expected her to send anything at all. In the midst of pondering the president's best wishes and wondering what might be appropriate to the occasion, Kate appeared in the living room with a champagne bottle in one hand, two frosty glasses in the other, and a toast for the occasion—"Here's to your final graduation. Actually, it's not your final graduation. It's your next-to-the-last one. The final one will be the great-graduation-in-the-sky, and I can happily wait awhile for that one to take place."

Saturday / May 17

"Are you feeling alright?" Kate and I asked each other the same question when we woke up around three this morning, both of us sweating, both of us suffering from heartburn, though it's not clear whether it was from too much champagne, too much pizza, too much wine, too much excitement, or all of the above. For a few minutes, I was so panicked by my rapid pulse rate that I thought my final graduation, the great-graduation-in-the-sky, might occur just a few hours after my termination from the university. In which case, I also wondered what kind of form letter the university president would write for that occasion.

Once my pulse settled down and I lay awake, resting from the panic attack, I thought about the president's letter again, wondering why it had upset me so much. After all, if I didn't want the department to do anything special for my retirement, and I didn't care enough about my self-chosen retirement/graduation ceremony to stay awake during the whole thing, why should I have cared whether the president sent me a form letter or not? At first, I thought it might be the result of having been a writing teacher for so long that I've become overly sensitive to the tactfulness and rhetoric of all the letters I receive, whether they come from the president of the university or from one of my children. But then I remembered a time some twenty years ago, when I knew a former president of the university so well that we were on a first-name basis—Sandy and I—and he'd send me congratulatory notes whenever I did something special that caught his attention. And that made me think that perhaps my irritation was the result of an irrepressible desire to be regarded as a person of special importance—so special that even the president of a large university like Iowa, a president who knows me not at all, might nonetheless single me out for special attention. Which in turn led me to think that perhaps it was aroused by a nostalgic desire to reverse the clock and be once again at the height of my professional powers. So many ways to explain my earlier distress that I could hardly sort through them all before I started dozing off. But just when I was on the edge of sleep, it occurred to me that I was probably aroused just by the natural desire to know that I had made a difference and my doings would not be forgotten—in which case, I realized, I've already had enough evidence that I don't need a presidential letter to set my mind at ease. Still, I can't help thinking right now that I continue to be more sensitive about retirement than is good for me or Kate or anyone else nearby. I hope the day will come, sooner rather than later, when I can shake off such a form letter with the flick of a finger.

The thought of being so thick-skinned was especially appealing after I met Dan's father—the retired military man—at Dan and Maura's graduation potluck this afternoon. A bountiful feast, given all the salads and desserts that people had put together for the occasion. But the main attraction was Dan's father, standing over a large outdoor grill, clad in a barbecuing apron and a chef's hat, turning out some of the most picture-perfect hamburgers and brats I've ever seen. And doing so with such a grand smile and take-charge style that it seemed to me he was virtually unflappable. After talking with him about his recent travels and adventures, as well as our Ohio backgrounds, I could also tell that he probably wouldn't have given that presidential form letter a second thought. He obviously had more important things on his mind, like turning the brats, turning the brats, until their skins were so brown and juicy and crisp that no one could ever forget them (or him).

Sunday / May 18

"I'll close the upstairs windows. You get Pip on the leash and get down to the basement. That's a tornado warning!" The wailing, shrieking whistle, just when I was beginning to sip on my predinner glass of sauvignon blanc. Just when I was about to start sautéing the delicate tilapia to go with the pasta salad that Kate had whipped up for dinner. The three of us hustled down to the basement laundry room to wait out the storm. And what a storm it turned out to be—the golf-ball-to-hardball-sized hail resounding on the Plexiglas of the outdoor cellarway, Pip whimpering and shuddering on the concrete floor next to my feet, Kate tuning her portable radio back and forth from one local station to another, while exclaiming upon the size of the hail (and worrying about dents all over the Jeep), and I trying to distract myself with the Sunday *New York Times* crossword puzzle. A scene that Kate and I have performed so many times over the past twenty-seven years that we could do a touring version of it for summer stock. Especially because the melodramatic possibility of an actual tornado has never yet come to pass. Then forty-five minutes later, back up to check on the damage and get some food on the table. So many little hailstones still melting in the yard that Kate quickly gathered them up as if they were pennies from heaven. So little damage in the gardens as to be a minor miracle. But then upon close inspection so many minuscule dents all over the hood and the front bumpers of the Jeep as to make me wonder what the roof of the house might look like.

A day of extraordinary weather, the temperature having risen to 87 and the dew point to 91 after a spring when it never exceeded the 60s, except for one day in the 70s and yesterday in the lower 80s. A day when Kate and her tree cohorts were sweating it out along county roads, checking out the potential tree-damage to come from a planned county road-widening project, while I was home hastily replacing all the storm windows with screens lest our double-brick home turn into a double-brick blast furnace. Such breathtaking weather, I'll surely never forget the day after the day after I retired.

Monday / May 19

This morning at last I started to clean out my office, beginning with the file cabinet by the door, and the first thing I ran into were all the records from the Institute on Writing, the million-dollar project that I designed and directed from 1977 to 1984, "to improve the teaching of writing at colleges and universities throughout the United States." The stress-ridden project whose files I've been holding onto the past fourteen years, even after submitting a final report to the National Endowment for the Humanities, even after publishing an award-winning book of model courses from the Institute, even after some ten years have passed without anyone asking for anything from the project. So I stopped down to see Hamilton, since he too had been on the Institute staff and might have wanted some of the files for his own purposes. But his reaction was so blunt it took me completely by surprise—"Let it go. Let it go. There's no point in hanging on to that stuff any longer. Just let go of it once and for all." I was also surprised because his advice sounded just like Kate's when I asked her about it yesterday. "Get rid of it all. It's over and done with a long time ago, and there's no point in looking back."

And that's the same thing she said when I asked her what to do with all the Ph.D. dissertations and M.F.A. theses I've been saving the past thirty-five years. How strange that I felt compelled to ask people what I should do with all those manuscripts, as if I weren't capable of making such decisions myself. I once felt obliged to save them for future reference, until I realized that they're all available in bound copies at the university library. It never occurred to me that I might have been saving all those theses just for the bittersweet pleasure of pitching them out one by one, as I did today, looking at the title page, looking at the name of its author, and thereby revisiting every one of the graduate students I worked closely with in years gone by, in a swift reprise of my entire career. No wonder I didn't get back to the Institute files.

Tuesday / May 20

Early this morning, when I should have been at the office again, packing things up and pitching things out, I was up here in our attic study, programming and reprogramming my modem, trying to figure out why the little message box on the screen kept telling me of an "error in the communications toolbox," as if I knew anything about such a toolbox, or where to find it, or how to correct it. The only toolbox I'm familiar with is on the landing of our cellarway steps, and nothing in it could possibly be of help, except in extremis, when the large hammer might be exactly what's called for. Not even the instruction booklet that came with the modem had anything to say about a communications toolbox, and neither did any of the printed directions I received from the university computer center, though I read them all from start to finish. Anything to get my e-mail at home, now that I'm about to lose it at the office.

By midmorning, when I headed off to the dentist's to have a couple of teeth filled, I was on the verge of hammering out my own solution to the problem. The only good thing about the error in my communications toolbox was that it distracted me from the needle in my gum, the cavities in my teeth, and the drilling in my mouth. But it didn't distract me from showing the dentist an unopened bill I discovered yesterday in the process of cleaning out my desk—a bill for six dollars that I received from his predecessor some thirty-four years ago for cleaning the teeth of my children, Hannah and Marshall, and he asked me, "Did you pay it?" And I couldn't remember.

What I won't soon forget is how I rushed back home from the dentist's and wasted another hour trying to fix the toolbox, which led me to do what I should have done in the first place—I called the university's computer help desk, where I hooked up with Peter, a genial-voiced instructor, who asked me if the software for my modem included a fax program and if so I should "deactivate it." Like an obedient student, I was eager to follow Peter's suggestion, though I had little hope it would make any difference, since I didn't know how to deactivate my fax program, until he told me "just uncheck the fax manager in your extensions file." So I terminated my fax manager, and lo! the error in my tool box was instantly corrected, which in turn enabled me to get my e-mail with the click of my mouse. Some terminations are more immediately productive than others.

With that thought in mind, I went down to the office for some more file pitching. This time all the stuff from the Institute that consumed some seven years of my life and almost my life itself, when the end of the project coincided with my heart attack some twelve years ago. And this time, I found myself reliving the entire venture in fast forward—from writing the proposal to organizing the sessions to meeting the participants to making the campus visits to editing the book of model courses to having the model heart attack. In the midst of such memories, I was delighted to see Dan, who came by to pick over the remnants of the Institute library to help stock a library for the department of writing where he's going to teach at Central Arkansas. Casting my books upon the waters!—I never imagined it might be so liberating an experience. By the end of the afternoon, though, after pitching a whole bunch of files that reminded me of colleagues dead and gone, I was hardly in a mood to do any cooking, so Kate and I went out for dinner, which taught me another memorable lesson—never to order a Chinese dish at a Japanese-Korean restaurant.

Wednesday / May 21

Two or three or more days of pitching out, packing up, and carting off before I'll be completely moved from my office to the emeritus suite. But already I've come to realize something about this office of mine that I should have known much sooner than this—that in many respects it's been serving as an archive for all the memorabilia of my academic career. All the way back to class notes from some of my undergraduate English courses. More than three-quarters of the place devoted to a remembrance of things past—to books I haven't looked at, files I haven't used, and notes I haven't consulted for longer than I care to remember. A museum of sorts, somewhat like a presidential library to the greater glory of myself, which I suppose everyone is entitled to, though it sure is a heavy burden to deal with come moving time. Heavy enough to outweigh the nostalgic impulse once and for all. No wonder my retired colleague Stavros always kept such a spartan office—his bookshelves almost empty, as if everything he needed was available in his head, a habit he must have acquired from wandering the Romanian countryside with his parents during the Second World War. I, on the other hand, have been so reluctant to let go of anything that I'm now confronted with a lifetime of folders and papers piling up in the hallway next to my door and in the corridors of my mind. And nothing to do but wait for the janitor and the passage of time to cart them away. Such an embarrassing spectacle that I'm suddenly eager to leave my office and move into the emeritus suite, where my temporary status should help to keep my pack-ratting impulses in check.

After a morning at home, planting up the annual side of the herb bed—basil, borage, burnet, dill, nasturtium, and parsley—I went down to the building, still in my overalls, and started setting things up in my new office, rearranging the bookshelves, the tables, the chairs, my desk, until everything was just so. Then for the first time this spring, I felt such a heady sense of starting a new life in a new place that I remembered the world of possibilities that seemed to unfold before me when I first opened the door to my office at Bowdoin College some thirty-eight years ago and began my full-time teaching career. So it was a pleasure to start carting books from my old office to my new one, from the fifth floor to the third floor, shelving all the essayists and other nonfiction writers in the bookcases closest to my desk. And each time I went back upstairs to fetch another load of books, I also pitched out another pile of stuff from ventures past—grant proposals to governmental agencies, departmental memoranda, textbook manuscripts—all piling up in the hallway outside my office, knee-high, like corn on the Fourth of July.

Thursday / May 22

A red-letter day at the university press, thanks to the arrival not only of bound page proofs for *Weathering Winter* but also the press's fall catalog of books, featuring the cover art from my book on the cover of the catalog itself. An author's dream, especially the detailed description of the book on the first page of the catalog. Even though it was just a paperbound set of page proofs rather than the hardback that it's destined to be, the preview I held in my hands was so distinctively shaped, a small, square format, that I imagined my little book might make a very big splash. But when I thought of all the books on my office shelves waiting to be given away or thrown away or boxed up and stashed away, I realized that *Weathering Winter* will probably go the way of most books. A brief flurry of attention and then a long and quiet life, gathering dust on the shelves of libraries around the country. A retirement of sorts that put me in the mood for a few more hours of digging through memorabilia, like an Institute snapshot from seventeen summers ago—my hair still dark, my body trim, my colleagues and I surrounded by the smiling freshman writing directors who had just finished their six-month stint with us in Iowa City, a few of them now gone the way of all flesh. And the framed reproduction of Georgia O'Keeffe's *Winter Road*, a voluptuous image that appeared on the cover of a textbook essay collection I edited some thirteen years ago, a book now gone the way of all texts. And all the student evaluations of my teaching that former chairs had told me to keep on file "forever." Narcissistic memories enough to create a nostalgic bonfire. But I was more interested in producing some fresh tomatoes before the first of July, so I hurried home in midafternoon to dig a few holes at the back of the lot for a few early-bearing tomato plants. Better to look forward than back, especially in an early summer garden.

Friday / May 23

Housecleaning all morning and early afternoon to get ready for the weekend visit of Amelia and Joe. A pleasant distraction from cleaning out my office. Better to confront a dirty toilet bowl than the detritus of an academic career. The only problem was the telephone, ringing with calls from people in Kate's tree mafia, and confirmations from our travel agent, and come-ons from telemarketing geeks, and at one point, when I was on the phone upstairs, a bellowing outside from our garden helper, Rebecca, who had ripped the seat of her pants and wanted to let me know she was going home for another pair. "No," she didn't want to borrow a pair of Kate's jeans, "thank you."

But it wasn't just the calls that were distracting me; it was the sense of being pulled in several directions. Cleaning house when I wanted to be outside planting the main crop of tomatoes, but also feeling I should be down at the office to finish moving before next Tuesday's deadline, as well as working on this journal to catch up with the last few days before I lose the immediacy of everything that's been happening this week. Is this what my neighbor Jim meant a few nights ago, when I talked about hungering for just a few spare hours to get my tomato plants in, and he said, "I know just what you mean. Ever since I retired, it seems like I'm busier than ever before." But what is the busyness, I wonder, that fills his hours and days? Or those of anyone who's fully retired. I hope it's not all the distractions I had to put up with today. Still, I can hardly complain, for by midafternoon I was free to put in the main crop of ten tomato plants, as well as the eight-foot poles to support them, and the compost to feed them. And with the help of Rebecca, I was able to do the job in just a few hours.

Perhaps I just need to be a bit more patient with the telephone, or better yet get a telephone answering machine. But an answering machine won't take care of the telephone that keeps ringing inside my head, calling me to deal with three or four different obligations all at once. The only way to silence that phone is by studying tranquillity, as I did after my heart attack—relaxing and retiring, relaxing and retiring, until nothing can reach me but birdsong and wind chimes and the rustle of wind in the trees.

Saturday / May 24

Thanks to the telephone, I was greeted this birthday morning by Kate's ever buoyant, tree-hugging compatriot Gert with the splendid news that "Life begins at sixty-five!" But at four this morning, when I was awakened by a sneezing fit so loud that it also roused Kate, I had the momentary feeling that my life might actually end before the sun had risen, especially when I went into the bathroom to blow my nose and bring the sneezing to a stop. For it persisted with so much intensity that my forehead was swept with hot flashes after every outburst, and I was swept with the chilling thought that a sneezing fit might be the onset of my final graduation. The great-graduation-in-the-sky. And then the seizures passed as quickly as they had started.

Some birthday present! Ominous enough to make me wonder what I might expect of this sixty-fifth year in my life, an age that's the product of such antithetical multiplicands as the mystical number five and the unlucky number thirteen. Hardly as promising as my sixty-fourth, which was so filled with bountiful multiplicands— twos, fours, eights, sixteens, and thirty-twos—that I managed to get one book published, another accepted for publication (and now in

page proof), another under way that I'm working on even now, not
to mention the completion of my academic career and the beginning of my retirement. So many accomplishments in a single year
that I lay in bed the next three hours, planning a full menu of things
to do on this single day, with a time set aside for each one. At eight
A.M., take the Mazda to Midas and have its muffler replaced; at nine,
come back and finish cleaning the downstairs before Amelia and
Joe's noontime arrival; at ten, catch up on the incomplete journal
entries of the last few days; at eleven, pot up a few of the patio tomato plants; at noon, make a lunch salad for four; at one, go down
to the office for an hour or two with Amelia to finish moving out,
and then come back for an hour or two of "R and R" before going
out to a local roadhouse for a classic Iowa steak dinner.

If birthday deeds are a measure of things to come, it looks like
this will be a year of eating, for as things worked out I managed to
do nothing on my list but lunch and dinner. But we did drive out to
the Rochester Cemetery twenty miles east of here, where Kate takes
me each year at this time for a trek through that splendid remnant
of prairie wildflowers and a haunting reminder of things to come.
And I did open a few surprising presents, including a lightweight
all-weather slicker from Kate, a pair of T-shirts with fish rubbings
from Amelia and Hannah, and a bottle of champagne from Rebecca. And I did enjoy the thought that having turned sixty-five, the
government-issue retirement age, I'm now officially retired in every
sense of the word.

Sunday / May 25

Sometimes I wonder why people are so eager to congratulate me
just because I've retired. Oh yes, I realize it's certainly not an occasion for the weepies, but the enthusiasm I've heard in their voices is
enough to give me pause, as it did a few days ago when our neighbor
Ann, a longtime secretary at the university, bowled me over with
congratulations as I was walking Pip around the block, and she was

walking her cocker spaniel. Our dogs were so surprised that they didn't even give each other their customary barks and threat displays. And it happened again this morning when Kate's cousin David, a television producer in Minneapolis, and his wife, Caroline, an executive secretary for a national merchandising corporation, joined us for brunch at one of the local bistros and toasted me as if I were an instant celebrity, as if I'd won the lottery or broken the bank at Monte Carlo. Maybe all the congratulations are just a convenient way of spreading good cheer, of hailing the old folks as well as the young. But the enthusiasm I've heard, tinged with sounds of genuine envy, makes me think that for many people their jobs are so oppressive and unrewarding that they hunger for retirement as if it were an escape from the prison of work, an entry into a world free of schedules, duties, meetings, time clocks, and all the other obligations and constraints associated with regular employment. And in a sense it is, as I've discovered just from the few weeks I've been retired.

The only problem I've noticed is that no matter where I go or what I'm doing, I can't get away from myself. I'm still enslaved by my habits and driven by my compulsions—to take a second helping, a third glass of wine, a fourth ibuprofen, as if I couldn't get enough of anything, not even of work, which I continue to work at as if I were still on the payroll. So whenever people congratulate me, I always smile a bit sheepishly at the thought that I'm traveling under false colors, that I'm retired but not actually retired and probably never will be until I've retired from life itself.

Monday / May 26

Memorial Day, and a memorable day it was. Chilly and rainy enough that Lib called off her annual trek to the family cemetery plot, giving Kate a much-needed day of rest after the weekend frenzy. I had no choice but to spend the day finishing the move from my river-view office to the emeritus suite before the upper levels of the building are closed at midmorning tomorrow. A more tedious and time-consuming job than I'd imagined. Boxing up several shelves of unwanted books and carting them down to the faculty library for giveaways. Packing up all the artwork on the walls and bookshelves and taking it down to my new office. Carting all the plants to the basement of the building to spend the summer hanging out with the secretaries. Boxing up all the desktop stacks of current letters, student manuscripts, and other business to be taken home for the summer. Packing up the computer and taking it down to the car where it will sit overnight until I can move it into my faculty study at the library. Making a list of e-mail addresses to log into my home computer. Nothing memorable in any of those chores, until I got to the few bits of tumbleweed and yucca pods I've been saving from a trip out west that Kate made some thirty-one years ago, a year before we were married. And the rust-colored bowl with the outline of a fish in the bottom of it that Amelia made some twenty years ago when she was in her last year at Scattergood, a Friends school ten miles east of here. And then the hand-lettered nameplate on my door that a graduate student penned for me some fifteen years ago. And finally the large poster on my door from an Audubon exhibit—a full-color photographic portrait of a barn owl peering out at the world, my alter ego past and present.

Tuesday / May 27

Mazda to the Midas Muffler shop. Computer to the library. And I to the Staff Benefits office for a meeting with Nancy, to find out why CREF hasn't yet established my IRA rollover account. Though she couldn't track down the problem, she assured me that it will all work out in time to receive my first payment from CREF in early July, when I'll no longer be receiving a paycheck from the university. And then back home besieged by sweats and dizziness and general exhaustion from all the rigmarole of the past several weeks. So at Kate's suggestion, I distracted myself by deviling some crab meat, fresh in from the Gulf, with a mixture of chopped onions, parsley, pepper, celery, Worcestershire sauce, cracker crumbs, lemon juice, and hot sauce—then baking it in the oven while I put together a composed salad of leaf lettuce, tomato wedges, black olives, and fresh garden radishes, dressed with a lemon vinaigrette, to be accompanied by a sourdough baguette and a bottle of sauvignon blanc. Now, maybe, I'm ready to start retirement. Or as Kate kept saying in soothing tones, "It's all over. You've done it. There's nothing more to go through. Just relax. Don't focus on it anymore." (And I didn't focus on it anymore, except to take stock of it here and then forget about it.)

Wednesday / May 28

This morning I focused on sleeping in, then on eating a leisurely breakfast while reading the newspaper without actually taking in the news. A studious form of inattention. Like training for tranquillity. Like imaging. Like savoring my cup of Kona coffee. And the aroma of freshly ground beans from Hawaii. And memories of our last visit to the Big Island, especially the tang of tangerines right outside our cottage window. A New Year's present to Kate and myself, two and a half years ago, a reward for finishing the vegetable book, and now all that's left are the beans and the memories, which made me think it might be time to drink that juice again next year as a reward for finishing this journal.

Then I focused on a few e-mails to catch up with last week's correspondence. Then a long and genial telephone call from my friend Mary, to confirm the schedule she's arranged for our readings next month from *Bloom and Blossom*. Then a spectacular bouquet arrived this afternoon from David and Caroline—a retirement gift that made me think they must have been reading my mind this morning. How else to account for all those Birds of Paradise and nothing but those Birds? A gaudy display of them like the ones bounding the walkway outside our Hawaiian cottage, just a few steps away from where the tangerines grow, their juice so piquant that I picked and squeezed them every day, even before grinding the beans and brewing the coffee.

Thursday / May 29

Another leisurely morning at home, so free of any professional obligations that for the first time this spring I'm beginning to feel relieved at the prospect of having no classes to teach, no students to meet—nothing but a few M.F.A. theses to direct this summer and fall. Maybe it's just my lingering sense of fatigue that makes me feel this way, and perhaps I'll be yearning for the classroom again this fall, when the students come back to town, full of the eagerness that marks a new academic year. For the time being, though, it looks like those Birds of Paradise could be a harbinger of things to come, once I get all the bureaucratic problems resolved. So at the library this afternoon, when Hamilton asked me how I was feeling about retirement, I told him that I was somewhere between exhausted and relieved and elated, which provoked him to give me a fascinating bit of linguistic information—that the Spanish word for retirement is *jubilación*. Such a surprising and suggestive word that I decided to follow up on it and discovered that *jubilación* is the Spanish word not only for retirement but also for pension—and that *jubilación* is derived from the Spanish verb *jubilar*, to rejoice. Such a fitting combination of definitions and derivations that it made me feel like jubilating a bit myself. But not for long, since it also reminded me that my *jubilación* is not complete, owing to the unfinished business of my IRA rollover. Which means that I shouldn't transfer any of my accumulations from one fund to another until the rollover has taken place. And what happens if the stock market plummets or soars in the meantime? Then I might be weeping rather than rejoicing, and my word for retirement might be lamentation rather than jubilation.

Friday / May 30

Late yesterday afternoon, just when I was in the midst of preparing a green grape, white wine, and lemon sauce for a sautéed filet of sole, I received a call from Jacqueline, the CREF representative in New York City who oversees my account, reporting that she doesn't know why the IRA rollover hasn't yet taken place. But she promised to give me an update late this afternoon.

Then as if to add a new twist to my mercenary concerns, I received a confusing letter today from the Social Security Administration, telling me that my first benefit check, due in early July, will be reduced by almost $150 to pay for Medicare coverage that I didn't request and don't need until August. So I called the local Social Security office and spent a half hour on the phone explaining the error and then got the dubious assurance that I'd soon receive a form to fill out and return in order to correct the error.

Then I called Nancy at the Staff Benefits office to bring her up to date on the rigmarole, which prompted her to tell me, "It sounds like your retirement is being eaten up by trying to get your retirement in order." But she also assured me that all the problems will soon be worked out and suggested that I not fret about anything this weekend.

And I didn't fret about anything until I was standing at the kitchen counter late this afternoon, waiting for Jacqueline's call. I had a pork tenderloin roasting in the oven, a French potato salad setting up on the kitchen counter, and a bowl of our homegrown radishes chilling in the icebox—everything in hand, so I'd be free to talk with Jacqueline when she called. But she never did call back, which made me wonder why I'd gone to the bother of preparing the whole dinner in advance. But I didn't wonder too long, especially after tasting the pork, fragrant with sage and thyme from the garden, and the potato salad, dressed with a white wine vinaigrette and herbed with chives and parsley. In fact, after munching on the first crisp radishes of the season, I vowed not to fret the red tape again this weekend (if I can keep myself from thinking about it again this weekend).

Saturday / May 31

The first sunny day this week and one of the few warm days the past several weeks. Such an abrupt change from the cold weather this month that today's mild temperatures had all of us in a wilt. Not only Kate, Pip, and I, but most of the spring vegetables, and even some of the perennials in Kate's flower border. How strange that an idyllic spring day should make me feel so uncomfortable that it was all I could do just to scrub a couple of large clay pots, fill them with a homemade mix of potting soil and rotted cow manure, plant them up with a couple of patio cherry tomatoes, and haul up some patio furniture from the basement. But even idyllic conditions can be the cause of pain, as I've been discovering from the palmy circumstances of my retirement. How else to account for the constipation I've been suffering the past few weeks and the return of the nervous rash on my right leg for the first time in almost fifteen years? Maybe all I need are a few more days (or weeks) of balmy weather, and all these nervous reactions will take care of themselves. But maybe what I really need to do is turn off the work-driven habits of a lifetime, the impulses that keep making me feel I should be doing something useful every minute of the day, even when I've committed myself to a long-term study of tranquillity.

Sunday / June 1

Sunday, a day of rest, but even today I couldn't turn off, couldn't just take the mild air on the terrace with a cup of coffee and the *New York Times*. No, I had to do my weekly recycling chores, and then spend the rest of the morning cleaning up all the stuff that's accumulated around the compost bins the past year or so—rotting corn stalks, rank pepper plants, crumbling tomato vines, dried marigold bushes, unused straw, ripped row covers, sodden tree stumps, and God knows what else. It all started when I was trying to uncover some old tree brush that I save each year to stake up the spring peas. By the time I was done forking all the recyclable stuff into a single pile and raking up the surrounding dirt, it was time for lunch, and I was too exhausted even to think about staking the peas, especially in the midday sun with the mosquitoes driving me back inside for an afternoon at the computer. At this rate, I'll never get adjusted to summer or to retirement.

But my troubles are nothing compared to Kate's—so dizzy and woozy the past few days that she canceled an outing with Lib and spent the afternoon reading, though it didn't make her feel any better. By late afternoon, I felt rested enough to stake up the peas, pull the row covers off the broccoli, cabbage, and cauliflower plants, and hoe up the surrounding soil, so the garden is beginning to look like a real garden, rather than a ghostly barricade against the elements and the deer. Now if I can give Kate a boost, I'd consider myself a specialist in restoration.

I wonder if she's having a delayed reaction to all the emotional ups and downs I've been going through the last several months, without my realizing how she might feel as a result of having to ride such a roller coaster, especially one that's not of her own choosing. How else to explain the note she left on the kitchen table yesterday: "You're writing a Me Alone book, a Me on the Edge of the Shore, and that's not true, not right. I'm here, have been and will be . . . world without end." When I first read that note, I immediately felt defensive, given how often she figures in my day-to-day entries. Now I'm beginning to think that it's one thing to include her in the story but another to be aware of what she's been going through from day to day on this self-centered voyage of mine.

A few years ago, when I was still teaching a course in the personal essay, I remember how uneasy I felt when I first noticed that E. B. White, George Orwell, and other male essayists I admire had almost completely excluded their wives from their essays and were writing

"Me Alone" pieces from start to finish. I vowed to break that chauvinist tradition in my own writing, without realizing what it really takes to resist the self-centeredness and effrontery that White acknowledged in the personal essay and that I now see in my own work, even in the midst of self-consciously trying to avoid it. Having said all of that, I'm not about to rewrite any of my previous entries, lest I put a face on things that didn't really exist. And I don't know whether my sudden awareness of the problem will enable me to overcome any of the self-centeredness that's inherent in a diary, especially one about retirement.

Monday / June 2

"Work expands to fill the time," or so I've often heard, ever since the theorem was first propounded during my undergraduate days at Michigan. But I've rarely experienced the truth of that maxim so clearly as today, when it took me almost seven hours to do a task that usually takes me three or four hours at most, namely, to pay the monthly bills. Oh yes, I was interrupted a couple of times by having to drive Kate to the doctor's office and pick her up again, since she's still feeling too light-headed to drive herself. But her doctor's appointment wasn't scheduled until 2:30 this afternoon, by which time I'd already devoted five hours to the bills. The task was also complicated by my trying to handle a few other business chores at the same time, like reserving a room in Ames this Sunday, so Kate and I can stay overnight after the joint reading with Mary, reserving a kennel at the vet's for Pip's weekend stay, filing an insurance claim for the dent on our Jeep, and filling out a form to amend the starting date of my Medicare policy. But those little tasks could hardly have taken more than a half hour. On the other hand, I spent an hour doing several errands around town, and I probably frittered away another hour checking on things in the backyard, to see how they're weathering the sun and the breeze and the mild air, as if they couldn't take care of themselves without my fretful oversight.

But why am I worrying about the way I spend my time, as if I were on some tight work schedule, with so little to spare that I didn't have the leisure to be as flexible as I'd like about the way I manage my affairs? Even if it includes some time to fuss over the well-being of my pepper plants. So much for the value of my five-year phase-in, which evidently didn't free me from the clock-driven world of work with all its bottom-line imperatives. No wonder I had a heart attack at the age of fifty-three. And now I wonder if Kate might be heading toward one herself, given the doctor's diagnosis that she might have high blood pressure. So he wants her to go on a no-salt or a very low-salt diet, as well as to start exercising more regularly than she has the past several months, to see if that brings down her blood pressure. Both of us are skeptical about the diagnosis, since it doesn't seem to account for her symptoms of light-headedness, nor does it explain the occasional sensations of weakness in her left arm, nor does it seem related to the chills and sweats she's been having the last several days. And besides, we've been on a low-salt diet for so many years that Kate could hardly be consuming enough of it to make any palpable difference in her blood pressure. I wonder if the doctor was thinking about some other patient when he was diagnosing Kate. On the other hand, I wonder what he'd think if he knew that for dinner this evening we had some very salty Polish hot dogs that Kate took out of the freezer before her appointment. But I prepared the rest of the meal without any salt, so our dietary sin was immediately balanced by expiation.

Tuesday / June 3

When Kate and I were on our pre-lunch walk this morning, I took her by the park to show her how much my retirement tree has grown—six to ten inches on all its branches. The minute she saw the tree, she told me, "You should be pleased with how well it's doing." And I was, but the more I've thought about the tree's new growth, the more I wondered how much I've grown during the past month since it went in the ground, and the answers were so dismaying that I felt a bit dashed by the comparison. For so far as I can see, I've not even grown an inch beyond where I was back then, except for a keen awareness that I'm more self-centered than I thought, and that I seem to be more wired for work than for play—even in my garden, which I've been fussing over the past few days as if I were still writing the vegetable book and wanted to have some upbeat news to report about it every day of the growing season. This afternoon, for example, I went out to plant a few salsa pepper plants at the back corner of the lot, but before I allowed myself the pleasure of putting them in, I forced myself to weed the entire raspberry patch right next to them.

As for my self-centeredness, today's news is not any better. For when Kate came back from a local nursery with a surprise flat of pepper plants to supplement some of mine that seem to be languishing, I greeted her gift with the report that she'd brought me a variety I rejected some twenty years ago because of its failure to produce much in our climate. What a cad! Especially given the way she's been feeling. But then again, when I took them back a while later, I did find a newer variety of peppers just right for our climate, and I also found some of the species poppies she'd been looking for. So, after all, I felt vindicated. But why do I need to be vindicated when all that really matters is getting on as decently and thoughtfully as one can? Now I'm beginning to see that it's easier to retire than to break the mental habits that come from a lifetime of work.

Wednesday / June 4

Now that I'm retired, I look forward to the mail even more than when I was working—partly, I suppose, because it's one of the few regular events that's left in my daily life, also because it might contain a pleasant surprise or two, like today's fan letter about the vegetable book, and the disks that came from my Internet provider to set up my Web browser at home. But most days, the mail consists of catalogs, advertisements, and bills, which make me feel that if it weren't for the e-mail that comes from friends and relatives, I might begin to think that the world out there perceived me largely as a consumer of things.

Now that I'm retired, I shouldn't care what the world thinks of me, especially if I'm studying tranquillity, especially if I've decided to be a lone ranger. But if that's the case, I shouldn't be writing this diary for all the world to read, creating and recreating myself every day in every piece I write. Retirement, it seems, doesn't really free one from the hungers of a lifetime, from the need for some kind of affirmation and recognition, unless one happens to be a thorough-going hermit or misanthrope. How else to account for the conversation I had this morning with my librarian friend Margaret, who's on phased-in retirement and has evidently been giving the subject a good deal of thought? We were standing by the card catalog, when she asked me in a serious but somewhat hesitant voice whether I've been writing about "affirmation" and how one seems to lose it (or lose the opportunity to receive it) in the process of moving from a career "of service" to the kind of "solitary work behind the scenes" that she finds herself in at the moment. A surprising question coming from Margaret, who's always seemed to be quite selfless and indifferent to public recognition. I told her about how I had grieved over the end of my teaching career, in part at least because I regretted the loss of affirmation that comes from a life in the classroom. And that little confession brought such a big smile to her face that I could tell she must have been looking down the same tunnel that I've been peering into, without any idea of whether there might be any kind of light at the end of it.

Thursday / June 5

After last week's musings on Hawaii, I mentioned the possibility of a return trip to Kate, and she quickly accepted the offer. The mere thought of a month in the islands next February or March, when I'd ordinarily be teaching, is enough to make me feel like a genuine card-carrying retiree. Ready to take off whenever the spirit moves me. And why not, since I've got enough frequent flier miles for a free airline ticket to Hawaii. There's a time and a place for every purpose under the heaven. The only problem is to find the places and times that seem to have been meant for each other.

This afternoon, the weather was so agreeable that it seemed to be meant for gardening, so I put on my overalls and spent a few hours outside seeding in some bush beans and ruby red chard, as well as transplanting a row of endive and escarole seedlings. Such a peaceable activity, it almost made me feel that I didn't need a Pacific lullaby to set my mind at ease.

Friday / June 6

I didn't get anything planted today, and I didn't get much written today, but it sure was a pleasure just to behold the overcast skies, the occasional showers, and to hear the distant thunder, sometimes to the west of us, sometimes in the east, but never nearby, as if we were at the calm center of a convulsive upheaval. Thanks to the weather, the lush peony display in Kate's flower border continues unravaged for another day. And thanks to the continuance of this genially cool spring, everything in her garden continues to be two weeks late and to remain in bloom almost two weeks longer than usual. A spectacle that led me to spend much of the day gazing out the back windows, when I wasn't walking around the yard, taking in all the sights and the tropical smell of the blossoming fringe tree.

Actually, I wasn't just gazing and smelling. I also wrote a few e-mails and took a few phone calls about this and that—textbook revisions, forthcoming readings, unfinished theses, and bookings for our trip to Hawaii. Work and play throughout the day. Yet much of the day, my mind was somewhere else, musing upon my brother on this his seventieth birthday. I called Marshall as usual and left a birthday greeting on his answering machine and thought about how he's always been so eager to be the responsible older brother that after our parents died he nearly killed me with kindness. He so good, and I so rebellious, that our relatives never stopped asking me, "Why can't you be like your brother?" A hard question that I never knew how to answer except with a shrug of my shoulders. A question, I now realize, that only served to make me as unlike him as I could possibly be, though I didn't recognize its insidious influence when I was making the choices that made me who I am (and who I've been). Choices that led me not to become a doctor like him (and my father and two of my uncles and two of my cousins). And not to live in Cleveland like him, nor to marry someone of our religion like him. And while he's forever been orchestrating family reunions, I've had little to do with our relatives all the days of my life. Now in retirement, while he continues to pursue his far-flung career of research and lecturing throughout the world, I continue to tend my garden and my solitary life here in Iowa City. If my aunts and uncles were alive today, they'd probably still be shaking their heads, wondering why I couldn't be more like my brother. But now at least I'd be able to tell them why—and thank them for helping me find my way.

Saturday / June 7

This morning Kate and I hit the road for the first of several readings from Mary's new gardening collection. Kate, feeling rested again, served as pilot, navigator, and hostess all the way to the bookstore in Des Moines, while I rehearsed several pieces that Mary had excerpted in her book. Journal entries about our lives two years ago at this time, when I was contending with a groundhog at the edge of my vegetable garden and Kate with a recurrence of cancer at the site of her previous mastectomy. A haunting remembrance of things past that I chose to lighten up a bit by focusing on my escapades with the elusive groundhog, given the darker pieces of their own that Mary and her friend Barbara had chosen to read, especially Barbara's memoir of her hardscrabble southern childhood. Comic relief—I've never taken that role before, but it worked so well with the forty people who showed up in Des Moines that I've decided to play the same part for the rest of our joint readings. Maybe I was meant to be a stand-up comedian or a clown or a court fool. The only problem is that I'm so unaccustomed to flashing a natural smile, that I can't imagine myself ever learning how to grin on cue. But the lush, checkerboard countryside, undulating to the edge of the horizon, sure did bring a smile to my face. And so did the fields of young corn, like fleurs-de-lis rampant on a ground of rich black soil. Such a lovely day on the road, it made me wish we were still heading west, all the way to the Rockies.

Sunday / June 8

Today began earlier than usual—at two in the morning, when Kate and I heard something that sounded like water dripping on the attic steps, just around the corner from our bedroom. And water it was, dripping from the rim of the attic fanlight, dropping onto so many of the steps that I rushed down to the kitchen to get enough pots and pans to catch all the water. And then back upstairs to place them below the drip spots and listen to the pinging sound of water on metal. And then back to bed, where Kate spent a few minutes fretting about the attic ceiling, about a cave-in, before she went back to sleep and left me sitting upright in bed, panicked and puzzled about the dripping, the pinging, the dripping, the pinging, wondering why it hadn't started much earlier with the heavy rain that fell yesterday afternoon. That question was answered by our neighbor Steve, a carpenter-contractor, who inspected the leaking area this morning, promised to patch it up before the end of the day (before the rain predicted again for this evening), and then explained that it probably began to drip only after the insulation and wallboard had reached "the saturation point." I couldn't help wondering just then what else in our lives might be approaching the saturation point. But my musing readily gave way to sightseeing, when we headed west again this afternoon for an evening reading in Ames.

Today's outing was even more pleasant than yesterday's, for I didn't have to rehearse, so I paid more attention to the landscape, the riverscape, the farmscape, glistening all the way in the wake of yesterday's rain. Puddles along the roadside, water in the fields, corn and beans, corn and beans. And then a busman's holiday of sorts at Iowa State University, where our overnight room at the Union looked directly out upon the nostalgic carillon towers and the red brick Victorian buildings of the spacious, tree-lined campus. So beguiling a spot I could easily have spent the whole cocktail and dinner hour walking the campus with Kate, getting a feel of the place, imagining what it might be like to study or teach there. But we had a reservation at Aunt Maude's Restaurant, and I had promises to keep at the Big Table Bookstore in Ames, where two dozen people turned out to hear us read, and I began to see that I probably couldn't endure the daily repetitions of a stand-up comedian, not even with a responsive crowd and a watertight room on campus.

Monday / June 9

Breakfast in Ames, lunch in Iowa City. Home, in fact, by midmorning, in time for a backyard chat with Jim about the deer in our gardens, the traffic on our street, and the rain in our attic. So many hassles at home I checked in with Ruth about our travel arrangements for Hawaii. Sometimes I wish we could settle in the islands and sup on lotus forever, especially after a day as hectic and scattered as this one. An early afternoon meeting with my graduate student Julia to discuss her M.F.A. thesis. A midafternoon meeting with Nancy to wrap up my retirement plans. A late afternoon tour of the garden, a quick constitutional for Pip, and then off to Hamilton's for his fifty-eighth birthday party, in the midst of which I had to leave for another book reading with Mary and Barbara. This time at Prairie Lights Bookstore in downtown Iowa City, for a genial crowd of 150 people, whose laughter turned me on so much that again I imagined myself taking to the stage or the lecture circuit, until I realized that it's one thing to perform at home, another to be on the road. And then back to Hamilton's and then back home to write up this entry and think of Hawaii even more longingly than before.

Tuesday / June 10

A full day in the vegetable beds, weeding the borders, cultivating the soil, hoeing in compost, raking the surface, and then transplanting the melon and pepper plants, as well as the decorative (and protective) rows of orange and yellow marigolds. So much fuss, so much work that I was exhausted by day's end, but the pressure's on right now to get things planted before the summer's under way and the big heat arrives—also before we go off for another book-reading jaunt this Thursday and Friday. Still, I'd rather have the focus of a day like this than the scatter of yesterday, especially after an early morning call from my brother with the grievous and shocking news that our cousin Joanne's forty-year-old son had just died of a heart attack. Grim proof of Kate's cautionary remarks late last night when I was fretting about the costs of the month-long vacation we're planning for Hawaii. "Just remember," she said, "this is it, and you can't take it with you, and you never know how much time is left, so there's no point in holding on to that money you've been saving for travel."

Wednesday / June 11

Another full day in the garden, transplanting the cucumber, eggplant, okra, pattypan, and zucchini plants, also the remaining pepper and melon plants. Now at last the summer garden is fully under way. But throughout the day, my mind was often somewhere else. At first on top of our house, when the insurance assessor inspected our roof and estimated that the recent hailstorm did so much damage that the insurance company will pay for a new one—an unexpected gift of the weather. Then my mind was suddenly back down to earth, when my friend Tom called, canceling a lunch date with the cryptic explanation, "Part of my therapy is saying no." I didn't want to pry, so I have no idea how denial or refusal might be part of his cure. Still, I couldn't help wondering how my own case might be served by saying no. What should I refuse that I'm now accepting, what should I cease that I'm now doing or planning to do? The trip to Hawaii? My gardening? The theses I'm still directing? The rest of our book tour? This journal? Or perhaps just the fixation on retirement that keeps me thinking and writing about it day in, day out? But no sooner was I contemplating those possibilities than Kate called me in from the garden, this time for a phone call from Mary, with the sad news that Barbara's mother had just died from an ear infection that suddenly went to her brain. So Mary and I will finish the reading tour without Barbara, which left me feeling less inclined to play the role of clown in the readings that remain. And more inclined to be grateful at dinnertime just for the simple fruits of my labors, like the fresh spinach salad from our garden and the last of our homegrown radishes.

Thursday / June 12

On the road again—this time to Madison, Wisconsin, another university town, where Kate and I arrived late this afternoon at the Edgewater, an *art moderne* relic, perfectly restored, overlooking Lake Mendota. Just a hundred and fifty miles from home, only a few hours away, but it feels as if we've been transported back some fifty or sixty years, thanks to the Edgewater's ambience and the university's nostalgic lakeside setting. It also feels as if we've been transported to some other world, thanks to the newsy dinner we had with Amelia and Joe, who drove in from their home some fifteen miles away, to hear the reading and join us for a post-reading repast at the Edgewater. And earlier this afternoon, it felt as if we'd suddenly been transported from one season to another, thanks to the bright sun and intense heat that greeted us in Wisconsin after driving through a cold spring rain, up and down the hills and lush green landscape of northeast Iowa.

But the high temperature was nothing compared to the low turnout for this evening's reading. Just a handful of people, plus Amelia, Joe, and Kate. Such a falling-off from the crowd we had in Iowa City that it momentarily seemed as if we were on a fool's errand. But then it occurred to me that for the first time in my life, I had an opportunity to perform for Amelia and Joe. And afterward it was a pleasure to be together with them on the brightly lit dock of the Edgewater in the refreshing night air, the water lapping softly at the edge of the wooden pilings. A wonderful change of scene that was itself transformed by the surprising appearance of my distinguished colleague Garrett, together with his wife and two young children, whose presence on the dock made me feel as if Kate and I and Amelia and Joe were in a magical landscape, where people might turn up from any time or place. Garrett, of course, was as surprised by my presence as I by his, so each of us felt called upon to explain how we'd come to be at the Edgewater this evening, rather than at home in Iowa City.

But no explanation could diminish my feeling that we'd momentarily been changed into imaginary characters, thrown together by the coincidental necessities of a fictional plot. Especially because Garrett, a brightly lit presence himself, delivered me a surprising bit of information, a revelation of sorts, when he told me that our former department chair, Ed, and he and several other colleagues felt that "something should have been done" to mark my retirement, even though I had requested that nothing be done. So I felt obliged to explain my reasons for not wanting anything, which moved Garrett to say something I'd never considered before—that "perhaps a retirement party would have been as much for us, for others, as for you." Such a different point of view from mine that it made me think I'd been quite selfish in my refusal to have any kind of retirement ceremony, as if I were refusing to share a part of myself with colleagues who wanted to share something of themselves with me. No wonder Kate accused me of writing a "Me Alone" book. Now I'm beginning to think I must be a closet misanthrope, hermit, or perhaps just a lone ranger.

Friday / June 13

Another day, another reading—this time in Decorah, Iowa, home of Luther College and of Vesterheim, the museum and cultural center of Norwegian-American life. But before our Scandinavian jaunt, while Kate was still asleep, I bade farewell to Lake Mendota, veiled in the mists of dawn—the dock empty, the tables cleared, the chairs stacked, all so different from the night before that I was momentarily surprised by the mutability of things. At breakfast, I viewed the lake again, this time through the mists of coffee and orange juice, fruit compote and Canadian bacon, and the bobbing head of a bejeweled woman who eyed us up and down, up and down, as she scanned her morning newspaper, while I in turn was scanning the mestizo waiters, so wide-eyed and broad-cheeked, so elegantly clad in formal black suits and vividly colored bow ties, so exquisitely well-mannered in the lily-white dining room of the Edgewater that it seemed as if the colonial world lived on, right at the edge of Lake Mendota. A few hours later at the university's arboretum, we scanned the trees, without any sense of cultural anxiety. A treat for me, a treasure trove for Kate.

Then westward over the lush countryside toward Decorah, marveling again at the intense green of the rolling landscape and the intense heat of the day. Suddenly it was summer, and suddenly we were crossing the Mississippi, and suddenly Kate wanted to visit the antique stores in the quaint old river town of McGregor, and I wanted to behold the effigy mounds above the river, but we had promises to keep and miles to go before we reached our bed and breakfast in late afternoon. And there on the door was a note to "The Carl Klauses" from Delores, who was baby-sitting and probably wouldn't be home until after dark, inviting us to come in, make ourselves at home, and leave a note telling when we'd like to have breakfast. A far cry from the Edgewater.

The full house at Skeates's bookstore was also a far cry from last night's turnout, especially because they laughed at all of my groundhog stories. Yet the best part of the reading, the best part of the whole day, in fact, was Charlie, whom Kate and I had never met before. Charlie, the voice of Vesterheim, Mary's good friend and fellow poet, who read a little piece himself, paid us some lavish compliments, and then took Kate and me to see his place in the country—a brightly remodeled two-story chicken coop on the grounds of the Jacobsen farm, a venerable Norwegian-American homestead that now belongs to Vesterheim. And there in the light of the setting sun, Charlie, the tour guide/performance artist/poet/raconteur, bounced around the rolling farmyard in his dark shorts and purple T-shirt, giving us a tour of the grounds and the home and the Jacobsen family's life from the time they first settled in America. And a tour of his own life too—from his big city childhood out east to the time he first arrived in Iowa City at the Writers' Workshop to the time he first settled in Decorah, appalled and then captivated by the small-town rural life and above all by "Nature," which he kept invoking like a poet and a lover as we sat around the table of his well-furnished chicken coop, drinking fresh water. And marveling at the irrepressible enthusiasm that sustained him even during the time several years ago when he fell through an open trap door in the Jacobsens' old kitchen, fell eighteen feet to a cistern below, fretting more about the loss of his keys than the possible loss of his life. So many wonderful stories that we didn't go to dinner until 9:30 and didn't get to bed until long after Delores had returned and left us another friendly note.

One more thing—just to make sure I don't ignore the nominal theme of this diary. There was a moment after the reading at Skeates's, when I was approached by a retired English professor and his wife, who asked me how I was enjoying retirement, and I told them that I've gradually come to relish it far more than I imagined just a few months ago. What I didn't tell them was how their question suddenly made me realize that for the first time in a long time I hadn't thought of it all day long—not until that very moment. And that realization made me wish just then that I could keep on traveling until I was so far away that no one would ever ask me about retirement, or until my mind was somewhere else, so far, far away that I might never think of it again.

Saturday / June 14

At breakfast this morning, we finally met Delores, who looked to be a few years older than I but went about her work so calmly that it seemed as if she might be a few years younger, and better still might never have thought about retirement. How else to explain her casually dishing up a full-scale breakfast of ham and eggs, sweet rolls and waffles, coffee and orange juice after a long stint of baby-sitting yesterday afternoon and evening? How else to explain her having bought a run-down nineteenth-century house just a few years ago, completely restored it, then turned it into a home for herself as well as a bed and breakfast, when she could just as easily have settled for an apartment, especially given a bout with cancer and other hardships she's been through in recent years? "I like to keep busy" is the way she put it, and she obviously has plenty of things to tend, with her baby-sitting, her bed and breakfast, her children and grandchildren, her antique collection, and her community activities.

Compared to Delores, I felt like a sluggard, having limited myself of late just to keeping this diary, tending my garden, doing a few readings, and overseeing the work of a few graduate students. What a falling off from all the things I was doing just a few months ago when I was still teaching, or a few years ago when I was still directing the nonfiction program. But just when I was getting all worked up about the work I used to do, it occurred to me that I was being silly to make such comparisons between myself and anyone else, or between myself now and myself back then, especially having committed myself to a long-term study of tranquillity. The old mental habits, it seems, are harder to break than I'd imagined, even on a little jaunt through the Iowa countryside.

And a pleasurable trip it was this morning, thanks to Mary and Charlie, who took us on a gardener's gallivant around the outskirts of Decorah. First to the Seed Savers Exchange, the fabled place where Diane and Kent Whealy have been saving seeds for some twenty-five years—eighteen thousand different kinds of flower, herb, and vegetable seeds from around the world now under refrigeration. And not only preserving them, but also "growing them out"—fifteen hundred varieties of peppers this summer, for example—to identify their distinctive habits and qualities, as well as to make them available to others. And not only that, but also keeping track of the seed companies and purveyors from whom these varieties can still be obtained. A prodigious Noah-like undertaking to preserve and disseminate the seed stock of the world. And all of it being carried on in the backyard and outlying acreage of a small farmstead by a former high school biology teacher and his wife. But it wasn't just the modesty of the setting and the people compared to the magnificence of the undertaking that caught my attention and admiration—it was also the deep connection between their livelihood and their living, their work and their way of being. So intimate a connection that it was impossible to imagine any separation between their personal lives and their professional activities. Given such a vocation, such a dedication, it was also impossible to imagine them ever retiring from their work, without also retiring from life itself.

Nor could I imagine Lee and Lindsay, the owners of Willowglen Nursery, ever retiring from their rural place, where they not only sell a large selection of perennial plants, but also allow folks to walk through their extensive gardens and see all those perennials planted and growing in the natural setting of their home, bounded by the wildness of the surrounding woods and streams. Again, I marveled at a life and a livelihood so completely integrated that one flowed seamlessly into the other, like their garden plots veering off into the woods. From a life such as this, it seemed, one might never retire, assuming, of course, that you could keep yourself focused on the plants rather than running off into the woods.

With that thought in mind, Kate and I headed back to our own piece of land, where I returned to find some rabbit-nibbled lettuce, deer-bitten sunflowers, and a wilting row of cauliflower plants. For a moment I wished to be someplace else far, far away, or just in the wilderness park a few blocks away, until it occurred to me that I was really right where I wanted to be—in my own backyard. The only thing I wanted to be far away from, I then realized, was myself.

Sunday / June 15

"Well, there's only one reason that people retire, and you know what that is. Unless you happen to be an actor or an athlete and a multi-multimillionaire." Hannah called this morning from California to wish me a happy Father's Day, but I was out doing my Sunday morning errands, so Kate took the message and then got into a conversation about my retirement, which led to Hannah's remark. Right after the call, Hannah headed off for a two-week vacation, so

I couldn't get in touch with her to ask what she meant by it. But Kate quickly satisfied my curiosity—"She was talking about people retiring because of getting old, and said she didn't particularly like to think about it." So I don't imagine she'll be eager to read this book. Sometimes, of course, I don't like to think about aging, but I don't ever remember feeling that I wanted to retire because I was getting old. Old? I don't ordinarily think of myself as being old, or getting old, or feeling old, or even looking old. Not yet, anyway. Especially not when I'm working in the garden, or walking with Kate, or surfing the Internet, or even when I'm writing this diary. But maybe Hannah thinks I'm getting old and just don't want to admit it. Maybe this is another case of my being in denial.

I wonder what Hannah would think about Keith, my art colleague and one of her former professors, who's sixty-three and planning to retire in a few years, so he can devote himself fully to his art. Given her own artistic dedication—she's at work in her studio at least four hours every day—perhaps she'd take Keith at his word and not think of him as retiring just because of his age. If I were Keith, I'd already be retired, especially considering his current project, which he showed us before dinner at his place this evening—an extensive watercolor series, depicting a *Hosta* "Grandiflora" in the various stages of its annual growth cycle, from the dried leaves of last year's growth to the flowering of this year's lily and then to the gradual aging and fading of this year's growth, until it reaches the withered state of last year's leaves once again. When Keith showed us the initial studies he's already completed, he told us, "Whenever I need to invigorate myself, there's nothing like turning my eye to something in nature and recording its growth cycle as close as I can. From beginning to end." So throughout the spectacular dinner that he spread before us and his other guests—from the smoked salmon and capers on shredded cabbage, to the Italianate coq au vin and pesto-dressed boiled potatoes, to the salad of mixed greens, to the decorative tart of kiwi, strawberries, and blueberries—throughout that splendid series of dishes, I kept thinking about Keith's "Grandiflora" series. And not just because a couple of the paintings were already framed and hanging side by side on a living room wall, a few feet away from the table where we were eating, but because they seemed to embody a beautiful and compelling evocation of the life cycle itself, beginning and ending appropriately with the withered leaves, the emblems not only of aging, but also of nurturing.

If I didn't know any better, I might be moved to think that only an aging person would attempt such a series, especially the vividly detailed studies that Keith has already produced of the withered leaves. But then again, I can't help thinking of how young Keats was when he wrote his sensuous "Ode to Autumn." Or Shakespeare when he wrote his autumnal sonnet on aging. Old? It's all a matter of how we look at things. So it's not in our bodies but in our selves that we are thus or thus.

Monday / June 16

Well, sometimes it is in our bodies, especially with the hangover I had this morning. But the rest of the day brought such pleasant distractions that I almost didn't feel like a withering hosta. The mail contained snapshots of the Hawaiian cottages we've rented on the Big Island and Kauai; as well as a letter from our friend Ruth, who lives on Oahu, promising to visit us while we're in the islands and inviting us to visit her in return; as well as a contract from a literary magazine that's publishing a segment of my winter book early this fall. Such harbingers of good things to come that it seemed as if today must be one of those special days when the manna is with me, so I decided it would be a good day to transfer the rest of my savings in the TIAA real estate fund back into the CREF growth fund, especially given the 3 percent gain I made on my previous transfer last week. The market's up and I'm up, despite the lingering effects of the hangover. So up that I was delighted rather than dismayed by an encounter with my neighbor Barb, who asked what I'm doing in retirement and when I told her about my various writing and editorial projects looked at me and laughingly proclaimed, "You're not retired at all, not with all the things you're doing. If it were me, I'd be thinking of all the ways I could pass the time of day without really doing anything—like swinging in a hammock or walking my dog or hanging out at the beach or just sitting cross-legged on the back lawn. Not even thinking about my garden." That last remark really hit home, as she probably knew it would. But it helped me to see that I'm not as lazy as I thought I was compared to those folks in Decorah. Then again, it also made me wish I could be as laid back as Barb or Jim. Most of all, it put me in such a divided state of mind that I was in exactly the right mood to appreciate the suggestive piece of art that Marilyn left on the front porch this afternoon with a thank-you note for my teaching. Just two squarish pieces of handmade brown paper, cut from a single piece and pasted on a white paper background, with slightly frayed edges along the top, and a slight strip of space between them, as if to suggest that they might be coming together or pulling apart, existing, as it were, in a perfect balance or an irresolvable state of tension. A work of art in the Japanese manner, set in a shiny black wooden frame, it now hangs on its own piece of wall directly below the second-floor landing, where Kate put it so I can see those two haunting pieces of paper suspended in midair whenever I'm walking downstairs and contemplate the Zen of my retirement.

Tuesday / June 17

"You're not retired at all!" That remark of Barb's has stuck in my mind, and I've been thinking about it ever since. For I've been saying the same sort of thing to myself now and then, though I've not really bothered to take stock of my reasons for feeling that way. Maybe it's because this month so far has been just like every other June the past fifteen years when I've not been teaching in summer school. I garden every day, just as I've always done in summers past. I write every day, as in summers past. I'm occasionally in touch with graduate students whose theses I'm directing, as in summers past. And I'm still living on my June paycheck from the university, as in summers past. All in all, there's not been much of a difference as yet between this summer and any other the past several years. Oh yes, I'm now a professor emeritus rather than a full professor, and I'm keeping this diary about retirement, and I'll start drawing all my retirement checks in a few weeks, and I won't be teaching again when the fall semester begins a couple of months from now. But until those big changes take place and I'm somewhere in the Canadian Rockies far, far away, I guess I'll feel like I'm somewhere in limbo, between one world and the other, waiting to be reborn. A strange feeling that I hadn't expected, but then again nothing about retirement has been quite what I expected, so why should this phase of it be any different from the rest? Like Dan said, there'll be rises and falls and complications.

I especially felt that way this evening, when Mary and I made the last stop on our joint reading tour—at the Oaknoll Retirement Home here in Iowa City, where Kate's mother has been living the past several years and some of the folks are old enough to be my parents. Like the former dean of the liberal arts college, who hired me some thirty-five years ago and was sitting in the front row with his wife, both of them smiling and genially nodding, whereas I remember both of them being much more starchy in years gone by. Such a haunting change, it made me wonder how I might be transformed in years to come, if I live so long. But it was hard to think of myself as being in the same boat as they and the others, though we're all retirees, so called. And it was even harder when Oaknoll's hostess asked me how I feel about being retired, and all I could say in response was that I didn't seem to be doing any better than my vegetables, which have recently had a little trouble adjusting to the sudden change from the cool weather of spring to the intense heat of summer. All of us wilting a bit the past few days, but we hope to be better adjusted a few weeks or months from now.

Thursday / June 19

Yesterday for the first time since I've been keeping this diary, I skipped a day and didn't write anything, not even a short paragraph. Nothing. I wonder if anyone noticed. I certainly did. It's the first time I've ever skipped a day in any of my journals—the sort of thing I never would have done before, despite the gentle proddings of friends, relatives, colleagues, my agent and editors to loosen up a bit and not feel so tied to the dailiness of things. My response to them was always the same—the sun doesn't skip a day, the vegetables don't skip a day, Kate doesn't skip a day, so how can I? But yesterday, something led me to resist that daily compulsion. Maybe it was the weather, so mild and sunny that I spent the whole day outside, tending the vegetables and the herbs, weeding and cultivating the soil, tying up the tomato plants, putting in a few more pepper plants, and inspecting the cool-weather crops—the broccoli and cabbage heading up, the snow peas almost ready for picking. Everything now on schedule despite the earlier delays, which put me in such a good mood that I didn't want to ruffle things up by writing about retirement, not even to suggest that perhaps things just fall into place in retirement, as in the garden, without one's even knowing it. Now that I skipped yesterday, maybe I'll skip tomorrow too, and maybe over the next few months I'll gradually wean myself away from this daybook until I'm entirely free of it. So free of it that I can work on my other writing projects, whenever the spirit moves me.

Friday / June 20

So much for my resolve to phase out of this daybook. But what's a reluctant diarist to do when a former textbook collaborator and retired English professor, whom one hasn't seen in six or seven years, pays a surprise visit in the middle of dinner? When I heard the knock on the back screen door, I thought it might be one of the neighbors, checking in about Sunday's potluck at the neighborhood park. So I was doubly surprised to see Brad, who lives in Michigan and whom I last beheld in New York City several years ago, when he, my colleague Miriam, and I were together for an editorial conference on the drama anthology. Brad's always been a fast talker from his days as a ham radio operator, also something of a showman, with an interest in theater and ventures in playwriting, but he's never been more dramatic than he was this evening, just staring at me, momentarily silent, on the other side of the kitchen screen door. And more dramatic still, when he refused my invitation to join us for dinner. No, he couldn't spare the time, seeing as how he'd come to Iowa City to spend the week in a fiction-writing course, trying to tighten up a thousand-page manuscript for a mystery novel he's been trying to get published the past few years. We talked briefly about his retirement some five years ago, about a subsequent stroke from which he's evidently recovered, and about his wife, Mary Lee, who's still teaching, and then he was off just as suddenly as he'd arrived, off to work on some short stories for a weekend course he's also taking before the novel-writing course starts next week. Though he promised to call back this evening, to let us know when he could come for dinner, the call never came, and I couldn't reach him by phone, which left me wondering what had come of him on this hot night in Iowa City, when I wasn't wondering about the mysteries of retirement and how it might have led him to produce a thousand-page manuscript for a mystery novel, and what it might lead me to create five years from now.

Sunday / June 22

Early this morning, Kate gave me my marching orders for today's neighborhood picnic. "It's time to get some of the younger men in the neighborhood to lug those picnic tables around. Besides, you shouldn't be doing it with your bad back and your heart and neither should Jim. And neither should I. We're all too old for that stuff." So I called Patrick, one of our younger neighbors, and he promised to set up the tables, which made me feel mighty good about handing off that chore. But a half hour before the potluck was scheduled to begin, Kate was fretting about the unmoved picnic tables in the park, so before Patrick could get his crew together, I jockeyed the tables into place myself, pulling at one end then the other until they were arranged in a neat semicircle. And then I sat down to catch my breath, wondering how I'm ever going to let go of the other things I shouldn't be lugging around, if I can't let go of the picnic tables.

But the picnic itself was a lively affair, with fifty or sixty neighbors who turned out and filled the tables with bean salad, lettuce salad, potato salad, pasta salad, purple cabbage salad, pickled ham, oven-baked chicken, carrot cake, chocolate cake, and fresh fruit galore. And good talk—about the neighborhood, the park, the cool spring, the suddenly hot summer, last month's hailstorm, last night's rain-storm, and what to do about my inoperable modem, which was evidently zapped by the lightning that accompanied the storm.

Later this evening, as I walked Pip past the neighborhood park, I thought about the picnic again and the young parents who came with their children and the handful of old-timers who are left and how I've evidently become one of them. What else could I think, when I remembered how several of the young people came up to me during the picnic and congratulated me on my retirement—"That's a real achievement." And I suppose it is, if you're looking at it from a great distance. But from my perspective, the real achievement took place just a few minutes after the potluck began, when Marianne and her husband, Michael, both in their eighties, deftly lifted one of those massive picnic tables and carried it into the shade.

Monday / June 23

I may be one of the old-timers, but I sure don't have it together like Marianne and Michael and never will if I can't get any better control of myself than I had today. It all started early this morning with a call to the hot line of my modem manufacturer and the crisp assurance of the answering chiphead, "Yes, you've probably fried your modem, and the warranty doesn't cover acts of God, but if you mail it in, we can get it repaired and back to you in two or three weeks for about $50 or $60." Not the assurance I wanted to hear, so I called one of the mail-order computer companies and discovered that I could get a new modem, same brand, for $99, delivered express mail to my front door tomorrow. Then just to check things out locally, I called the university computer center and discovered I could get one there today for the same price. So I drove down to campus, only to learn that the version I wanted to replace actually costs $169. A sizable difference, but I wasn't fretting about cost when I could have a new modem in hand immediately. Then I hurried back home, unplugged the fried one, hooked up the new one, clicked on my e-mail icon, and lo! my computer screen lit up with a special message, the same damn message I'd gotten all day Saturday and Sunday when I was trying to activate the old one—"Looking for the modem. Is your modem plugged in? Is it turned on? Is it set at the right speed?" By this point, I was sweating with frustration—and the escalating temperature and the panicky sense of things beyond my control. Oh yes, it occurred to me that I didn't need to be on the Internet, except to keep in touch with Miriam at her summer home in Stratford-on-Avon, and even that need could be taken care of by the department's fax machine. But I wasn't in the mood to heed that inner voice. I'd just bought a new modem, and I wanted to know why it wouldn't work. So I called up the manufacturer's hot line again and got another disarming response— "It's quite unlikely that the modem is defective. It's more likely that you've fried the modem port on your computer, which you probably can't get repaired without replacing the entire motherboard. Just to be sure, I suggest that you hook the new modem up to a different computer and see what happens." Just then, I noticed my spare computer from the office, sitting on the window seat, so I hung up and started another hectic cycle of unplugging and plugging, this time dismantling everything on my work desk and reconstructing things to hook up the new modem with my spare computer. But just when I had everything hooked up and ready to test, it occurred to me that my office computer wasn't equipped with any of the software to get me on the Internet from home. By lunchtime I still hadn't tested the new modem, though I did at least have the printer up and working with the spare computer. After lunch and after installing some Internet and e-mail software and after reconfiguring everything to work with the spare computer, I did finally get my new modem to work, only to discover that I hadn't received any new e-mail over the weekend. And even if I had, it surely wouldn't have been worth the stress of this morning.

But I did get a batch of regular mail that set me off on another frenzy, when I discovered that the first of my rollover IRA payments had been deposited in my bank account a week early and without any of the tax deductions I'd requested (or thought I'd requested). This time, thank God, it took only a single call to discover that I'd not submitted the tax deduction form and that I'd not specified that the deposit be made on the first of the month. No wonder that most of the retirement books are devoted to managing one's money, especially on days like this.

Wednesday / June 25

Kate and I had a few dinner guests this evening—my retired colleague Oliver, his wife Joy, and Brad, whom we finally got in touch with a couple of days ago. And no sooner were we sitting around the cocktail table in the living room, munching on Kate's marinated mushrooms and roasted red peppers, than our chatter quickly turned into a conversation that surprised all of us. Kate started it off, when she mentioned the "gray heads" she'd seen the week before shopping in the Amanas—"nothing but people over retirement age." I chimed in, asking what we could do to deal with all the retirees who roam the countryside in their campers and RVs, swarming through the vacation spots all year long. The minute I finished my question, Oliver looked at me with an impish grin on his face and said, "I'd get me a steamroller and drive it down the sidewalk, squishing them dead like ants, just like that." Joy let out a gasp, while Brad chuckled in agreement with Oliver. "Exactly so," he said, "Exactly so."

Though Brad and I were laughing at Oliver's devilish sense of humor, I wonder now if we weren't also venting some of the hostility that seems to be so deeply ingrained in the culture that it's seething even in those of us who are retired. And if that's how we feel about our retired compatriots, I wonder how it is with all the people who are younger than we. Still working, still paying into social security, still waiting their turn, which Congress pushes back a bit each year, while we draw our monthly benefits, take to the highways or the airways, and head off to vacation spots around the country and around the world. If I thought it were just material envy, I could easily understand it and accept it. But I think there's more to it than that, especially when I look back and think of how I sometimes felt about some of the older people in my younger life, as if they were really out of it, and I didn't ever want to be like them, or think like them, or look like them, or anything of the sort. A fear of age and therefore a rejection of it that's fiercer today, given the segregation of youth and age that's rampant in our country, what with senior centers and retirement homes on the one hand, singles bars and disco clubs on the other. Maybe that's why I was uneasy about retiring and leaving the building this spring—not wanting to be consigned to a monoculture of the aged, wishing instead for a world that's more like an extended community than a network of age-segregated ghettoes. Sometimes when people ask me how I feel now that I'm retired, I want to answer that question by telling them about all the people inside me—not just the sixty-five-year-old retiree, but the six-year-old orphan, and the twelve-year-old Hebrew student, and the fifteen-year-old rebel, and the twenty-one-year-old grad student, and the twenty-two-year-old gardener, and the twenty-three-year-old father, and the thirty-two-year-old divorcee, and the thirty-five-year-old bridegroom, and the forty-two-year-old professor, and the forty-seven-year-old institute director, and the fifty-three-year-old heart-attack survivor, and the fifty-five-year-old writer. And so many others that I sometimes feel like I'm living in a tower of Babel.

Thursday / June 26

A full day of writing—the thing I've been waiting for all spring, without a worry about the garden, now that it's all planted; or about the modem, now that it's working; or the computer, now that it's being repaired; or the retirement income, now that it's beginning to come in as expected; or the house, now that I spent all day yesterday cleaning it up for last night's dinner party.

Such a carefree day that I wish it were the norm rather than the exception, and then retirement would be ideal. But from what I've seen so far, it's hardly a panacea. Deer still roam the backyard every night and sometimes during the day, my computer still crashes from time to time, and I'm still the victim of all my compulsions. A free lunch, after all, is not a guarantee of happiness. Still, it sure is a pleasure to write all day, without having to worry about a monthly paycheck.

Saturday / June 28

Another full day of writing while Kate and our neighbor Mary-beth went antiquing in Amana. But today's most important story didn't take place until late afternoon, when Kate and I went to a nearby dairy farm to look at some young kittens. "I'll pay you a quarter for every one you take," said Eldon, the farmer, his ruddy cheeks breaking into a wide smile. Then his wife, Joanne, emerged from the side of the barn, a clutch of kittens right behind her, a black, a calico, and a spotted gray, followed by a dark nondescript mother cat, and then a few minutes later by a few other litters emerging from other nooks and crannies around the edges of the barn. I could see why Eldon wanted to unload a few kittens. Kate discovered them a few days ago when she went out to pick up some fresh Guernsey cream for the dinner with Brad, and ever since then she's been carrying on a low-key sales campaign for a "brownish tiger" that reminds her of our former cat Phoebe, a twenty-year-old who died of cancer two summers ago.

So much talk about a new cat that I went out to the backyard this morning to look at the spot behind the old apple tree where we buried Phoebe, and for the first time in two years I couldn't find it right away, thanks to the grass having filled in the boundaries of her grave and my grief. A sign, I thought, that maybe it's time to get the cat that Kate's been angling for the past two years, usually by appealing to the needs of Pip—"Pip needs a young companion for his old age, to keep him perky, just like the vet said." I wonder if the vet would recommend the same thing for me. Sometimes, in fact, I've wondered if Kate herself wouldn't like a young critter bouncing around the place just to make me a little more perky. But no sooner did I imagine a kitten bounding around the house than I began to think about all the trouble of training it—first the food bowl and litter box routine, then the regimen to make it an indoor-outdoor cat, not to mention the emotional challenge of getting Pip to accept its companionship without going into a deep funk. No wonder my feet were dragging all the way out to the barn. Yet the minute I saw all those kittens, I could hardly resist, especially the mushroom-colored male with spots all over his flanks and his white belly, also the female with two or three different shades of gray in her coat. The brownish tiger reminded me a bit too much of Phoebe, and I don't want to be mourning an old cat when I'm just starting to raise a new one. So now we're torn between the spotted male and the gray female, which makes me even more uneasy than before, lest we wind up getting two kittens when I was worried just about taking care of one. Already the propaganda has begun—"They'll keep each other company!" But if that's the case, I wonder what's in it for Pip, except to be paired with an old geezer like me.

Sunday / June 29

My daughter Amelia, nurse and cat fancier, is a straight shooter, so I knew when I called her this morning for advice about house training a new kitten that she'd also have some ideas about getting one kitten or two. "I'd definitely get both cats, Dad. That's the way Joe and I have always done it. They'll keep each other company. Every creature needs one of its own kind to be with, so we're seriously thinking of getting another dog to go with the one we have. Just think of how you'd feel without Kate, and you'll see what I mean." I didn't figure she'd cut so close to the bone with that remark about Kate. I also didn't figure that I'd be so haunted by my recollection of the time, some twenty years ago, when Kate and I did have a couple of cats—Phoebe in her early years and Calliope, our calico, in her dotage, strutting her stuff but also teaching Phoebe how to patrol the backyard and hang out on the terrace in the summer heat—a time when Kate and I were so much younger, untouched by either heart disease or cancer, that the future seemed unclouded by harbingers of mortality.

Even though we hadn't decided how many to get, Kate threw herself into preparations for the new kitten(s) as if she were buying a layette for a newborn child. And after several hours of shopping, she came home with elastic for a neckband and cat bells to tie on it, a food bowl and food, kitty litter, litter box, litter scooper, and deodorizer. Everything to civilize the beast(s), except a few toys. Then we talked some more about the question of one or two, I fretting about the double responsibility (and costs), Kate fancying the double pleasures and spicing the debate with a favorite refrain, "If you spend so much time worrying about this and that, you'll never have time for life itself." But we did agree on our preference for the spectacularly spotted tiger and a spectacularly composed salad of crab, shrimp, snow peas from the garden, cooked then chilled, and sliced tomatoes on a bed of our homegrown lettuce. And then the day ended much as it began, with another long-distance phone call, this time from Kate's longtime friend Glenda, who lives in California with her menagerie of horses, dogs, and cats, urging us to get both kittens, "so they can keep each other company." And so to bed.

Monday / June 30

An early call to the vet's to get a specialist's view of the matter found all the doctors occupied with their patients, so we made the decision ourselves and settled on one, especially when Kate started to consider all the hassle of training and caring for two. And then out to Eldon and Joanne's to pick up our spotted kitten and take it to the vet's to start the cycle of de-fleaing, de-miting, de-worming, and other de-pesting (and depressing) routines. Before we parted, Eldon and I had an amusing conversation about our heart attacks, bypass operations, and diets. I can still see the smile on his face when he said, "The doctor advised me to limit my ice cream to once a week, but nowadays it seems like every day is once a week for me." His ruddy-cheeked smile, in fact, was as broad as when he offered to pay me twenty-five cents for each kitten I took off his hands.

But the kitten didn't seem to be smiling a few minutes later when he found himself on a metal examining table, being inspected with a flea comb by our longtime vet, Bill, who gave us a plastic bag of so-called goodies, containing a packet of drug brochures and a small sample of kitten food, available only from vets, but no sign of a toy. And then we left the critter there to be bathed, sedated, injected, and started on all the other procedures that will turn him into a plump, sophisticated city cat rather than a thin scrawny farm kitten with oozing eyes, pulled away from its mother's breast at nine o'clock this morning. "Come back around four," said Bill, "and we'll have him ready for you to pick up." Somewhat like a newly bought car, I thought, all polished up and ready to go.

No sooner had we left the vet's than the name game began, each suggestion inspired by the striking array of dark spots on his white belly and his mushroom gray coat, somewhat like a diminutive jaguar or ocelot. So Kate wanted to call him Jag or Ossie, whereas I favored Bob for bobcat. Tyge for tiger also seemed like a possibility. Thank God, we couldn't think of any more spotted felines to name him after. In fact, if it weren't for a duplicate retirement check from TIAA-CREF that arrived in this afternoon's mail, I'd probably have become obsessed with naming the kitten. But the unrequested check led me down another path that wound up with the delightful news that it was mistakenly issued because I'd asked TIAA-CREF to change the deposit date of subsequent checks when the first one arrived ten days early, which made me wonder how many more surplus retirement checks I could get just by asking to change the date of my payments once every month or two.

Late this afternoon, we picked up the cat, and Bill gave it his beaming approval, then gave us a batch of ointments, pills, eyedrops, and a few parting words. "He looks like a bright one. You'd better keep your camera ready, because the changes are going to happen much quicker than you can imagine." Pip took the change much better than I imagined, licking him eagerly, circling him busily, then shambling off to his basket, where it was unclear whether he was sulking, thinking it over, or just sleeping it off. The kitten meanwhile had his first meal of dry food, mixed with some canned fish, water, and a little milk, while we had a celebratory dinner of grilled steak, French potato salad, sliced tomatoes, and fresh greens from the garden. All things considered, I'd rather be an old dog than a young cat.

Tuesday / July 1

Early this morning, Kate headed off to a meeting of the county board of supervisors, in hope of saving some century-old trees from a destructive road-widening project. That left me to baby-sit the kitten, which spent most of the morning snuggling, sleeping, and purring in my lap, while I, still in my pajamas, tried to catch up on this journal, wondering if this is what retirement is all about. By eleven, I'd had enough of the still unnamed kitten, so I put it in the downstairs bathroom (which is doubling as its one-room apartment), and headed back upstairs to shower, shave, get dressed, and get lunch ready for Kate and me.

By the time I finished dressing, Kate had returned so stirred up from the board meeting and so delighted (as I was) to discover that the kitten has learned to use the litter box during its hour alone in the bathroom that she wanted to go out for lunch. So we dined at a downtown bistro, where she had a dish of fresh tomato pasta with shrimp in a basil-wine sauce, and I had a grilled halibut steak served over a bed of steamed greens with rice cakes and a salsa of black beans and corn—everything so piquant it made me think that perhaps this is what retirement's all about.

But early this evening, when I was tying up the tomato plants with Pip by my side, I noticed that he's been scratching a sore on his back to the point that he's knocked off the scab and irritated it even more than before. Which made me wonder if this is his response to the new kitten, his way of dealing with the threat of suddenly being a retired pet—without even the courtesy of a phased-in retirement.

If I didn't know any better, I'd say it's just like the nervous rash that erupted on my leg a few months ago when I first started wondering what retirement is all about.

Wednesday / July 2

The kitten, whom we've decided to call Jag, is learning by such leaps and bounds that Kate found him sleeping on the windowsill this morning, four feet above the floor, without any apparent way up, except by vaulting from the litter box to the toilet to the counter and the sill. Nothing shy or retiring about him! But the speed of his scamper also leaves us delighted that we only have one to contend with. Late this morning, for example, when Kate was shopping and I was baby-sitting, reading a newspaper on the living room couch, he managed to sneak around the barrier at the foot of the living room stairway by leaping through the balustrade and up the carpeted steps to the second floor. When the vet's monthly bill arrived this afternoon with the fee for Monday's full service inspection and overhaul, I was even more delighted that we only have one to take care of.

Yesterday afternoon, Jag met a few other members of the family, when Lib, her cousin Donna from Wichita, Donna's son, John, and his two sons, Josh and Jason, came over for a short visit on the back terrace. Lemonade all around and a general round of oohing and aahing over Jag. But the talk quickly turned to work and retirement, for I was curious about John's current job at an airplane manufacturer in Wichita, and Donna, a former English teacher and high school principal, was curious about my retirement and how I feel about it. I told her about my mixed feelings, especially about leaving the classroom, and told her about keeping this journal, and told her how I'm now trying to work my way out of the journal by forgetting about retirement whenever I possibly can. But nothing I said sticks so clearly in my mind as Donna's parting shot when I asked her how

she felt about retiring and leaving the classroom several years ago—
"I haven't missed it a bit, and neither will you when you discover
how much you can do now that you've finally gotten out of school."
Say, like baby-sitting a new kitten and mollifying an old dog.

Thursday / July 3

Thanks to getting my first full retirement checks from Uncle Sam
and TIAA-CREF, I'm now living entirely on funds from my various
retirement accounts, which means that I'm now completely retired.
No sooner had I given that upbeat report to our friend Linda, who
called this afternoon from Chicago, than I began to feel creepy
about marking the onset of my retirement in such blatantly financial terms. Linda also seemed a bit disconcerted by my report, for
she quickly asked, "But do you find yourself feeling any different or
living differently?" And without hesitation, I found myself talking
about a pleasurable loss of obligation. No deadlines, no duties, no
dissertations.

But the minute I finished talking to Linda, I also began to feel
creepy about defining my existential condition in such negative, es-
capist, terms, as if retirement had nothing positive to offer me. So
I've been thinking some more about that conversation with Linda,
and I'm now beginning to feel more comfortable about it, though
not perhaps for the reasons that I had in mind when I was talking
with her this morning. I've been thinking, for example, that if it
weren't for my various retirement accounts, I wouldn't be completely free to go my own way, to follow my own star, to forget about
all the obligations of employment. And if I weren't completely free
to go my own way, I wouldn't have the opportunity to live quite
differently from the way I've been living the past forty years of my
life—bound, as I've been, by the servile need to earn enough for our
living and save enough for the future. No wonder the Spanish words
for pension and retirement are one and the same—*jubilación!*

Now, for the first time, I'm beginning to feel as if living well were all that mattered. Not as the means to an end, but as an end in itself. A way of being that I've never really considered before except in connection with the world of art or the acquisition of knowledge—like a Grecian urn or a liberal education. To live in such a way seems such a strange and extraordinary opportunity—so different from the way I've been trained to be—that I can hardly imagine myself doing so. Yet now that I've come to envision such a possibility, I can hardly imagine anything else worth doing in the time that now remains. It's "the last gift of time," as Carolyn Heilbrun puts it in her splendid book about life beyond sixty. So, if Linda were to call me now and ask how I'm feeling about retirement, I'd tell her right off that I certainly do find myself "feeling different" about life, though I haven't yet started living as differently as I hope to live in the days and weeks to come.

Friday / July 4

Independence Day, and I spent the first half of it cleaning up Jag's bedroom and litter box, then the kitchen, then all the bowls and crocks that Kate used last night to make her pepper-cabbage salad for Alan and Kris's Fourth of July picnic this afternoon. If this is freedom, I'm not sure it's for me. But the picnic this afternoon was something else altogether. And it wasn't just the keg of Leinenkugel's Ale that Alan and Kris provided, nor their platters full of charcoal-roasted beef, ham, and turkey, nor the potluck table of salads, nor the rich array of desserts that followed—the chocolate cakes, white cakes, fudge squares, fruit tarts, and fresh fruit. Nor even the extraordinary weather, like May or June in the midst of July—crisp air, gentle breezes, and a partially overcast sky. No, it was something else about the picnic that I only realized when we were on our way home, driving down the gravel road, and it suddenly occurred to me that I'd spent the entire afternoon talking with people, none of whom asked me about retirement. No wonder I had such a good time. The freedom from having to talk about retirement was so liberating that it made me feel as if I'd been traveling in some new mental territory, as spacious and liberating as the expansive grounds of Alan and Kris's hilltop place outside of Iowa City. The only problem is that Marshall just called from California, wanting to find out about my CREF account right in the middle of the city's fireworks display, when the bright orange chrysanthemum rockets were blossoming so high in the sky that I could see them from our attic windows two miles away, so dazzling a sight that I too was blooming with a renewed sense of my freedom from thinking about retirement. I wonder why my brother keeps asking me about my CREF account, especially when he remembers my having explained it to him once or twice before, especially when he's a financial wizard compared to me, especially when he's been retired the past five years and by this point, I imagine, would have found his way around all the nooks and crannies of retirement financing. Maybe it's because he likes to fuss over things even more than I do, or because he wants to control his nest egg and spend as little of it as possible. Whereas I just want to get as much living and pleasure out of the money as possible. And otherwise not think of such things anymore.

Saturday / July 5

Maybe I'm fated to keep thinking about retirement. How else to account for my reaction to a visit today from my former graduate student Katie and her husband, Joe, the creator and master of my Web site? They're back in Iowa City for the weekend, having driven nonstop from Memphis, where both of them are working in the world of the Internet and imagining a future life when they're both freelancing somewhere in the dreamscape of northern California—a far cry from the high school teaching that Joe gave up this winter and the newspaper reporting that Katie stopped doing this spring. They came over this morning to see the garden again in high summer, and Joe also came to talk about updating my Web site with links about the winter book. But all the while they were walking around the yard, gawking at the cabbages, tasting the snow peas and the shell peas, admiring the lilies and lithrum and yarrow in Kate's flower border, I was admiring the genial fluidity of their lives and their work. How relaxed and unconstrained they seem compared to the way I went at things when I was their age, doggedly pursuing an academic career that I could never imagine myself forsaking except in occasional moments of frustration or fantasy. The one-track career, the one-track life—we were all schooled to believe in it when I was growing up. Now, thank God, it's largely a thing of the past, and maybe, by extension, the retirement problems I've been coping with—so tied to one job and one place of work that giving it up has sometimes felt like abandoning the very ground of my being. I wonder, on the other hand, what it might feel like to have worked at several different jobs in several different places, like Katie and Joe. Would retirement, then, be less troubling? Would one even be retiring or just continuing a nomadic life? And what would be wrong with that? One could do far worse, I think, than be a vagabond.

Monday / July 7

A couple of graduate students called me late this afternoon to report that they've just finished their theses, one for the M.F.A., the other for the Ph.D., and to remind me of the meetings they've scheduled next week to defend their dissertations. Nothing unusual, except for the brief time to read their manuscripts, and even that's not so unusual during the summer session when the schedule's so compressed. But for some reason, I was put out by the calls, even though I knew in advance of the upcoming meetings, even though they involved a couple of my favorite students, Angela and

John, whom I've been working with the past several years. Maybe it's because they called when I was in the midst of cooking dinner, the sacred hour, shelling fresh peas and shrimp for a saffron and wine-flavored dish I was concocting to serve over spaghetti. Maybe it's because I'm feeling pressed for time these days, given all the unanswered correspondence of the past several months and this Friday's deadline to submit my share of the instructor's manual for *Fields of Reading*. Maybe it's because I spent most of the day up here in the attic, starting to get rid of all the outdated correspondence and manuscripts and canceled checks and bank notes and income tax forms and quarterly reports from TIAA-CREF that I've been accumulating the past thirty-five years, and it looks like I'll be at it for the rest of the week. But I also have a hunch that I'm beginning to get so accustomed to the freedom of retirement—the late evenings, the leisurely mornings, the languid afternoons—that I don't want to be bothered by any kind of academic obligation, even the ones I'd been longing to continue just a few months ago. Now I'm beginning to understand why some of my retired colleagues moved out of the building without looking back. A clean break, a new path, a fresh field of play.

Thursday / July 10

I wonder what Kristin, my St. Martin's editor, thought when she called this afternoon to find out how I'm doing on my share of the instructor's manual for *Fields of Reading*, due tomorrow, and I told her that I haven't done any work on it and probably won't have anything done until the end of this month. I've never been so blunt about breaking a deadline—so blunt that Kate raised her eyebrows as she listened to me talking on the phone. Even I was surprised when the words came out of my mouth without a second's thought, especially when Kristin asked if there was something she could do to help, and I said, "No, it's just life, taking its course. Besides, it's hard to get serious about an instructor's manual, especially during the summer. The book is one thing, but an instructor's manual is another." She didn't raise any objections. In fact, she sounded cheery about it, as if she too had recently retired. I wonder what she'd have thought if she knew that I'd actually spent the last few days up here in the attic, trying to simplify my life by getting rid of all the outdated documents I've been saving, including a bunch of correspondence and manuscripts from previous editions of *Fields*. I wonder what she'd have thought if she knew I was working on this diary rather than the instructor's manual for the book.

Friday / July 11

All week long I've been feeling like a deranged pack rat, wading back and forth between the heaps of old documents I've been piling up on each side of the attic floor. But every once in a while I've also been feeling like a literary wastrel, especially in the wake of a conversation with Dan, who told me, "You should be saving all that stuff for a personal essay or memoir about the past thirty years of your life, or at least a piece about throwing it all away after all those years of saving it." Even before he put it so bluntly, I'd been having a few pangs about casting away all those records, all those aids to memory, those sure ways back to the past that I'd not thought about for so long they might as well have been lost forever. Every canceled check a spot in time, like the cocktail party that Kate and I threw some twenty-six years ago for my longtime friend and colleague Bob, from whom we bought this house. Or the beige pinwale corduroy suit that I bought at the Brooks Brothers store in St. Louis, twenty-five years ago this November. Or the former neighbor who roto-tilled my garden twenty years ago this spring, a robust young man with a wife and five children, who was dead of cancer two years later. Or the boat trip we took up the Wailua River in Kauai, fifteen years ago this spring. Or the train trip we took to Denver to visit Kate's brother, thirteen years ago this December, two months before my heart attack. So many checks, so many spots in time, I could've spent another thirty years recalling them all, savoring every one of them to the fullest, which may be why Kate said, "It's time to move on," when I told her of Dan's suggestion. But even before she told me to get on with it, I knew it was the right thing to do, because I couldn't stand the clutter of all that stuff closing in on me, in on me, like a narrowing tunnel.

Sunday / July 13

Kate and I took Dan and Maura out for a farewell dinner last night, before they head off to Arkansas, where he'll be starting his first full-time teaching job and she'll be finishing her doctoral thesis. A festive evening at a Greek restaurant in Cedar Rapids, from the flaming saganaki, to lamb shish kebab, Greek salad, and a taste of Dan's custardy dessert. Such a celebratory evening that Dan caught me by surprise when he asked if I planned to hold a meeting of our essay study group before everyone leaves town. During the last several months, I've not given much thought to our collaborative project of the past several years—six graduate students and I tracking down, reading, and discussing an extensive body of material about the personal essay with the intent of putting together a collection of such pieces by twentieth-century essayists. But once Dan reminded me, I could hardly refuse. He's going to arrange a get-together, but I'm now beginning to wonder how many collaborative projects and graduate students I can sustain and still have time for my own work and the different kind of life I've been thinking about. After all, I'm now committed not only to the collection of essayists on the essay, but also to the drama anthology that I'm helping Miriam to revise, and the freshman anthology of readings for which I still haven't finished my share of the instructor's manual. As things now stand, it's hard just to keep up with this diary, even though it's no longer a daily chore. So I can hardly imagine how I might finish my book on the personal essay, or start the one about food that I've been wanting to write, much less imagine doing a travel book that Kate has in mind. No wonder my neighbor Jim keeps talking about how busy he's been since he retired. Maybe our true work only begins once we're free to do the things we've always yearned to do.

Friday / July 18

"Professor emeritus"—today for the first time I referred to myself as that most distinguished thing. What better way to get some action from TIAA-CREF on my request to have them restart one of my monthly retirement payments that they mistakenly canceled? Now if I can also get them to withhold federal and state income taxes from another of my monthly payments, I'll have all my retirement affairs in order—at least for the time being. The only problem is that I still don't feel like a retired professor, especially not after this week, when I found myself writing a last-minute letter of reference for Vanessa, lunching with my former graduate student Hope, chairing the exam for Angela's thesis, sitting on the exam committee for John's thesis, and meeting with the essay study group to plan our collaborative anthology. If it were just a matter of time-consuming meetings, I could easily disregard this week as being atypical, since it's the only one this summer that's been filled with such academic affairs. But as the week unfolded, I found myself repeatedly behaving like a professor, or at least like someone who's still wired to ask students the challenging questions, to draw out the implications of their answers, to prod them into revising their work as carefully as possible. In fact, at each meeting I found myself getting more stirred up as the discussion unfolded, try as I might to keep myself above it all, like someone as stately and wise as a professor emeritus. Maybe Kate was right when she told me, "You're still trying to teach them something." And maybe I shouldn't fight the impulse, since I've been doing it for almost forty-five years. Some things, I guess, are so deeply ingrained that one cannot ever stop doing them. So, maybe I'm a professor emeritus on the one hand, and a professor forever on the other.

Sunday / July 20

Come to think of it, maybe I'm not a professor of any kind, but a gardener plain and simple. Or so I've been thinking, ever since Vanessa gave me a tote bag earlier this week, with a picture of George Bernard Shaw on the side of it and a Shavian quote directly below the picture—"Gardening is unquestionably the only useful job." I'm not sure I'd describe my current occupation quite so boldly as Shaw (especially if I were speaking professorially), but the garden must have some kind of powerful hold on me, else I wouldn't have been attracted to it this week when the temperature's been in the mid-90s every day and the humidity too. Sometimes, I think it's just the taste of all those fresh vegetables that's kept me working in the garden the past forty-five years. I certainly felt that way this noon, when my mouth was zinging with the chilled gazpacho that Kate concocted from the vegetables she harvested this morning. But I wasn't even thinking about gazpacho or anything else to eat when I found myself drawn into the garden early this morning just as I was about to do my Sunday recycling routine. Before I knew it, I was lost amid the cucumber vines, the squash bushes, and the pepper plants—so carried away that I completely forgot about the empty wine bottles and the plastic cartons and the old newspapers in the trunk of the car. And I didn't pick a single thing. My mind was elsewhere, transfixed by the rampant growth of all the bushes, plants, and vines. Then distracted by a few weeds around the tomato bed. Then beguiled by the unruffled water in the lily pond. Then compelled by a flat of parched basil plants. Then amused by the spectacle of myself tending things and beholding their response, as if I, and I alone, were in control of the garden. An illusion momentarily as satisfying as to think that one is what one does to keep one's self employed—a professor, a gardener, a writer, a diarist. A ruminator, chewing on the cud of his identity. The occupational hazard of retirement.

Tuesday / July 22

Today, after three years of swearing I'd never buy a laptop computer—too difficult for me to work the little trackball and keep my eye on the cursor—I bought myself a laptop computer. How else could I keep track of things during our trip to the Rockies? How else could I record my ruminations anywhere in the world without a laptop computer? And how could I resist the opportunity to buy one for less than a third of its original price just twelve months ago? A Macintosh Powerbook, with an easily workable trackpad, an easily visible cursor, and a ninety-day warranty. Who could ask for anything more? Now all I have to do is learn how to work it without working myself into a frazzle.

Monday / July 28

Six days without writing anything in this diary! A new record and one I might be pleased with, if it hadn't started with my feeling a bit depressed last Tuesday, but for reasons I couldn't put my finger on, because I'd gotten up early with a fresh resolve to start work on the instructor's manual in time to finish it by Friday. Kate said, "It's probably the heat and humidity and drought we've been going through. It's enough to get anyone down." But Monday morning last week brought us some relief from the heat wave and a little overnight rain, so I couldn't blame the weather, and I couldn't blame the diary, given all the days I've skipped this month. The only way out, I decided, was to stop procrastinating and start the manual, hoping it would distract me from the depression. But the manual wasn't any help, because the first thing I had to do for it was to write a series of answers to the questions I'd asked about an excerpt from Anne

Frank's diary. Reading her work and thinking about her tragic situation some fifty-five years ago made me ashamed of my own diary, dedicated as it is to fretting about the trivial ups and downs of my luxurious retirement, like having to work on the instructor's manual.

Then, to make things worse, the heat wave returned with temperatures and humidity so high that the heat index was running between 100 and 125 for three consecutive days. The only good thing about the heat was that it forced me to stay inside our air-conditioned house and work on the instructor's manual, except in the early morning, when I was outside watering the vegetable gardens, the herb beds, the flower bed in the neighborhood park, and my retirement tree. What would it mean, I wondered, if my retirement tree, my swamp white oak, were done in by a drought, like the cucumber vines shriveling up in the garden?

Bad omens, alright, but nothing so bad as what I saw Friday morning as I riffled through a drawer of old snapshots, looking for a mug shot of myself to give the publicity folks at the press. Thirty-five years of unsorted snapshots, ranging from the time when I still looked like my son, Marshall, dark-haired, lean, raunchy, and young, to the present-day specter, gray-haired, jowly, pouchy, and glum. Worse still, when I did find the black-and-white shot I'd been looking for, up here in the attic, a shot of me standing in front of our cedar tree, clad in a button-down shirt and a shetland sweater, looking middle-aged and preppy as ever, Kate said, "You don't look that way anymore. Not at all. That's the way you looked twelve years ago." So, after all, I settled on another shot I found in the attic, another black-and-white, with thinning gray hair, a quizzical eye, and a short-sleeved summer shirt, taken eight years ago, which Kate said I should use because "That's how you look now." The only consolation of sorts came in a note from Linzee, the publicist at the press, who told me, "You don't look any different now," so "rest assured that no one will notice the difference between you now and you back then." If Linzee's right, then perhaps I've been standing still for the past eight years, or better still I'm ageless, at least for the moment.

Tuesday / July 29

No sooner had I settled into a couch at Janusz's birthday party last night than I was congratulated by a couple of other guests who had heard about my retirement. "That's wonderful," said one. "That's just wonderful," said the other. And I wondered, as usual, why I deserved their congratulations, except for having lived long enough to cash in on my annuities. But I managed to keep those thoughts to myself, lest I insult them both for their well-intentioned remarks, occasioned no doubt by their own impending retirements. I can still remember how eager I was to retire when it was somewhat in the distance, as if it were a goal to be reached and prized for itself alone (as well as its luxurious benefits). Though I don't feel that way anymore, I do sometimes think about former friends and colleagues and acquaintances who didn't make it all the way—victims of accident, affliction, suicide, war, or some other mortal circumstance. Musing upon their fates, I sometimes find myself thinking that "they didn't finish the race"—such an old and inappropriate expression that I'm embarrassed to find it lurking within me, a residue no doubt of my childhood days, when our lives were marked out for us like a footrace with a series of distinct goals along the way. When I told Kate about those thoughts at lunch today, she—the poet, ever on the watch for overused expressions—surprised me by saying, "It is a race of sorts, and you either finish it or you don't." (I guess they were still using the same old metaphors when she went through grade school ten years after me.) I didn't think she was trying to reassure me, and she certainly didn't, for the moment she made that remark about finishing the race or not, I couldn't help wondering what she meant by finishing. Living long enough (and accumulating enough money) to take retirement? Or living long enough within retirement to savor its peculiar pleasures before one goes into a debilitating decline? And how long might that be? It all depends, I guess, on how voracious one is for the feast of life. Maybe that's why I was thinking last night that the person who really deserves congratulations is Janusz, and not just because he's still energetic at seventy-eight, nor just because he recently finished one memoir that's been accepted for publication and has started work on another, nor even because he can outlast almost anyone when it comes to downing straight shots of vodka. But because some fifty years ago he survived four and a half years in a Russian gulag and another year in Siberia before going to Moscow, where he trained to become the internationally distinguished surgeon that he was when our university's faculty regulations forced him into retirement at the age of seventy. Comparing myself to Janusz, I can't help thinking that I've run the race on tiptoes, whereas he has run it vigorously, never breaking his stride, thanks no doubt to his years in the gulag. I certainly don't envy him those years, but I do occasionally find myself thinking that extreme hardship of some sort may be a better teacher than anyone I've ever encountered in the classroom.

Thursday / July 31

If extreme hardship is a good teacher, then a comfortable berth, like my retirement, is probably a lousy way to learn anything, especially how to keep calm when things go wrong, as they have the past couple of days. First it was the insurance company trying to short-change me on their estimate for repairing our hail-damaged roof. Then it was a repairman at our university computer center mistakenly telling me that the new computer I bought last January wasn't under warranty. Then it was TIAA-CREF not yet having reactivated the annuity that they mistakenly canceled in June. Then it was my textbook editor calling to report that the publisher of Anne Frank's diary wants $10,000 for permission to reprint just a dozen or so pages from her book. Then it was the repaired computer so badly reconfigured by the repairman that I couldn't get the modem to work, so I couldn't check on my e-mail or log on the Internet or do anything else of that sort. And then in the midst of trying to activate my modem, it was the sudden realization that I was about to be late for a thesis conference with my graduate student Mary, and that I hadn't yet made a reservation for the going-away lunch I'd scheduled with Angela. No wonder I still haven't had the nerve to unpack my new Powerbook.

The weather yesterday morning, when it all came to a climax, was idyllic, especially for late July—crisp mountain air, temperature in the high 70s, gentle breezes—but I was sitting at my computer, sweat pouring down my cheeks from the stress I was feeling. And it didn't get any better when Kate came up the attic stairs, asking me to help her find a missing document from the Heritage Tree files, scattered at the other end of the room. Oh, for a sense of humor at such a moment, or just the common sense to distract myself by looking out the window at my tomatoes almost to the top of their seven-foot poles—anything to break through the frustration and anger and hysteria building within me. Now, twenty-four hours later, I've got the computer reconfigured, so my modem is working again, but otherwise everything else is still out of whack. And the weather is turning hot again, and the humidity is steaming up again. Yet none of that stuff seems important enough to have let myself get heated up by it as I was yesterday morning. Perhaps what I need to do is study tranquillity more assiduously than ever before, make it so much a part of myself, a way of my being, that nothing can raise my temperature, not even a wonky modem or a missing retirement check.

Friday / August 1

Thanks to predictions of the biggest El Niño in fifteen years, and thanks to the winter book, which touches on the most recent El

Niño of 1995, and thanks to the ever-resourceful Linzee, I'm finally on the verge of having my fifteen minutes (or fifteen seconds, or fifteen kilobytes) of fame. I never imagined that the bizarre ups and downs of a three-year-old winter might still be newsworthy today. But now with an even more extensive and convulsive El Niño beginning to take shape, all the media are gearing up for the big story, looking for meteorologists and others who might know something about it. Why else would MSNBC post an urgent request for El Niñoists on "Profnet," a Web site where anyone can find academic specialists on any subject. I'd never heard of Profnet until Linzee told me about it a few days ago, shortly after she contacted MSNBC and sent them my name, telephone number, page proofs, and a press release about the book.

"Fame," as Milton once said, "is not a plant that grows in mortal soil." And in keeping with that solemn truth, my fame will grow on MSNBC's Web site, according to Bobbi, the reporter who called this evening, interviewed me, and raved about the book, especially when I gave her a list of all the pages that refer to El Niño. Bobbi also asked me to do a short reading and told me that she'll include it, along with a snapshot of me, and a link to my Web site in her feature story for the MSNBC Web site. So, next month, when I'm in Canada, my sound bytes and my image will also be somewhere in the ions, waiting to be found by millions in Bobbi's story of El Niño. It never occurred to me that I might be in so many places at once, but then again I never imagined that my fortune cookie might really come true—that when winter comes the heavens will rain success upon me.

Saturday / August 2

A few days ago at the university's computer repair shop, I ran into Carolyn, a former graduate student, and our conversation led to the familiar question of how I feel about retirement. But before

I could answer we were both distracted by the repairman's verdict that her broken-down printer wasn't worth fixing. I offered to e-mail her the name of my favorite low-price computer store, and today she sent me an e-mail with some of her own thoughts about retirement. "In some ways," she said, "it must be like moving without going to another place." Such a paradoxical and disarming perception that it took me by surprise, especially because it spoke directly to the sense of dislocation I've been feeling ever since February. Carolyn said she'd been thinking about how it might compare to "the large and long jolt" she experienced after a long-distance move she made several years ago. But I also have a hunch that her long bout with premature arthritis, which abated a dozen years ago only to return the past few years, must also have something to do with her keen sense of how one can feel dislocated, displaced, disoriented, without changing one's location at all. And the past few days, I guess I've been feeling more dislocated than usual, as I've said goodbye to Angela and then to John, whose departures remind me in more ways than one that I am, indeed, moving without going to another place.

Tuesday / August 5

Today was Lib's eighty-third birthday, so we took her on a picnic to the county park, a picturesque spot in a rolling patch of Iowa countryside. A place apart, surrounded by thousands of trees with a doglegged lake running the length of it, pathways and hillsides around the lake, and gazebos, benches, antique bridges, and lookouts throughout the park. A special place for someone whose emphysema and osteoporosis have kept her inside during much of this hot and humid summer.

At the retirement home where she lives, there are so few men compared to the number of women that I'm always a bit surprised by the imbalance, as I was again today, even though I've long known about the different longevities of men and women. It's one thing to read about the differences, but another to see them so clearly visible as they are at Lib's place and Aunt Ada's. Those aging women who greet me in the hallway with their gentle smiles are more haunting than they can possibly imagine, for they remind me as nothing else can of what the future might have in store for Kate and me. But Lib's been living with that reality for almost thirty years, so why should I be fretting about it, especially after such a blessedly mild day in the country, the air suddenly cooler and drier. Perfect weather for a picnic dinner like the ones she served in summers past. Back then, there were always five or ten of us gathered around the oak table on the back porch, passing the plate of fresh vegetables from her garden and the dish of homemade mayonnaise and the potato salad and the roast pork tenderloin and the bowl of fresh fruit. Today, it was just Kate and me and Lib (in a wheelchair)—and a solitary bird, twittering away in a nearby grove of trees. And all those unvoiced memories. But it made her so happy to be outside again, taking the air and the sun and the sights and our picnic dinner in the shelter of a little gazebo that I wish I could have enjoyed it all as much as she did.

Thursday / August 7

I'd just come back from Chipper's, the Irish tailor we've been taking our clothes to the past thirty years, and I was telling Kate how much trimmer he looks than the last time I saw him a year ago, so much so that I couldn't resist an admiring question about how he lost all the weight. "Fell off a high ladder—that's how. Painting my house. And damaged my legs so bad I lost thirty-five pounds. I wouldn't advise it. Wouldn't advise it." I was also curious about his age, and again he answered me in his forthright way. "Sixty-eight and still at it!" So, when he asked me what I was up to, I felt a bit sheepish about admitting that I'd retired in May. But more than that, as I stood there looking at him looking at me over his Ben Franklins, I was surprised—almost shocked, even—at how the years had passed since I first met Chipper when he was still a young man, newly arrived from Ireland. He's still as cheerful and vigorous and cocky as his name, and he's still got his lively brogue, but he's clearly not a young man any longer. And somehow on this bright August morning, I couldn't stop thinking about his age, his age, as if the fall had done it to him in one fell swoop, until Kate helped me understand my disquiet—"It's like looking in a mirror, the mirror of memory. Only you wind up facing reality."

Friday / August 8

Sarah, the press's marketing director, turned up at the front door this afternoon with some fifteen hundred postcards, featuring the woodcut from the cover of the winter book. An attractively over-sized card, almost the same size and shape as the book, announcing its publication. A pleasure to behold, at least for the moment. But before we leave for Canada a few weeks from now, I have to address several hundred cards to announce the Prairie Lights reading here in Iowa City, shortly after we return in late September. And then I'll have to address several hundred more postcards and do several more readings and signings around the Midwest, all of which makes me wish it were enough to write a book, without also having to hype it. A writing life, like the academic life, seems filled with onerous duties.

Sunday / August 10

"Just think, a month from now we'll be in Canada!" We were leaning over a bridge, looking at the Iowa River stretching out beyond us and the campus all around, when Kate made that exuberant announcement. Canada was not on my mind just then, for I was thinking about the start of classes only two weeks away, trying to decide whether the pleasure of not having to get myself in harness again was greater than the sadness of not ever holding forth in a classroom again. I guess it was our walk by the dorms and the first sight of returning students that set my thoughts in motion. Also the cool, overcast day and the premonitions of fall. I must have been so lost in thought that Kate asked me if I had heard what she said about being in Canada, and then suddenly I realized the silliness of pondering a question I'd resolved a few months ago, especially considering the prospect of hiking again in the Canadian Rockies, looking down upon rivers and lakes so glacially turquoise, so different from the greenish cast of ours, as to make me feel I'd been transported to some other world, a loftier place by far, where such questions might never arise.

Monday / August 11

Oh, to be in the Canadian Rockies when the United States mail arrives, especially when it contains a form letter from John J. Callahan, the acting commissioner of Social Security, asking me to fill out a three-page form reestimating my 1997 earned income from wages and self-employment, "because we want to make sure that we are paying you accurately." After last month's mix-up, I thought everything had been squared away, especially when this month's check arrived containing exactly what I expected. But now Mr. Callahan and his colleagues want to do a little fine-tuning for the rest of the year.

The form contains only five simple questions about my date of retirement, my projected wages for 1997 and 1998, my estimated number of months when I will earn $1,125 or less, and my estimated hours of self-employment each month. Such a simple form that I almost finished it within the government's estimated completion time of ten minutes. The only problem is that I had to fudge on the question of how many hours I expect to be self-employed each month. As a self-employed writer, musing upon the run of my personal experience, I'm sometimes at work almost every hour of my waking life—in other words, about 16 hours a day, for a total of 480 hours a month. But my musing, on the whole, probably averages out to no more than 8 hours a day, for a total of 240 hours a month. Still a troubling thought, especially when I know that Mr. Callahan doesn't want me to be self-employed any longer than 45 hours each month. But if I tried to explain the nature of my self-employment, I'm sure it would lead to an interminable set of problems beyond resolution. Faced with this absurd predicament, I obeyed Mr. Callahan's advice "to put something down for each month," so I estimated 40 hours of self-employment per month from January through April, 45 per month for the rest of the year—in other words, about 1½ hours of musing and/or writing per day. Then I signed the form, quickly folded it up, and put it in the return envelope, hoping that once I put it out of sight, it would also be out of mind.

But now four hours later, I'm still thinking about that question and my answer, which means, of course, that I've far exceeded my government allotted self-employment time for the day. And that doesn't include the time I spent writing this entry, which puts me way over my quota for the day, which means that I shouldn't say anything about the dill-broiled salmon filet, the spinach linguine with garlic-flavored olive oil, and the garden tomato salad that we had for dinner.

Wednesday / August 13

Today for the third or fourth time in a week, I didn't shave or shower until late afternoon, when I began to feel so uncomfortable with a day's worth of growth (and sweat) that I couldn't stand it any longer. I wonder what it means that a fifty-year-old habit—shaving and showering every morning, shortly after breakfast—could begin to break down only three months into retirement. Am I going to seed? Or just getting into the leisurely pace of retirement? When I announced to Kate that I was going to shower and shave, she quickly issued a word of caution—"Don't rush into anything." Nothing so blunt as her announcement last week that "those pants you're wearing are an embarrassment. They're so spotted and worn around the pockets and fly that I think you should go downtown and get some new ones while Land's End is having its end-of-summer sale." And I agreed, but I still haven't done anything about getting new pants and hiking shoes for our upcoming vacation. I wonder whether I'm suffering from a retirement-induced inertia or a resistance to making myself presentable when I'm no longer on display.

My recently broken shaving habit has been bothering me so much that I couldn't even keep it to myself when I was talking to David, an acquaintance I've known only from his occasional work on our antique glass light fixtures. We were standing in his driveway this afternoon after he'd loaded a pair of fixtures into my car, when he looked at me with a gleam in his eye and asked me the now familiar question, "So how are you liking retirement?" I think he wanted me to say that it's wonderful, everything it's cracked up to be, since he's just five or six years away from it himself. But I hemmed and hawed, went into my spiel about ups and downs, and then told him about not even having shaved until a few minutes before I came over to pick up the light fixtures. David's always seemed so fastidious about his appearance that I thought he'd look upon my belated shaving as a matter worth fretting about. So I was completely surprised when he broke into a big smile and said, "But why even worry about it?" A question that left me more troubled than the broken habit itself. Why worry about it, indeed?! And then as if to give me further food for thought, David told me that from what he's heard, "it takes about two years or so to get into the rhythm of retirement." By that point, I might have a beard down to my beltline!

Thursday / August 14

"I was downsized in 1993." So it was that Craig, our dinner guest, spoke of the corporate trimming that led to the end of his managerial career in computer engineering. Craig had driven down from Wisconsin with my son-in-law to do some remodeling at the home of our gardening friend Rebecca, and we were all sitting around the table, savoring Kate's homemade mushroom and spinach lasagna, listening to Craig talk about how he had gone from being a midlevel manager to being an independent jack-of-all-trades.

The first time I heard him speak of being downsized, I was somewhat puzzled because he didn't show any signs of being diminished either in his stature or his sense of self-assurance. But as dinner wore on, and Craig continued to talk about himself, I came to feel that in some sense he must have felt profoundly diminished by the corporate downsizing that ended his twenty-year career. Still, in talking about the experience, he didn't seem to betray any sadness or disappointment whatsoever. So I wondered what might account for his composure and self-assurance, since he's now juggling a wide range of different jobs to support himself and his family. And at that point he launched into a detailed explanation of how he completely changed his professional outlook from pursuing a "single career" to having a life of "projects" as a tax assessor, a carpenter, and a nurse (which he's also training to be). When I asked him how he felt about the radical change in the relationship between employers and employees—from a paternalistic and protective one to the bottom-line mentality that produced his downsizing—he quickly replied, "I think it's better for the workers. They're on their own, with no illusions that the corporation will ever look after them, so they have to look after themselves. From here on out everyone's on their own."

Listening to Craig's reflections, I realized that during the past fifteen years my kind of career has almost become an anachronism. Nowadays, I suppose, most people wouldn't even dream about the possibility of working thirty-five years for the same employer, much less of being provided with such an ample and secure retirement as I've received. But then again, perhaps I'd have been better off in the long run—more adaptable, more resourceful—if I too had been forced at some point to leave the protective world of the university and make my way as a lone ranger in a lifetime of projects from which I might never retire.

Friday / August 15

Amelia breezed in from Wisconsin today, in time for us to celebrate her birthday this evening and for her to drive Joe home from his remodeling project tomorrow. She came, as usual, bearing a few heads of garlic from her garden to barter for several peppers from mine. A fair exchange, given the trouble she has with peppers and I with garlic. But the best trade of all took place at the dinner table, when she asked me how retirement was going and I in turn inquired about her current working arrangements. Amelia, who's thirty-eight today, has already made three career changes, each of her own choosing, which have taken her from agricultural journalism to corporate communications, and most recently to nursing. Such a varied professional menu that I'm dazzled by her ability to move from one venue to another without losing her balance or her sense of humor. And today she again took me by surprise when she talked about the possibility of becoming an emergency-room nurse and working part-time at two or three different hospitals. Why would she want to juggle three part-time jobs and give up the benefits of full-time work? "So I can have more say in arranging my hours on and hours off, even if it means giving up all the benefits that might come from a full-time job." When I mentioned how grateful she might be some twenty-five years from now for the benefit of a secure retirement income, she quickly countered by telling me about the many people in her generation "who want to create the kind of lives for ourselves that give us more freedom than we'd have in a full-time job, eight to five." If Amelia and Craig are at all typical, many working people these days seem to be defining their professional lives in phases, or in bits and pieces, so they can break free of the monolithic strictures and structures that dominated the lives of people in my generation. Strictures and structures that make little sense in the free-form world of retirement, a world that seems to be refreshingly free of boundaries or schedules or obligations except those we choose to create for ourselves.

Saturday / August 16

A surprise visit from my former graduate student Laura led to a pleasant lunch downtown and a conversation about her recent visit to Prince Edward Island, the site of a team-taught course that she plans to offer in Nova Scotia next year with one of her colleagues from Michigan State—a project that will combine her special interests in journal writing, nature writing, and island literary culture with his special knowledge of natural resources, particularly in the area of marine biology and island ecology. Talk about moving beyond conventional boundaries! The prospect of offering such a course on Prince Edward Island was almost enough to make me wish I hadn't yet retired. Especially when I thought about mingling travel and teaching with an opportunity to learn something about one of my favorite creatures, the north Atlantic mussel—a dish of which I ordered for lunch just to savor the thought of Laura's forthcoming venture.

I didn't expect that our upcoming Canadian venture would be of comparable interest to Laura, until she reported that she has a research leave this semester and would welcome the opportunity to spend a month in Iowa City, tending our gardens, our house, and her writing. Laura, it seems, has a special affection for Iowa City, so if she can find someone to tend her pets and her new house in East

Lansing, she will tend our place while we're off in Canada. Now if only I can learn to be as venturesome and improvisational as Laura, Amelia, and Craig, I might find a way to savor retirement as much as I enjoyed the steamed mussels steeped in a sauce of fresh tomatoes, garlic, white wine, thyme, and parsley.

Monday / August 18

Today was the first day for moving back into our offices now that the summer remodeling is done. A move that I approached with mixed feelings, still eager to have a place within the community of my colleagues and former students, but not wanting to awaken any of those old yearnings for the classroom. Thanks to all the unpacked boxes and unshelved books that I carted to the emeritus suite last May, I suddenly wondered why I had ever wanted to keep an office in the building, especially when it meant that I'd have to unpack everything just when my mind is elsewhere (or I wish it were elsewhere)—on our upcoming vacation. But after a few hours of shelving books, filing folders, throwing out boxes, moving in a few comfortable chairs and my plants, it gradually began to look like a place that I could muse in, write in, pleasurably hold forth in, plausibly act the part of a professor emeritus in, without ever hungering to teach another class in. Perhaps I've found the place I've been looking for ever since I started this journal back in February. The only thing that needs to be done is to have my computer "touched," as they put it, by one of the university's computer specialists, so that it's programmed for our new local area network. Maybe I could also get myself touched at the same time, so that I'm programmed for our upcoming trip to Canada.

Wednesday / August 20

A few days ago the Jeep started acting up—an abruptly racing engine—leaving both of us unnerved about what else might go wrong when we're on the road. And it didn't help any when the service department fixed the problem, but also did something that produced a glitch in our electrical system that they won't be able to repair without ordering a special piece of equipment that'll take a couple of days to arrive.

Meanwhile, back at home, the garden is so filled with ripening vegetables that we're eager to can or freeze or juice or pickle or eat that our vacation now seems a bit ill timed. Also because Pip and Jag are getting on so peaceably and playfully that it seems unfortunate to cage them up for a month-long stay at the vet's. Also because the weather has turned so balmy and breezy that it's hard to imagine a place I'd rather be right now than my own backyard. But then again, I wonder if I'm just looking for reasons to avoid a full-fledged break with the past, to be here as usual when the new academic year begins, sitting in my office, waiting for classes to start.

Friday / August 22

Laura called this morning to confirm her intention of staying in the house, and the Jeep service department called reporting that they fixed the electrical problem. But the real news of the day is that Kate and I had lunch outside on the terrace of the Union, watching the students amble along the banks of the Iowa River, without my having any sentimental feelings about the onset of classes next week.

Sunday / August 24

"You haven't yet produced your syllabi?" We were eating dinner this evening when Kate asked me that question in mock disbelief. To tell the truth, I hadn't even been thinking about my syllabi, though I might well have been doing so if I were getting ready for the first day of classes, which begin tomorrow. A good sign that I'm getting over my desire to keep teaching and all the ritual activities connected to it, which always begin with planning one's courses and producing one's syllabi—the day-by-day, week-by-week schedules for the whole semester—in time to have them ready for the first day of class.

Given my bad habits, I never did start working on my syllabi until the last week of summer vacation, and then I was so stressed out by everything else connected with the start of classes that I usually didn't have them ready until the last minute, right before I walked into the first class of the semester. But even before classes begin each fall, there's always the first department meeting of the year, always scheduled for Sunday evening, and that's what I was thinking of when Kate asked her mock question. I was thinking of all my former colleagues down at the building, listening to announcements and to Dee's opening remarks for the year, whereas I was at home on this departmental Sunday for the first time in thirty-five years, savoring a grilled veal chop with mushrooms sautéed in red wine and fresh basil. I was gloating, a habit that seems to develop more quickly than I'd imagined.

Tuesday / August 26

"Are you having withdrawal symptoms?" That's the way I was greeted this afternoon by Scott, our lawn mower, when I came running out to gather up the weed piles and leaf prunings I'd left around the yard before he scattered them with his mulching mower. I didn't understand him at first, but then I remembered visiting my colleague Carol yesterday afternoon and talking about how quickly we became addicted to teaching, because it gratified our instinctive need for admiration.

Actually, the past two days I've been so involved in cleaning the house before Laura arrives that I've hardly had a moment to think about teaching, retirement, or anything but how to get through all the chores that need to be done before we leave on Saturday morning. Yesterday it was the basement, today the attic, tomorrow the living room and the guest bedroom for Laura, Thursday the TV room and kitchen, Friday our bedroom, the dining room, and the two bathrooms. By the time we leave, the house should be fully cleared out and cleaned up for the first time since we started our golden years projects last August. And by that time, I should be so fed up with housecleaning that I won't have any withdrawal symptoms when we hit the road.

Wednesday / August 27

Late this afternoon, Sarah turned up at the front door with the first copies of *Weathering Winter* in hand. And I was transfixed by the evocative winter scene on its cover and the comfortable feel of it in my hands. The thing itself at the moment of its completion, a moment that passes all too quickly. So I wanted to savor it and toast it, but Sarah didn't have time for festivities. I, on the other hand, couldn't resist the impulse to run out and get a couple bottles of champagne—one for Kate and me to have with dinner, the other for Sarah and her cohorts at the press.

Friday / August 29

Our last day in Iowa City before heading west, and I spent it in such a frenzy of activities that I was ready for a vacation just to relax from getting ready for the vacation. The unfinished housecleaning would have been enough to fill an ordinary day, but I also had to pay the September bills, pick up my pants at Chipper's, e-mail Miriam about the drama anthology, check my mail at the office, check in with Sarah about arrangements for a book reading in Dubois, Wyoming, harvest all the surplus red peppers and sell fourteen pounds of them to my neighbor Steve, who manages the produce section of the co-op. Doing business with Steve is always somewhat like visiting over the back fence, a sociable occasion for exchanging neighborhood news and haggling a bit over the price of my produce. But by the time I hit the co-op in midafternoon, I was traveling at such high speed that I was eager just to unload the peppers for whatever Steve offered. No wonder he felt "we didn't haggle enough." But we did compare notes about our previous trips out west and agreed that it's always a pleasure to be on the road, especially when it's heading toward the Rockies. Laura arrived a bit later, in time to take a quick tour of the garden and then to join us for dinner at a local Japanese-Korean restaurant, where my fortune cookie provided a memorable conclusion to the meal, the day, and the summer— "Time is prime for changing your profession."

Saturday / August 30

Kate identified my new profession and how to do it, just as we were leaving Iowa City this morning. "I'll do most of the driving, so you can take notes. And don't worry about trying to make anything of them right now. That'll come later. Right now the only thing that matters is to keep a record of things that catch your attention the minute you see them, so you don't forget any of the important details. That's what you have to do if you want to be a travel writer." So I quickly started taking notes in my spiral stenographer's notebook, recording the important details. Like the image of Laura, standing at the top of the driveway, waving us on our way with a big smile on her face, while I was thinking how strange it is for someone to be standing in our driveway, waving us on our way. And the rain falling, falling hard, washing us on our way. And the bumper sticker on a truck coming out of a small town grocery, declaring, "Work is only for people who don't go fishing," which made me wonder why I haven't gone fishing this spring or summer, especially when I noticed the farm ponds beckoning me all along the way. And the long stretch of driving in midafternoon on a two-lane highway so devoid of traffic it seemed as if we were the only ones traveling amid the corn and beans, corn and beans, all the way across Iowa. But then the bizarre spectacle of a farmhouse set back from the road with a host of trucks surrounding it, all the way around, which made me think that all the missing traffic was concentrated on that farm, until Kate set me right by announcing, "That's a farm auction. That's something you wouldn't see on the interstate." We were heading west on blue highways all the way across Iowa, the vistas so spacious all around that I gradually came to feel a greater sense of release than I had all summer. "Feeling free," as Kate said in late afternoon, "is like being a prairie dog who's gotten out of the burrow. You can stand up on your hind legs and look around." And that's what we were doing all the way to the Mulberry Inn, our bed and breakfast in Yankton, South Dakota.

An eighteen-room red brick Victorian Gothic house, built in 1873, with ten gables, six guest rooms, two parlors, parquet floors, a massive front door, and a brass plaque announcing its inclusion on the National Register of Historic Places. The minute we entered, we were greeted by Millie, the manager and joint owner, who explained that the inn was swarming with guests for a fortieth anniversary dinner party, which put me in mind of our own wedding thirty years ago on a Saturday afternoon right before Labor Day. And the local roadhouse-steakhouse, where Millie advised us to eat, was also bustling with a pair of newlyweds and their wedding party, including a country rock group, got up in solid black outfits and glittering black cowboy boots. So it seemed that we too should also be strutting our stuff. But we didn't stay for the free shortcake, since our anniversary doesn't actually take place until September 2. We returned instead to our book-lined room at the inn, where I finished writing up these notes on my new portable computer, while Kate watched late-night TV, transfixed by the breaking news of Princess Diana's automobile accident and then of her death and the death of her lover, Dodi Fayed.

Sunday / August 31

"Well, you gotta do something. You can't just sit around, especially if you used to be an ambulance driver." Jerry, the joint owner of the Mulberry Inn, sat in the back corner of the breakfast room, explaining what led him and Millie to buy the place and restore it. "When my boys were younger, they wanted me and Millie to buy this old house and move everyone into it. All the relatives. Now, of course, the boys are grown up and moved away, but we did finally manage to get the house. And now we can't get free of it. You can't ever leave a place like this, even when you're away from it. So it's a strange thing—I'm retired, but I'm not any freer than I was eight years ago when I was still driving an ambulance." The minute I heard that Jerry had been an ambulance driver, I thought he'd be eager to talk about the death of Diana, waiting so long for an ambulance to come that she couldn't have been saved by the time it arrived. But Jerry hadn't yet heard about Diana and Dodi, nor had Millie, nor had any of the guests. So I felt like an unwelcome messenger delivering bad news, except for the blank faces, the bland reactions, of everyone in the room, which left me wondering whether they were shocked or just indifferent. It's a long way from Paris to Yankton, but I never imagined the possibility of getting so far away from it all just by driving a few hundred miles west of Iowa City. Which also made me wonder what it might be like when we reach the Black Hills this afternoon and check in at the State Game Lodge of Custer State Park.

But before the Black Hills, there was the farmland and the farming from one end of South Dakota to the other, changing, it sometimes seemed, with every passing mile. Soybeans one minute, sorghum the next, then sunflowers, yellow to the horizon, then short grass and rolling prairie, then corn, then soybeans again. "It's funny," Kate said, "how you come over a little hill and it's all changed." A transitional landscape without any transitions, changing as abruptly as the solemn midmorning radio program on Diana followed by the tinkling words and melody of "It's a lovely day today for whatever you want to do." And it was a lovely day, except for the temperature edging into the 90s when we stopped for a picnic lunch under the shade of a cottonwood grove at the Binke Lake State Park. By midafternoon, the flatland of the Rosebud Reservation was sweeping out on all sides. Fields of grass with only an occasional pond or tree or anything else along the way. Hardly anything to distract one's eye from the land. The land itself. An ocean of it without a ripple. Virtually untraveled on this Sunday afternoon, and seemingly unsettled too, except for a few Kwiktrips and a few hardscrabble settlements.

But then heading north (on US 385), how about Hot Springs?! A community built entirely, it seemed, of red sandstone. Redstone hotels, redstone banks, redstone stores, redstone gas stations, and redstone homes. Maybe they should have called it Redstone. And heading upward toward the Black Hills, how about the buffalo grazing and reclining in the meadow just a few hundred feet off road?! So carefully dispersed, it seemed to Kate as if "the rangers must have assigned them separate spots along the way to make sure they'd be just right for snapshots and sightseeing." So in late afternoon, we eyeballed the buffalo in Custer State Park while listening to a BBC overview of Diana's life. Which put me in mind of the Movietone newsreels I watched as a child, images of Hoover Dam alternating with shots of Hitler. And then we checked into our specially reserved room, the Eisenhower Room, with a brass plaque on the door announcing that "Dwight D. Eisenhower slept in this room— June 1953." Right next door to another room with another brass plaque announcing that "Calvin Coolidge stayed in this room— Summer 1927." The whole summer, including the whole White House staff. Seems as if Cal must've known more about retirement than any president before or since.

Monday / September 1

Labor Day, which I celebrated by continuing to work at my new job as a travel writer, noting, for example, that the Eisenhower

Room is nothing to write home about—just a modestly sized room so crammed with a four-poster bed, TV console, tall dresser, dressing table with faux brass handles, and swag draperies that Kate and I could hardly move around in it without bumping into each other. I wonder if Mamie stayed in Washington when Ike slept here. But the Pheasant Eye restaurant last night was something, especially the walls festooned with stuffed pheasants and my plate with a sautéed pheasant breast in plum brandy sauce. Almost enough to take my mind off the solemn promise of Dan Rather, still ringing in my ears, "to bring you the best American coverage of Diana's life." But not even Dan's grandiloquent commentary on the media's creation and undoing of Diana could match up to the grandiose buffalo pies this morning on the front lawn of the State Game Lodge. So, after all, it was a pleasure to get a breath of fresh air as we headed upward to behold the Needles—the Needles!—the rock outcroppings featured in all of our guidebooks.

A narrow road up with sharp turns, one-lane tunnels, and evergreens more and more dense all around us—a claustrophobic ascent—and the Needles gradually coming into sight. But when we stopped to view them, to walk amid them, to touch them, to look through them at the vistas beyond and below, it wasn't just those granite spires spiraling above us that caught our attention but the cool air, the fresh breezes, rustling, whistling through the cottonwoods, the lodgepole pines, and the spruces. And the glitter of fool's gold, the glow of wildflowers, and the taste of wild raspberries. And suddenly both of us reduced to nothing but exclamations. "Look at the fool's gold!" "Look at the wildflowers!" "Look at the wild raspberries!"

We were also exclaiming in Deadwood a few hours later, and not just at all the gambling joints cheek by jowl on both sides of the main street, but also at the three gold bars that turned up on my first chance at the slot machines. Too bad I was only playing for quarters.

Too bad I couldn't resist a few more tries, so I wound up with only twenty-five of the thirty quarters that I won, which moved Kate to inform me that "gambling is a real problem with the aged." I didn't have any problem with it at all, except for a second or two, when I wanted to have a few more tries with one of the dollar machines, just to see if I could make enough to cover lunch and maybe dinner too and possibly a bottle of champagne to celebrate our anniversary tomorrow. If they hadn't replaced the old-fashioned arm-pull with a newfangled push button, I might have given it another try, but somehow it didn't feel right—didn't feel as if the press of my finger could make as much difference as my arm used to make, pulling the one-armed bandit.

From Deadwood to Billings, everything seemed to be telling us that we were heading toward the fabled world of Big Sky Country. Black hills giving way to high plains, evergreens to grassland, wildflowers to sagebrush. So many changes, so many transitions that I almost lost sight of my own, until the waves parted at the Radisson Hotel and I found myself staring into the face of a bellman who was staring back at me as if he were thinking the very same thing that was running through my head—that we look the same age, but he's still at work, pushing a luggage cart for a living. I kept my thoughts to myself, and so did he. What could either of us say that might bridge the gulf of a lifetime?

Tuesday / September 2

Our thirtieth wedding anniversary, and it began with both of us absorbed by TV reports of massive crowds throughout Britain, bearing witness to their grief for Diana, who now seems on the verge of being anointed with her self-chosen title—the Queen of Hearts. A better title by far than the Princess of Wales. And then the first news of the driver's alcoholic blood levels, and the continuing talk about the guilt of the paparazzi, as if they were the exclusive cause of a much more complicated chain of events. Better, I thought, to savor a few recollections of dinner last night at the Rex. Like the steamed clams in cilantro and hot pepper broth, the baked king salmon, crusted in crushed pistachios, the wild rice, the sautéed zucchini and tomatoes, the fumé blanc.

Better still to hit the road again and keep heading northwest, toward the high plateau, toward Helena. Baled straw dotting the land like environmental art. Cylindrical in one field, rectangular in another. Beige bales in one field, green in another. Beige fields in one place, green fields in another. Beige on green, green on beige, green on green, beige on beige. A checkerboard landscape, as endless in its severities and its variations as the barbed-wire fences and gates that bind it and frame it for miles on end. But no sooner did I form those impressions of the land and the farming than they were called into question by outcroppings of rock and evergreens, beehives, and even a few cornfields. Then a river valley of pine, cottonwood, and Russian olive—studies in gray and green. Then sheep grazing in one field, cattle in another. Then mountains faintly visible in the distant haze, grassland giving way to sagebrush, alkali, and antelope. So much for the simplistic image of Big Sky Country.

A world as richly varied as White Sulphur Springs, a very small town with a very tall graystone mansion, looming over the village like a castle at the top of its single hill. So how could we resist a tour of the two-towered Castle Museum Carriage House? Especially given the porkpie hat, the green T-shirt, the beet-red cheeks, and the nonstop spiel of Harold, the tour guide who greeted us as we entered the place. "I was a teacher here in town. Taught school for thirty-five years, and that's the whole story of my life. If it hadn't been for the World War, I'd never have left here. I taught elementary school, then high school, then became principal, and now I'm doing this. And I've got plenty of time to do it. Time, that's what I've got more of than anything else. The man who built this house made a fortune in no time. Made it in gold, and lost it just as quick in bad investments. The story of this state is like the story of this house. Towns coming and going almost overnight. People coming and going, like the Ringling Circus family that built a place by the creek at the other end of town. And the sawmill that left here a year or two ago."

So we toured the Castle, as it's locally known, and looked at photographs of B. H. Freeman, the mine owner who built it, and admired the clothes and artifacts of local Indians who frequented the medicinal mud baths and hot springs before they were turned into a stagecoach stop that aspired to become a world famous spa, a Rocky Mountain Baden-Baden. But none of the photographs or the native art and artifacts were quite so compelling as the antique shepherd's wagon, housed right outside the Castle. Kate thought it was "as snug as a ship's cabin," complete with built-in cabinets, pullout tables, counters, and a sleeping loft. I couldn't resist the stepladder leading into it, and for a minute or two I was transported to a world more inviting and invigorating than a castle or a spa, a place where one could truly get away from it all. A Big Sky hideaway without any hokey pretensions. The only problem is that I couldn't imagine how I'd tend my flock, my self, and my writing, especially without any water or electrical outlets.

The shepherd's wagon was still on my mind a few hours later when we checked into the Sanders, "one of the 100 best bed and breakfasts in the U.S. and Canada," a Teddy Roosevelt–style place, complete with high ceilings, oak paneling, matching antiques, and a brass four-poster in our honeymoon suite (which looked to Kate as if "it might have been a servant's quarters or children's nursery tucked in under the eaves"), with a full-length mosquito canopy draped around the bed, a TV facing the end of the bed, and a large bathroom with a spacious walk-in tile shower, with two shower heads facing each other at opposite sides of the space. I was also thinking of the shepherd's life during a chilly pre-dinner walk to the

State Capitol—a Greco-Roman sandstone edifice, topped by a dome of Montana copper, where we beheld the manifest destiny of the West depicted in a massive painting: "Lewis and Clark Meeting the Flathead Indians."

Wednesday / September 3
Heading north this morning, just outside of Wolf Creek, we found ourselves on a long stretch of road without any animals or people in sight. Just undulant grassy upland, foothills in the middle distance, snowcapped mountains far off, and a glistening creek directly below the road. A Rocky Mountain cliché, but some clichés are irresistible. Like the golden wheat, glowing in the midmorning sun, so striking against the big blue sky that we stopped by an unfenced wheat field so I could pick a few stems and for the first time in my life feel the staff of life. Its stalk stiff, its head firm and tightly braided. A better thing by far than the men's urinal at Choteau City Park, where Kate mistakenly washed the veggies for our lunchtime picnic—"I've never been in a men's room before, so I thought it was just a strange looking sink." Better also than the oil pumps outside of Oilmont, the salt flats outside of Sweetgrass, and our first taste of Canada, where the customs officer confiscated the two pepper sprays that Kate had purchased for each of us to protect ourselves from grizzlies. "They're a dangerous weapon up here," he sternly informed us, "but if you fill out a form in the office we can hold them for forty days, so you can pick them up on the way back." Assuming, of course, that we'd be coming back that way and that a bear wouldn't attack us in the meantime. Not even the favorable exchange rate of $1.35 Canadian for $1.00 American was enough to placate the growling Kate, especially when she heard about a recent grizzly attack ("That could've been us!") and then discovered that the Canadian police carry pepper sprays for crowd control ("Why them and not us?!").

Canada. Our destination, or so it seemed when we were planning the trip. But now that we're here, I've begun to think our destination may be an illusion. Not because of what we lost at the border but because of what I found the past few days—in White Sulphur Springs, in Helena, in Deadwood, in Billings, in Custer State Park, in Yankton, and at the crossroads this morning where I picked those stalks of wheat. The staff and stuff of life. Extending so far toward the horizon that to think of any single place as one's destination may be as deceiving as the notion of manifest destiny. Better, perhaps, to consider the possibility that every place one stops, every thing one sees, might be a destination, fraught with surprise, with the rewards and risks of travel—a jackpot in Deadwood, a holdup at customs. A never-ending journey.

Such a heavy trip to lay upon this festive getaway trip! But ever since I've been thrust into the role of travel writer, I've been feeling that it's not enough just to describe the passing scene or report the day's events. I have to "make something of it," as Kate said a few years ago when I was starting my winter journal. The rage for meaning never dies. So I've been wondering what to make of my daily notes about the story of Diana, or why I feel obliged to take note of it every day. Why couldn't I end this entry just by writing about our dinner at Anton's, "the finest restaurant in Lethbridge," where the impeccably mannered waiters served us such exquisite braised spinach salads, twice-baked potatoes, zucchini sautéed in tomatoes, grilled tenderloins lightly sauced in mushrooms, and fresh strawberries with Grand Marnier that we were floating on air when we returned to our room at the Hotel Heidelberg? Why do I also feel obliged to mention the continuing media coverage of Diana, now having focused on the royal family's royally inappropriate silence about her death? Kate keeps telling me, "You just can't ignore it, as if it didn't exist. It's in the air, it's part of what we've been going through and living with every day of this trip." And I keep wondering why we don't just turn off the TV and ignore the newspapers. But this evening when we returned safely to our hotel, without any incident, and heard yet another replay of Diana's fatal accident, I suddenly found myself thinking about a meditation by John Donne, a calligraphic version of which I gave to Kate some ten years ago, now hanging on our living room wall. A daily reminder that "No man is an island, entire of itself. Every man is a piece of the continent, a part of the main."

Thursday / September 4

Today is the day I've been waiting for ever since last spring—the day that we finally arrived in the Canadian Rockies, almost five years to the day after we first beheld them on our twenty-fifth wedding anniversary, vowing that we'd return again someday. Talk about heavy trips to lay upon a trip! Today was more weighted with expectation than any of the past few days, for today's destination, I felt certain, would offer us the same breathtaking vistas we'd seen before. And better still, we'd be staying at a special place by the side of a mountain road that would bring us as close to the mountains as could possibly be. So as we headed out of Lethbridge, driving directly into high winds and wide open spaces, I pushed in a tape of Bach partitas, certain that its driving harmonies would bear us relentlessly to our manifest destiny—the mountains in the far distance. And we did, indeed, enter them in early afternoon, just as I'd expected. But not before getting lost in a seemingly endless web of beltways in and around Calgary. So many suburbs and exurbs on every side of the urb itself that Kate was growling as never before about urban sprawl and the dangers of overpopulation. Hardly the setting for Baroque music. But the radio wasn't much better, given the updated reports from England about the Queen's forthcoming announcement of royal grief, and the commentators' sloganizing the story as "a conflict of people versus protocol." No man is an island, alright, especially not in the hyped-up world of a sound bite. Eventually, though, we did get free of Calgary, in one rise and fall of the highway, much as I remembered us suddenly leaving the city five years ago and just as suddenly driving through a high grassland plateau with the snowcapped mountains in the background. And then the grasslands gradually giving way to forested foothills. And the big clouds and the blue skies overhead, just as before. And then the mountains themselves, gradually enfolding us, embracing us, rising higher and higher beyond us and around us, just as before.

The only problem was that we couldn't easily find the Lady McDonald Country Inn, where we were booked to stay, because we couldn't find the Bow Valley Trail, where the inn was supposedly located. Probably because we couldn't imagine that the so-called trail, when we finally found it, would be more like a newly developed strip, filled with newly built, Disneyfied versions of Rocky Mountain lodges on both sides of the road. Probably we should have known better, given the fact that we were booked into something called "the honeymoon turret room." But when our travel agent Ruth told us about the place several months ago, she was talking about "an old-fashioned sort of inn with a tower by the side of the mountain." There is, in fact, a mountain behind our recently built nostalgic-looking inn, and our room is indeed built in the shape of a tower. The only problem is that our turreted windows look directly across the street at a partially built version of another towered inn, with a crew of carpenters busily framing it in. The destination and vista of our dreams!

Friday / September 5

We were sitting by a floor-to-ceiling window in a restaurant at the Chateau Lake Louise, looking out at the picturesque lake, framed on each side by the forested mountainsides, backed by a snowcapped range, bordered by a rainbow of flowering perennials, having an exquisite little lunch of oriental duck salad, with chilled noodles, julienned carrots, ginger, bean sprouts, and bok choy in a ginger-soy sauce, when Kate asked me a question I never expected to hear from her lips—"Would you ever like to take a bus tour?" She seemed a bit uneasy just then, as if she were worried that I might say yes. So I wasn't surprised by her quick announcement—"I don't think I'm ready for that." I was already thinking the same thing, as I beheld the spectacle that occasioned her remark—a group of exuberant people, most of them visibly older than I, gathered together on a three-tiered platform to pose for a collective picture of themselves standing in front of the fabled lake. I've never been a "joiner," never had much of a taste for the canned commentary of tour guides, and never been a lover of busses, no matter what their destination. But as I watched the old folks enjoying themselves, I began to wonder whether there might be something wrong with me for scorning their pleasure, and then I realized there was something else arising from the depths, swimming right below the surface of my thoughts—a fear of dependency that I'd never confronted before. So, as I dined on the rest of my lunch, it was difficult to look at the lake without thinking of the years ahead, especially given the claque of old women I'd seen at the Lady MacDonald Inn, earlier this morning, celebrating the fortieth anniversary of their collective friendship. But then again it was also difficult to look at the lake without remembering the Alpine horn player we heard during our lakeside walk, dedicating a performance of "Amazing Grace" to "that amazing princess." Nor for that matter could I forget the TV image of the Queen, whom we also heard this morning, finally expressing her royal grief in chilly double entendres.

Still, perhaps the most memorable part of this day was our arrival in Jasper—the northernmost point of our Canadian trip and the point of departure this Sunday for our train to Vancouver. I was completely surprised at the Jasper Inn to find us booked into the Elke Sommers Suite, the best accommodation in the house, because our room had already been given to others. But Kate said, "You're overreacting," when I first entered the suite, gawking at the oversized couch and chairs, the fully equipped kitchen and wet bar, the spacious balcony, the stone-faced fireplace, the dried flower arrangements, the king-sized bedroom and the king-sized bed, the marble- and granite-lined bathroom with the king-sized shower and king-sized Jacuzzi, and the autographed picture of Elke herself, inscribed with king-sized words of gratitude to the inn, as the place where she had "found a new life" (and a new love). The minute I saw those words, I wondered if I too might find a new life in Jasper. Perhaps this might be the destination of my dreams.

Saturday / September 6

A few years ago, when I last taught a course in the personal essay, one of the readings that stuck in my mind was a piece about travel by Cynthia Ozick, especially because of her striking observation that travelers regain the "ghost-seizing brightness, eeriness, firstness" of childhood. And that's what I was expecting today when we went to visit two of the spots that had captivated us five years ago—Maligne Lake and Maligne Canyon. No one could fail to be haunted by the reach of that turquoise lake, the largest glacier-fed body of water in the Rockies, and the second largest in the world, snaking its way further and further back into the surrounding snowcapped mountains, further than the eye can see, even with the aid of binoculars. So we were expecting to be seized again by the eerie beauty of the hidden lake beyond the immediately visible lake, reachable only by means of a cruise and a tour guide—the secret lake with the diminutive island and the solitary evergreen, where Kate had spotted an osprey five years ago. The only problem this time around was the ghostly fog that so engulfed the scene we could barely see the inner lake, much less its solitary island and evergreen, or an osprey, even if one had been perched there.

Maligne Canyon, on the other hand, was visible from start to finish, so we hiked through its scalloped canyons, each one leading us deeper and deeper into its misty waterfalls and channels and bridges, each one bringing us closer and closer to the wildness of the mountains that had seized me five years ago and that I sought to feel again this time. But what I felt this time as we hiked back up along the steep ascent was a greater and greater sense of fatigue, bringing me closer and closer to the limits of my endurance. When I finally reached the end of the trail and was catching my breath on a bench outside the Maligne Teahouse, a stately woman walked by, looked at me briefly, compassionately, and said, "Time does have a way of doing such things."

I wonder what that stately woman would have said if she heard the impassioned tribute of Diana's brother at the funeral ceremonies today in Westminster Abbey—so passionate, so loving, so angry and genuine that it made me feel more deeply involved than at any other time since the first reports of Diana's death. Listening to her brother, I also heard again the words of Donne—"Any man's death diminishes me, because I am involved in mankind; and therefore never send to know for whom the bell tolls; it tolls for thee."

Sunday / September 7

At one o'clock this morning, grief week having finally come to an end, we were shuffling our clothes from one suitcase to another, trying to decide what to pack for Vancouver and what to leave behind in the Jeep, parked at the Jasper Inn for our return trip south. So many clothes for so many different climates and settings, both of us having schlepped them in and out at each stop along the way, that I wondered if Kate might be having second thoughts about this marathon of a vacation, if she too might be ready to park herself for awhile in a single place. But I decided to keep my counsel, especially at one in the morning when we only had five hours to sleep before getting up and dressed and down to the station for the Rocky Mountain Railtour's eight o'clock departure.

The minute we boarded the train and discovered that each car had an attendant who doubled as a tour guide, I thought of our conversation two days ago at the Chateau Lake Louise, wondering if we too would be turned into a jovial group of oldsters, posing for a group shot at the end of the ride. But Kate insisted, "This is not the same thing at all!"—her voice so assured I thought she might also be trying to convince herself, given the prospect of a slow train ride, taking eight hours today and eight tomorrow to cover a total of five hundred and fifty miles.

The ride was slow alright, slow enough to savor all the sights along the way—from the eleven glacier-topped peaks of the Premier Range to the three-hundred-foot cascade of Pyramid Falls—the train carefully making its way along mountainsides, over trestled bridges, through tunnels and box canyons, all bearing witness to the extraordinary feat of engineering that produced this culminating stretch of tracks in the Canadian railway system. And our attendant, William, who looked as clean-cut as a modern romance hero, was not just an articulate source of knowledge about the ecology and history of the changing scene, but also a philosopher of sorts, his informative remarks often resonating with the overtones of a meditation upon time, change, and mortality. He began, for example, by giving us a poignantly detailed account of the salmon's life cycle and survival rate, from four thousand eggs laid to an average of two hundred young fish that reach Alaskan waters to a dozen or so mature salmon that return up river to one or two that finally reach the spawning site, their bodies decomposing, their teeth jagged, their flesh falling away to feed the next generation. Then he told us about the Canadian entrepreneur Charles Hayes, who first envisioned and planned a cross-country Canadian railway system, then obtained financial backing for it by traveling to England, only to lose his life on the return trip aboard the Titanic. So many *memento mori*, including his remarks about the waning glaciers, that I began to wonder if William too had been reading the works of Donne and meditating upon the demise of Diana.

But no sooner did I imagine him following the track of my morbid thoughts than he took me by surprise, spotting a salmon here, a bald eagle there, like a biology professor on a wildlife field trip, whereas I, like a beginning student, was so concerned with taking notes, that I never spotted anything, not even the passing scene.

Monday / September 8

After yesterday's experience, I decided to give up my detailed note-taking, forget about being a travel writer, and return to being a diarist plain and simple—writing up each day at the end of the day, relying on my short-term memory (and Kate's) to recall the things that matter. Why spoil a picturesque train ride with a spiral notebook in hand? And the same goes for our upcoming days in Vancouver, when I can hardly imagine myself jotting down notes as we make our way through the streets and parks of the city. Besides, if this is a celebratory retirement trip, why should I be training myself for a new vocation?

Today was more pleasurable than any of the days just past, for my eyes were completely free to take in the passing scene. And the scenes were so striking that I don't think anyone would need a notebook to remember them, especially with the help of William's running commentary. At first I was carried away just by the spectacles themselves. Like the juncture of the Fraser and Thompson Rivers—the Fraser murky, the Thompson clear, its glacially blue waters having rippled beside our tracks most of the way south, and then suddenly a turbulent roiling as the silty Fraser, rushing in from the northwest, started to discolor the Thompson until the two were so indissolubly blended into one murky river that the Thompson was invisible while the Fraser continued to flow south along the same path as our train to Vancouver. The more I thought about that watery spectacle, the more it seemed as if the entire landscape and everything within it was bearing witness to the ancient truths of Heraclitus. Especially when the path of our tracks along the Canadian National line suddenly crossed the river directly above the crossing tracks of the Canadian Pacific line, each railroad taking its own course, yet both roads passing through an inexorably changing environment, from alpine to subalpine to semiarid to lush river valley to the oceanside setting of Vancouver itself. So, in the spirit of Heraclitus, I continued to feel that the world is constantly in motion, that everything is in a state of transition, everything in the process of becoming, myself included, traveling a course that was taking me I know not where, except perhaps toward places that might be as different and distant from my former life as Vancouver from Iowa City. Kate, who has long been preaching to me from Heraclitus's maxim that "You cannot step twice in the same river," also viewed the conjunction of the Fraser and Thompson Rivers as another example of how "Dirt always wins out," so she helped bring me down to earth from the philosophical heights I was climbing just then. And so did William, whom I thanked on our way off the train by suggesting that he had the makings of a great teacher, whereas he let me know that the ski slopes were more to his liking.

Tuesday / September 9

We were sitting in our apartment at the Sylvia Hotel, an ivy-covered relic, savoring our view of English Bay—taking in the barges and the bridges, the sailboats, the tugboats, the tour boats, and the speedboats, the beach walkers and the rollerbladers, and the Asian couple in the balcony of the apartment across the street, taking their tea and tai chi. A delicious morning scene, so different from everything else the past few weeks, or months, or years, that it seemed as if I had finally gotten away from it all. Found my Shangri-la in an old hotel with ivory drapes, overstuffed chairs, dark red carpets, and a friendly, wood-paneled bar with a spacious view of the bay. Kate and I visited the bar yesterday afternoon right after we checked in, and I was contemplating a return visit today right after our tour of the nearby park, when the phone rang, jolting me out of my reverie.

An early morning call could only be from someone far away, from my other life, and sure enough it was Laura—"I'm sorry to bother you, but a woman called wanting to interview you for a piece about the last vegetables of summer." How strange, that I'd only been away from the garden for ten days, but I felt so out of touch with it and everything else in Iowa City that I wanted to say no, wanted to preserve the delightful experience of being on the margins, at the edge of the continent. But no sooner did I start to refuse than Laura told me, "It's a woman named Marty, who says she did a couple of pieces about *My Vegetable Love* and now she's working on this one for the Sunday *New York Times.*" Such a flattering opportunity that I could hear the cynical author assuring me it would only be a single call from Marty, whereas the retired English professor was imploring me to remember that "The world is too much with us late and soon." A mental debate that I didn't know how to resolve, except for Laura's surprising eagerness for me to say yes. So I did, and then vowed not to think about it again until Marty calls tomorrow morning.

And I kept my vow thanks to Stanley Park, a thousand-acre peninsula of cedar and Douglas fir, a dense forest stretching along the bay with a network of trails and a host of attractions from one end to the other. A rose garden, an aquarium, a miniature steam train, a cormorant nesting site, a children's zoo, a grove of totem poles, and a hidden pond called Beaver Lake almost in the center of the park. Actually, the pond isn't hidden, but we had so much trouble finding it, despite a detailed map of the park, that by midmorning I began to feel we were taking part in a treasure hunt and that all the trail markers were designed to lead us astray. From Lovers Walk to Thompson Trail to Lake Trail, we threaded our way from one path to the next, without reaching the lake until at last we were led there by some other folks who had also been lost in the woods. So many people lost in the forest, like characters in a Shakespearean comedy.

The biggest surprise of all was the lake itself, a sun-filled clearing in the midst of the forest, covered with pink and yellow water lilies, a site worthy of Monet, without a beaver in sight or any sign of one. But there were roses in the rose garden, totem poles in the totem area, and an open-air luncheon near the aquarium. So we spent the whole day walking and gawking in the park, seven miles in seven hours—long enough to get away from it all and to earn ourselves another visit to the Sylvia bar, where we watched the sun set on English Bay and then headed off to dinner at a local bistro, where I had a grilled tuna steak served over mashed potatoes over blanched spinach in a fresh tomato sauce topped by a ginger salsa. Such an elaborate construction, such a tower of food that it reminded me of the totem poles—in more ways than one.

Wednesday / September 10

Even before Marty called this morning, I was feeling like one of last summer's vegetables, probably because of all the walking we did yesterday after all the riding we've done the past two weeks. And it wasn't any better when I tried to answer her question about why I fuss so much over my eggplants, peppers, and tomatoes, trying to keep them going each fall as long as possible. Rather than talking about my hunger for homegrown produce as long as possible, and the bond that grows from devoting so much time and energy to the plants, I wish that I'd spoken to Marty about my irrepressible desire to postpone the onset of winter, a compulsion so strong that I sometimes feel as if it's not only my plants but my self that's ultimately at stake when the first killing frost arrives. But my thoughts just then were as sluggish as my legs.

Breakfast at a neighborhood coffeehouse was a surprising restorative, as was the brisk pace of an elderly couple who passed us on foot, both so nattily dressed, so far beyond us in age, that they looked like models of how to endure. The whole day, in fact, was a study of endurance, from the historic neighborhoods we explored in Chinatown to the restored warehouse district of Gastown, where we spent a few hours and few hundred dollars at a Native American gallery before sauntering through the Sun Yat-Sen Gardens, the first classical Chinese garden built outside of China. But the place that sticks in my mind more than any of the others is the ancient scholar's study we toured in the classical Chinese pavilion. When we started the tour, Kate whispered in my ear, "You won't find a computer in here." I also didn't find any scrolls or any other evidence of a scholar's habitation beyond a single lacquered table. What I did find was an array of potted trees—flowering, evergreen, deciduous, and bamboo—and an ambience so airy, so tranquil, so fit for contemplation that it hardly surprised me when the guide announced at the end of the tour, "By this time you should be thoroughly relaxed."

Too bad we didn't find a similarly relaxing ambience at the Five Sails restaurant this evening, where my leek and portabello stuffed chicken breast arrived at the same time as an overblown dinner party of twenty- to forty-year-olds at the tables next to ours, filling the psychic space with their boisterous drinking, their noisy conversation, "like a herd of braying jackasses," according to Kate. A four-star restaurant with a four-star panoramic view of the bay, and no one had the nerve to complain—neither Kate, nor I, nor the prim young couple on the other side of us, nor our elegant Italian waiter, nor the maître d'hôtel. Why is it, I wonder, that all we could do was to sit in stunned silence, poking at our food, looking at each other with raised eyebrows? Kate claimed that all of us were too well mannered to make a scene. Perhaps, perhaps, but I have a hunch that the sprightly old couple who passed us this morning would know how to tame such a group.

Thursday / September 11

Our last day in Vancouver. But it was far from El Dorado or Shangri-la, thanks to my foolish quest for a corduroy jacket, which consumed most of a rainy morning in downtown Vancouver. Why didn't I heed the words of a bright, young clerk, at a tweedy-thatchy men's store, who blushed when he told me, "My father's been looking for one for a year or two, just like you. It must be your generation." And it wasn't any better when we rode the sky train to the edge of the suburbs and back again, trying to consume the whole city in a single afternoon and then went looking for a bus to Granville Island, hoping to savor its arty delights before the departure of our sunset train back to Jasper. We were looking for something in Vancouver—travelers are always looking for something, of course. But we never did find it, except in fleeting moments during a beery lunch at the Steamhouse Pub and Restaurant, beside the bay in Gastown, and later during a quick dinner at the Boathouse Restaurant, just a block from the Sylvia, where I savored a heaping pot of West Coast clams and mussels, and Kate an order of lightly fried calamari. Maybe we should have spent the whole day at the Sylvia bar, beholding the bay and whatever it was that beckoned us from afar.

Friday / September 12

A strange day, neither here nor there, our Canadian Via Rail train running three hours late, slowly tracking its way toward the alpine landscape of Jasper, my body running at least three hours short of sleep from the overnight ride in a reclining seat, somewhere between dozing and waking all night long. Via Rail, the common carrier across Canada—a different dish from the luxuries of the Rocky Mountain Railtour four days ago, when we rode only during the day and were put up overnight at a hotel in Kamloops midway between Jasper and Vancouver. Still my head was alert enough, or perhaps it was just my eyes, to notice that this train was populated not only by retired folks heading toward the mountains, but also by a host of teenagers and young adults, so many of them that I wondered what they were doing aboard the train, rather than being back at school, on campus, at work, or anywhere else but in this world of retired vacationers. A strange conjunction of youth and age, both groups being served by everyone in between—the train conductors, the tour guides, the waiters and waitresses. Everyone looking at everyone else with a hint of suspicion—or unease. And Diana's face still beckoning us all, thanks to all the weekly and monthly magazines having picked up her story where the newspapers and TV reporters dropped it off last week.

And then a rainy arrival at the Alpine Village so late in the day that it was all we could do just to unload our bags, wash up, change clothes, dine at Becker's Roaring Rapids, where we stayed five years ago, and then return to our cabin, where we built a fire and watched it gradually burn down until I was musing on Shakespeare's autumnal sonnets and vowing "to love that well which thou must leave ere long." Such a heavy burden to lay upon a few dying embers that I threw on a few more logs, just to keep my thoughts from turning more somber than they already were on this chill and rainy eve.

Saturday / September 13

On the Icefields Parkway this morning, heading south from Jasper to Lake Moraine, I was shivering or shuddering or heaving or weeping with each new sight along the way. At first, I thought it was the freshly snow-covered mountaintops that were touching me, but then I noticed the yellowing aspens and thought it might be them, or the reddening plants along the roadside, or the dandelions in the uplands, or the glistening rivers, or the clouds hovering over the mountains, shot through with sun. "I don't know what's getting to me," I said at one point, and Kate answered so swiftly—"It's the beauty of the earth!"—that it seemed as if she must have been pondering the same thing herself and just arrived at that unerringly simple conclusion. Whatever the case, I couldn't help thinking and feeling just then that everything else, or almost everything else, was beside the point. And I felt that conviction so strongly that I wished it had been possible for me to announce it to the entire world. "Drive south on the Icefields Highway from Jasper to Lake Moraine," I wanted to declare, "and you will never be the same again." But a few minutes later, I found myself thinking that it probably helps if you're driving in a Jeep Grand Cherokee Limited, listening to a tape of John Denver singing the glories of his Rocky Mountains in a voice as pristine as the world we were traveling through. Who knows what accounts for the state of one's feelings at any moment such as this?

I wish I could account for it as easily as I could explain my pleasure at the Post Hotel dining room this evening, when I first tasted the delicately dressed butterhead salad, or when I first cut into the caribou striploin surrounding a wild rice risotto in a pear Armagnac sauce, or when I first beheld my tall dessert glass of fresh red raspberries, blueberries, and boysenberries. Later in the evening, when Kate was in bed reading and I was up writing this entry, she said, "I hope you're recording today's experience of aging," which took me by surprise, and then she added "of mortality," which also puzzled me momentarily, until she added, "Why else were you in tears?"

But then again, why wasn't I also in tears when I first saw Lake Moraine this afternoon from the terrace of our room at the Moraine Lake Lodge, with the ten peaks ranged directly behind it, and the sun glittering on its exquisitely calm, turquoise water? Maybe, after all, it was John Denver and the Jeep.

Sunday / September 14

No tears today. The morning rain and fog and chill at Lake Moraine put a damper on everything but our desire to head south to the Waterton Lakes National Park and our room at the Prince of

Wales Inn. Eight hours of driving through lush green valleys, by dense forests, along mountain streams, before we suddenly found ourselves in high prairie and wheat fields golden in the setting sun of southern Alberta, and then just as suddenly found ourselves heading back into mountainous terrain at the beginning of the Waterton–Glacier International Peace Park. A mountain hidden, it seemed, in the midst of a wheat field, and within the mountain a fabulous lake, and at the edge of the lake on a barren windswept headland a fantastical piece of nostalgic architecture, piled high with eaves, with balconies, with turrets, and crowned with a very tall steeple. The Prince of Wales Inn, its dark wood paneling, its burgundy carpeting, its high-ceilinged common room looking out upon the long symmetrical lake, all evoking the ambience of a royal Scottish hunting lodge or a set for *Brigadoon.*

But nothing could have prepared us for the view of Waterton Lake from our wood-paneled bedroom, the mountains sweeping down to the lake on both sides, the lake stretching out seven miles to the peaks at its end. And then after sunset, the nearly full moon illuminating the water along the wilderness side, while the lights of Waterton village on the other side make it look like a glittering jewel in the lake. Such a weather-haunted lake that it deserves to be called a loch—clouds suddenly whipping up over the mountains in the background, obscuring the moon and the stars, then thunder in the background, then the clouds just as suddenly passing away. A place apart with its own interior climate, changing, it seems, from hour to hour, sometimes from minute to minute—the inn creaking and rattling like a wind harp in response to every breeze.

Monday / September 15

"I never learned much in a classroom, not anywhere near as much as I've learned by being outside in places like this, just doing things and watching things closely." So it was that our Waterton

Lake tour guide responded to my question about whether he'd ever considered a teaching career. I wouldn't have asked him such a question if I hadn't been captivated, as was Kate, by his wide-ranging knowledge and stand-up comedian's wit as he discoursed upon the flora, fauna, and geology of the lake, while his silent compatriot steered the boat down the full length of it. But his clear-cut rejection of teaching made me wonder about the value of my own career, so my thoughts just then were not particularly comforting, except for the fact that I was now some fifteen hundred miles away from the classroom and the distance increasing every day.

This morning, for example, before the boat ride, Kate and I took a hike up one of the mountain trails surrounding the lake, a hike that led us up a moderately steep path, by pine and spruce and aspen and birch, by berries and wildflowers, by rocks and peaks, until we were standing so high above the lake that we could see its length and shape more clearly than from the majestic vista of our baronial lodge—or from the picture postcards on sale in the innumerable tourist shops. And then we continued on, until we reached a waterfall, whose sound had been luring us toward its source from the moment we heard it, a mile up the mountainside. The lake was no longer in sight, so far had we gone along the forested mountain path, and then we came upon the rushing stream that seemed to be the source of the sound, and of the falls itself, until in the distance Kate saw yet a slightly higher stream, falling from a somewhat higher source, which seemed to both of us to be the source we'd been seeking, especially since we were feeling pressed by time to return down the path, lest we miss the boat tour, and also miss the chance to grab some lunch before the tour. But when I said we still had a few minutes to spare before having to turn back, Kate pressed on a bit longer, until we came upon a spectacular upheaval of rocks from which was flowing an even steeper and swifter and fiercer waterfall, and beyond the bridge from which we viewed it a path that would lead us to an even higher source, several miles away, from which the falls began. But time compelled us to turn back, though not regretfully, for I was already so inspired by the sights I'd beheld and the height of land we'd attained that I felt closer to the peak of things—and the source of things—than ever before, and also to the recognition that with every peak one attains there are more beyond it and more beyond those, world without end.

I didn't dare mention such things to our no-nonsense guide, but I did tell him about the ruffed grouse that Kate noticed on our way down, a bird that neither of us had ever seen before, sitting in a tree below the path, ruffling its feathers at one moment, silent the next, motionless, an apparition in the woods, as much a spirit of the place as the waterfall, the weather, and the lake itself. A few minutes after spotting the bird, we met another pair of hikers coming up the path, so we pointed them to the bird and then to the falls and thus became a pair of guides ourselves, schooled by the place, though I didn't realize how much it had taught us until my conversation with our guide.

Tuesday / September 16

"Rough Road"—the first sign we encountered after passing through the American port of entry, where the beefy border guard, his thighs thick in his taut blue pants, his arms crossed behind his back, his eyes focused on me, asked us the usual questions about what we were bringing across the border and then waved us on. Little did we realize that the sign might be an omen of what we'd encounter on the well-paved surface of the "Going-to-the-Sun Road," the only highway through Glacier National Park, across the Continental Divide. Falling temperatures, rising fog, rain, sleet, snow, and the suddenly erratic behavior of our Jeep—its engine momentarily racing without moving the car itself—made us wonder if we'd make it up and down the steep, twisting path of the spectacular mountain road that Kate had evidently been looking forward to since the beginning of our trip, without revealing that it was the destination of her dreams until we were enveloped in the treacherous weather that made its sublime vistas almost invisible. How surprising that Kate, ever the realist, had invested so much in a single mountain pass—"I came all this way to see it again, and I couldn't even see the turnoff to the overlook!"

But the trip from West Glacier to Missoula was a pleasure from beginning to end, thanks to the surprising orchards of the Flathead Valley, and the striking vistas of Flathead Lake, and the mountains visible in the distance along both sides of the valley, and the rain alternating with the sun all the way south. And finally as if to signal the climax of it all, three rainbows in the final two hours of driving, the last of which seemed to arise from the middle of a fire at the edge of the foothills, just a few hundred yards from the highway, a fire whose smoke we'd been tracking for some twenty miles before the rainbow suddenly appeared in the big Montana sky. "There's a rainbow in the smoke," was Kate's immediate reaction, followed swiftly by her command: "Get us the hell out of here. This is not the way reality is meant to be. And besides, that fire's too close for comfort." But I couldn't help thinking of that strange conjunction as an emblem of the day, of the trip, and of all I've been going through the past several months.

Missoula, by contrast, looked exactly as expected—mountains in the background, office buildings in the foreground, and a beltway straight through the middle of it. But then we spent a half hour driving around the spot where our inn was meant to be, unable to find any sign of it, until I drove into a gargantuan motel, looking for directions, only to discover that the motel and our inn were one and the same, thanks to a name change that had taken place several months before. And then upon finding our room, it turned out to be one of the most comfortably appointed places on our whole trip, with a balcony overlooking a mountain-fed river, and a solitary woman on its banks fly-casting for trout. A rainbow in the smoke, a mountain in the river, a peak in the valley.

Wednesday / September 17

Right after breakfast, Kate and I spent a few minutes by the riverside, gathering rocks for the dripline of our gazebo, then stopped at a nearby service station for a quick diagnosis of the erratically spinning engine—no apparent cause other than some moisture in the distributor cap—and then headed off for our first day of interstate driving (and hopefully our last). But we did get away from it for a few back-road adventures. First, to visit Three Forks, where the riffled waters of the Jefferson, the Madison, and the Gallatin Rivers join to form the start of the Missouri River—an alluring place where I imagined myself fly-fishing the Madison for a trout or two to serve us for lunch. Then, we drove a few miles south to dine at the Willow Creek Inn and Saloon, where the sassy proprietress and mother of two proudly informed us, "I've never been outside of Montana, except for a few years in Salt Lake. My husband took a job there, but we couldn't stand it, so we came back here and bought this place and don't ever plan to leave Montana again." I didn't want to leave either, especially not the Willow Creek Inn—a well-lit place where the split pea soup, the turkey sandwiches heaped with fresh vegetables, and the big draft beer had me thinking that Kate and I could open a bistro like this in another back-road town like this and live out the rest of our days in the Big Sky Country of Montana. A beguiling dream that lasted no longer than a windblown walk around the corner to look at the handful of other places struggling to survive in Willow Creek. So we returned to the interstate and continued heading east, until we spotted a sign pointing to a prairie dog town, a place more heavily populated than Willow Creek or Three Forks, though the residents were much less welcoming. No inn, no saloon, nothing but a few village guards and lookouts, standing atop their holes, yipping to alert their comrades against all predators, foreigners, sightseers, and other peeping toms. No wonder we were delighted by the gracious welcome we received awhile later at the Pollard Hotel in Red Lodge, a restored showpiece on the National Register of Historic Places, where the manager carried in our luggage—a place that once played host to Calamity Jane and Buffalo Bill, and on this particular evening seduced us with a table d'hôte meal of steamed artichokes, medallions of ostrich in a wild mushroom sauce, braised Belgian endive with a grated orange dressing, radicchio salad with dried tomatoes and olives, and an apple-walnut Charlotte in fresh mint sauce. A dinner fit for a national register of historic menus.

Thursday / September 18

A lavish breakfast at the Pollard, featuring stewed fruit compote and crème fraîche. A brief stop to check on the distributor cap. A short drive to the edge of town for an update on the Beartooth Mountain Highway—"the highest highway pass in Wyoming and one of the highest in America," according to our guidebook. The highway that some have called "the most scenic route in America" and others have called the most treacherous, given the blinding snow flurries that suddenly arise at its elevation of 10,947 feet above sea level. But everyone at the Pollard says "it's a must," and so does our friend Trudy, whom we're going to visit tomorrow, and so does Kate, not to be thwarted by yet another spectacular mountain pass. And the highway patrol sign at the edge of town says that it's open, so we start our ascent, Kate at the wheel, graced by a double rainbow as she enters the first hairpin turn. (So many rainbows in Montana, I'm beginning to think that it, rather than Hawaii, should be called the Rainbow State.) And the rainbow remains visible through the next few turns of the ribbon-shaped highway, each twist, each turn leading us to more panoramic vistas graced by the widening arc of the rainbow. The Jeep moves effortlessly up the highway, the engine doing its thing without any racing or spinning. Midway up, a few clouds begin to appear, and then a few more, then mist, then drizzle, then rain, and soon it's hard to believe that the sky was clear just a few turns back. And harder still to believe we were driving below a rainbow, especially when the rain turns to snow and the snow turns to sleet, as I watch our outdoor thermometer drop from 67 to 31 by the time we reach the top of the mountain—so windswept, cloud-covered, and snowblown it's almost impossible to see the nearby peaks, much less the road itself. But the road is still open, a walkway nearby, and I'm determined to be king of the mountain, to command the peak of the highest pass in Wyoming—at least for a moment, long enough to behold the alpine starkness of the nearby mountains through my pocket binoculars, also to get a snapshot or two of Kate, walking amid the clouds. Kate pulls off the road, and we take to the path, both of us thankful that we're wearing our Rockport hiking boots. The only problem is that I can hardly keep my footing along the wind-whipped walkway and neither can Kate and neither can the other people who arrived just a few minutes after us. So I can hardly object when Kate says, "Let's get the hell out of here before they close the gates on us."

Then down we drive, no longer through hairpin turns, no longer through panoramic vistas, but a gradually descending loop that takes us to a subalpine level of rock and evergreens, of crystalline pools and rippling streams, everything stunted like a bonsai landscape, like a Zen garden on high, exquisitely spare but intricately wrought, so dwarfed by the weather that it makes me feel a bit larger than life as I walk up and down its diminutive mountainsides, wondering what compels me to measure myself against each passing scene, each dazzling vista—why I cannot appreciate the place just for what it is, in and of itself. But my gargantuan sensations last no longer than it takes us to reach the Grand Canyon of the Yellowstone, when I suddenly feel dwarfed by the height of the waterfalls and the magnitude of the cavernous space carved by the volcanic and glacial upheavals of ages past and now by the ceaseless flow of the Yellowstone River.

By the time we reach the wide-open spaces of the Hayden Valley with a buffalo herd grazing in the near distance, and then Old Faithful erupting just as we drive into the parking lot, and then Lake Yellowstone Hotel, "the second largest wooden-framed building in North America," and then our lodge overlooking Jackson Lake, I'm so exhausted by the sight of so many sights—the steam spouts, the bubbling mud, the sulfur cauldron, the dragon's mouth—that I can barely stand to look at (or smell) another spectacle or measure myself against anything but my overwhelming sense of fatigue. And the Jeep, it seems, isn't doing much better, given the engine's momentary fit of motionless racing on an upward stretch of highway near the end of the day's drive. So it was hard to take much pleasure in my blackened trout bathed in a cilantro cream sauce, even though it was unquestionably the best trout I've had since we've been in the Rockies, even though (or perhaps, especially because) I ate it in a dining room looking across Jackson Lake to the snowcapped peaks of the Grand Tetons. Now, at last, I know what it means to be so utterly sated by experience that I'd just as soon have dined upon a can of sardines in a windowless room with nothing to distract me from the barrenness of my immediate surroundings.

Friday / September 19

"Next Wednesday is the earliest we can work you in, but you can probably make it to the Jeep place in Casper from the sound of what you're describing, and they can probably fit you in next Monday. No assurances, of course, but if you've made it this far, you can probably make it to Casper." So it was that the service manager of the Jeep place in Jackson put my mind at ease when I called him early this morning. With a "probably" this and a "probably" that—the word I've come to put more stock in these days than anything more certain. But it certainly was comforting to get a definite appointment at the Jeep place in Casper for Monday afternoon at one. And then it sure was a pleasure to have breakfast directly across the lake from the Grand Tetons, only a few scattered clouds obscuring the tips of their peaks. So delightful a scene that I didn't realize at first how much those splendid mountains had been domesticated by the resort from which I was viewing them—sailboats bobbing in the water at the bottom of the big picture windows, right below the mountains at the top of the window frame. Only after we finished breakfast, checked out, and were driving south toward Jenny Lake did I begin to see them unobscured by anything but the windshield of our Jeep. And not until we reached Jenny Lake and walked down to the shore of that pellucid spot did I finally see the Tetons unde-filed by anything—except, of course, for my own jaded perception of things. Still, it definitely was a pleasure to take lunch today at the Jackson Lake Lodge, again right across from the Tetons, especially since I was rested enough not only to savor another view but also another trout, this one smoked in a mixed green salad with a lime vinaigrette.

But the most striking sights of the day were yet to come, probably because we weren't expecting anything special, especially after beholding the Tetons from so many different angles. Oh yes, we were looking forward to the weekend with Trudy, a weekend away from it all at her log cabin retreat, 8,500 feet up in the mountains outside of Dubois. But no one told us that the fifty-mile ride from Jackson Lake to Dubois would take us from a lush green upland meadow, vividly sunlit, with rail fences along the road and a river snaking through the meadow and horses grazing on the hillside, to a heavily forested pass at the height of the Continental Divide, so dense, so green that it seemed to be lit only by a falling snow that made us feel as if we'd suddenly been transported from late summer to early winter. The Great Divide. And then just as quickly to a balding, sage-covered upland, with candy-striped badlands in the distance.

Such a variegated array of vistas in fifty miles, in less than an hour, I could hardly imagine that anything else might catch my attention, especially after yesterday's overdose. But I hadn't considered how moved I might be by the sight of Trudy standing in front of her black Jeep Wrangler, just as planned, in a gravel clearing right next to a ramshackle store and gas station. The familiar person in a foreign landscape. "The shock of teapots," as Cynthia Ozick puts it. Trudy—whom I've always associated less with Wyoming than with her eastern seaboard upbringing, her years in Italy, her graduate study at Chicago and Columbia, and her time at the Institute on Writing—displaced to a hardscrabble western setting, and my head was spinning. And it continued to spin as we followed her up the hairpin turns of the narrow washboard road to her cabin, sitting so far off-road that I couldn't see it until we were nearly upon it, set all alone on a hillside of sagebrush, surrounded by evergreens, so far away from it all I was momentarily overcome by the remoteness itself. And within the center of that remoteness the glowing presence of her log cabin, standing some twenty feet tall on the side of the hill, the peeled pine so shiny it could've been varnished just yesterday, though it's evidently been glowing there since it was built some twenty years ago. Wilderness and architectural sophistication in such a sharp juxtaposition that I was momentarily breathless at the spectacle, and breathless too when I stepped out of our Jeep because I'm not used to the thin air at this height above sea level. Trudy, on the other hand, was apologizing for the mist and the cloud cover and the invisible mountains surrounding her place—"If you could only see what it really looks like," which I thought I was actually seeing, as we looked at the surrounding hillsides. And Kate was chiding her for the invisible wildlife—"But where are the elk you've been promising us and the moose and the bighorn sheep?" And I was wondering if it ever gets any better than this, especially when Trudy handed me a lavishly detailed review of the winter book that had just appeared in the local newspaper along with a notice of tomorrow's reading. But Trudy was still hoping that we'd "get to see what it really looks like," which made me wonder whether we ever get to see what things really look like, especially after what Kate and I had seen and not seen during our past few days of sightseeing.

And then upon entering her cabin, I was overcome again, not just by the glow of all the varnished logs, but also by the spaciousness of the place—by the large living-dining-kitchen area that fills almost the entire cabin, as well as the ample sleeping loft at one end of the cabin and the study directly below it. A place for everything and everything in its place. Barging into her study, I was drawn to the built-in worktable along one end of it, desk-to-ceiling bookshelves framing each side of the table with a window in between, looking out upon the sloping hillside of sage and evergreens. Who could ask for anything more, with a sleeping cot along one wall, a file cabinet along the other, and the amplitude of her library, filled with contemporary essays and nature writing? I imagined myself working there, and was momentarily so captivated by the idea that I didn't ever want to leave, but a few minutes later I was caught short again by the thin air, also by the thought of the thirty-minute drive down the hillside and into Dubois to keep myself stocked with provisions. And then at last I was awed by the challenge that Trudy's taken upon herself, having chosen to live in this spectacularly remote place, the center and ground of her nature writing. If I couldn't make it in Willow Creek, I'd never survive up here.

But then I was so beguiled by the red wine and the big pillows and the buoyant talk of peaks and passes, and Trudy's festive dinner of elk sausage, wild rice with pine nuts, and yellow peppers stuffed with chopped tomatoes and anchovies that again I was imagining myself at home in this place. Especially after she lit up the entire room with antique clear-glass oil lamps and then left us to contemplate her shining world, while she walked over the dark hillside to bed down in an absent neighbor's cabin.

Saturday / September 20

A cabin in the Rockies, the morning after. At six o'clock I awoke, short of breath again and worried about the day ahead. A reading to be given this afternoon at the Two Ocean Bookstore in Dubois, and I hadn't chosen the pieces, much less rehearsed them. And I hadn't finished yesterday's entry. So I couldn't imagine how I'd get ready for the reading, go hiking this morning with Trudy and Kate, and keep track of things for today's entry without forgetting the leftovers from yesterday. No wonder I was short of breath—and wishing I were done with this diary.

But today, after all, worked out much better than I supposed, probably because things usually turn out better than they look at six in the morning to someone sucking on thin air. Today, in fact, was more like a dream than a nightmare—from a walk in the woods by a rippling creek, a mile down the road from Trudy's place, to the reading at Anna's bookstore in Dubois, to a post-reading party at Anita's Café just down the street from Anna's. I'd never gone hiking with Trudy, never seen a wood or any other patch of nature through her eyes, so I followed her like an awestruck student, admiring her ability not only to identify almost everything we saw—trees, shrubs, rocks, wildflowers, wild fruit, weeds, insects, birds, hoof prints, droppings, and God knows what else—but also to explain their intricate ecological connections. We never saw a live animal of any kind, but Trudy did spot some fresh moose tracks, which got another rise out of Kate—"Tracks are one thing, the moose itself is another." And the skies never cleared, which brought another apol-

ogy from Trudy—"If only you could see what it's really like." And I
was still short of breath, wondering when I'd get adjusted to the thin
air. But by that point, I figured, the script had been written, and we
were just playing our parts.

So I was doubly surprised by this afternoon's festivities, especially by the turnout of thirty people, most of them women, who listened so attentively that I could see it in their eyes and hear it in their
laughter (at all the right places) as well as in their questions about
everything from journal writing, vegetable gardening, teaching,
and retirement, to my predictions for the winter to come. I'd like to
think it was the author and his book that produced such a lively and
thoughtful audience. But I also know that Anna and Trudy beat the
bushes to publicize the reading, as did Norma, the newspaper editor, who featured it in yesterday's paper. How else to account for
such a relatively large group from a small town of five hundred? Possibly the appeal of a visiting author, especially for the first full-
fledged reading at Anna's bookstore, especially given the generous
hors d'oeuvres that Anna served before the reading and the ample
spread that Anita served afterward. And the wine and the good fellowship on an overcast Saturday afternoon.

But from start to finish, there was something else in the air that
transcended the food and the fellowship and the performance of a
visiting author—something that resonated in almost everyone I
talked with. A sense of adventure, of risk, that had drawn almost
every one of those women from somewhere else in the country to
live, like expatriates, in and around Dubois, looking for something
they evidently couldn't find elsewhere in their lives. Yet Dubois on
the face of it doesn't seem to be the community of anyone's dreams,
considering all the cabins, trailer homes, and small framed houses
that I saw on the way into town this afternoon, and the long
L-shaped main street with its false-front western buildings, some
authentic, some aspiring to look like the real thing, and the candy-

striped badlands in the distance rather than the majestic peaks of the Grand Tetons. It's just a small town, far away from it all, ringed, according to Trudy and our guidebook, with mountains in all directions, and the Wind River winding its way down a spacious valley where horses graze in irrigated pastures and luxurious homes are beginning to dot the hillsides. A place where the logging industry has given way to tourism, and some of the women are worrying about gentrification (even though they are in part responsible for it). But here in this conflicted spot, the mere presence of all these energetic women—artists, journalists, merchants, ranchers, environmentalists, historians, writers, and homemakers—made me feel I'd entered a special world, even if it was still too cloudy for me to see what it's really like. The jar of homemade sauerkraut that Annalee gave me after the reading—sauerkraut with a hot red pepper at the bottom of it—was a clear enough sign that there's something very special about this place, even though I haven't fully tasted it yet.

Sunday / September 21

This afternoon I saw another part of Trudy's world when she drove us into the badlands east of Dubois, to do some more hiking, to see a different kind of habitat, and to get another angle on the surrounding mountain peaks. But the clouds were still hanging in, and the road was too muddy to risk it all the way up, so we settled for a walk up and down several gullies, our eyes on the ground, on the short grass, on the flowering buckwheat, the empty beer cans, the weeds, and the cattle bones. Such a bleak array of things that I couldn't help thinking about the severities of this place, especially when we came upon a little grave at the top of a bluff overlooking the town—a pile of rocks with a weathered gray cross lying on the rocks and a dog collar nailed to the back of it. Some kind of critter had evidently been pawing at the rocks and exposed part of the skeleton, which made me wonder what else might be going on in the badlands. Not the sort of image I'd soon forget, but just to make sure, I picked up a bleached cow rib on our way back to the Jeep, while Kate plucked a rusty-colored sprig of buckwheat, and Trudy a few unknown plants that she planned to identify back at the cabin. "Now we all have our specimens," as Trudy said, "so it's time to go home." And back we went to Trudy's place, where we arrived at dusk just in time to watch a family of mule deer coming by the front of her cabin to settle in for the night. A cozy scene so different from this afternoon that my head was spinning between one and the other, but then I thought about the deer that've been ravaging our flower and vegetable gardens, and the scene didn't seem so cozy after all. So I couldn't resist muttering with Kate that "deer are one thing, moose another." But the glow of Trudy's oil lamps—and the glitter of her conversation with Kate about "the ambushes of family life"—distracted me at least for a while from all the animals living and dead.

Monday / September 22

This morning before Trudy arrived for breakfast, the clouds lifted enough for us to see most of Union Peak and part of Warm Springs Mountain, and a bit later for Trudy to show us the top of Lava Mountain, but we never caught the entire panorama unobscured. When we left a while later, Trudy made us vow to return so we could see what it really looks like, and we agreed, with the proviso that she'd also have all the missing animals on display—the elk, the moose, and the bighorn sheep—otherwise we wouldn't be able to see what it really looks like.

No sooner were we back on the highway, heading east out of Dubois in the midst of a downpour, than Kate said, "Look back over your shoulder, there should be a rainbow," and sure enough there was, thanks to the sun shining in front of us. And then we began to see things we hadn't seen before. Like the beauty of the badlands in a majestic sweep of red sandstone, rising and curving right along the side of the highway. And a bit later, the austerity of tableland and sagebrush, fanning out on all sides of us, punctuated now and then by fields of alfalfa and gatherings of antelope in the midst of the sage. "So this," I thought, is "where the deer and the antelope play." To which Kate replied, "No, this is where you wouldn't want the Jeep to break down." And I agreed, particularly when I noticed the tableland giving way to gullies and arroyos, without a tree or an antelope in sight, which made me think, "This is where you really wouldn't want the Jeep to break down." We were heading east toward Casper, both of us counting the miles and the minutes until we'd be safely in the hands of the Jeep service department. But when the land leveled out, and the sage returned, and the mustard-colored grass, and the rusty-colored weeds, and the pale yellow flowers, and the antelopes, I could see why someone, somewhere, might still be singing, "Home, home on the range." But then again, when we finally reached Casper and were waiting for the Jeep to be repaired, I found myself even more enchanted by the substantial old homes just a few blocks away, which made me think I'd probably seen enough of the range and the Rockies to quell all my fantasies of a life out west. Especially after we saw a dead antelope on the road outside of Orin, and a miles-long chain of coal cars just south of Shawnee, and the town of Lost Springs (population 4). So, after all, it was a strangely comforting sight when we rolled into Lusk at dinnertime and discovered that the Covered Wagon Motel, where we were booked to stay, didn't look like a covered wagon or anything else out west—just a one-story, U-shaped corridor of rooms, spread around a courtyard parking lot. A white clapboard place, clean and well-lit, like the Fireside Inn, a mile down the road, where we savored our grilled steaks and the salad bar and the beer and the friendly chatter of all the locals in this county seat of Wyoming's least populated county. So few people and so much land that according to the guidebook, there's an average of 520 acres per person.

Tuesday / September 23

"It's like turning the page of a book. You turn a corner, go down a road, and it's all behind you. The mountains, the sandhills, and now our vacation." Kate and I were dining at the Norfolk Inn in eastern Nebraska, relishing our salads in balsamic vinaigrette and musing upon the reach of balsamic vinegar, when I mentioned how suddenly the landscape had changed just an hour or so before, from the rolling sandhills to the far-reaching sweep of corn and wheat. And my remark provoked her to carry things further than I'd intended, though our vacation was clearly behind us. Actually, I thought it had ended somewhere in eastern Wyoming, several miles outside of Lusk, where I saw a few more gatherings of antelope grazing in the midst of the tableland, and then no more. But Kate was so beguiled by the ghostly landscape in western Nebraska—pine trees and rocky hillsides shrouded in heavy fog—and then by the extraordinary reach of the sandhills, "the world's largest area of grass stabilized sand dunes," that we drove all day through mist and rain and buffeting winds to stay in the heart of those fabled hills, to make a pilgrimage to the world of Mari Sandoz, where I too was captivated by the wild grasses and the yucca and the profusion of wildflowers growing in the midst of the dunes. A haunting world, especially on this early fall day, when the chill and driving rain seemed to be marking the end of summer as well as our trip. At the eastern edge of the sandhills, at sundown, with Kate at the wheel, speeding to reach our destination in Norfolk, we were picked up by a county sheriff, who seemed to me to be a friendly old man, with his genial smile, his apologetic manner, and his reduction of the fine from seventy-five to twenty-five dollars, "because you're out of state and it's obviously been a hard day of driving in the rain." But Kate was miffed and let me know it as she drove off muttering: "The old geezer stopped me just because that young guy was with him. And besides, what kind of county is it that only holds court every two months?!" It was just a few miles later, I think, that she turned a corner, went down a road, and it was all behind us.

Wednesday / September 24

But it sure was a pleasure today just to be on the road on a sunny fall day. Even the familiar farmscape of field corn and soybeans seemed pleasing to the eye, everything ripening off on schedule, the cycle of life clearly visible in the yellowing fields, in the reddening sumac, in the crow feeding on roadkill, entrails dangling from its beak. We were on our way to Atlantic, Iowa, for an overnight visit with Kate's cousin Mary, a retired high school teacher, and her husband, Larry, a stock brokerage executive. But before Atlantic, we decided to visit the DeSoto National Wildlife Refuge for one last bit of sightseeing. No moose or bighorn sheep in sight, but I did see a bluebird, Kate spotted a turtle sunning itself on a log, and both of us admired the Great Blue Herons—crook-necked and hunchbacked, like geezers standing along the shore of the river. But sharp of eye, quick of beak, and extraordinarily graceful in flight—so quick to launch themselves that I spent an entire roll of film trying to get a close-up shot of a single heron in repose.

When we arrived in Atlantic late this afternoon, Larry was still at work, consumed as he's always been by the responsibilities and the excitement of managing a brokerage that serves a large portion of western Iowa. For a moment just then, I was brought up short by the realities of the workaday world that I'd not been thinking about the past several weeks. I had, after all, gotten further away from it than I imagined, which made me wonder how it'll be when I go down to the building again and classes are in session but I'm not in session myself. So I was curious to see how Mary was dealing with her first time away from the classroom in thirty years, especially because she'd been as devoted to her journalism students as Larry to his numerous clients. I could see that she enjoyed the task of training her new schnauzer, teaching herself the art of drying roses, and learning her way around the intricacies of planning and building a grand new home for herself and Larry. But I also wondered how she felt about giving up the classroom, and as usual she was quick on the draw. "I don't miss the deadlines, don't miss the schedules and the paperwork, but I do miss the kids. They could always make me laugh, even when I was feeling down. They're so buoyant, so resilient that I remember them coming in tearfully in the morning with stories of how they'd broken up the night before and by noon they'd be in love with someone else. I miss that sometimes, but I don't miss the hassle and the work." Just then Larry arrived, ready to regale us with a tour of their new home and dinner at the country club. And I could see from the look in his eyes and some memories of my own that a part of him was still down at the office.

But no sooner were we touring the framed-in spaces of their new place on the edge of the city, overlooking a hillside with cattle grazing in the distance, than I could see that part of Larry was also looking toward the future. Especially when he took us down to the basement and showed us that it will not only include bedrooms and a bath for his full-grown sons whenever they come to visit, but also a full-scale kitchen and family room for a live-in couple to care for Larry and Mary (now just in their late fifties) if ever they can't care for themselves. The ultimate golden years project! A little while later at the country club, when we were talking about retirement, he also announced, "You just don't want to give up and do nothing. I want to keep going, stay vigorous," and I could hardly disagree.

Thursday / September 25

Before we left Atlantic this morning, Mary took us to visit her mother—Kate's ninety-one-year-old Aunt Esther—at the retirement center where she's been living the past fifteen years. I hadn't seen Esther for several years, so I didn't know what to expect. But I didn't look forward to visiting someone who had once been a professional journalist and then an exuberant gardener on her five-acre hillside in Des Moines—always on the lookout for new varieties, new growing techniques, and new ways of cooking and preserving the fruits of her harvest—but who now in the wake of several strokes was unable to walk, unable to write, and sometimes, reportedly, unable to speak. So after we wheelchaired her outside for a bit of fresh air, I was pleasantly surprised to see Esther still bright-eyed and alert enough to share her recollections of Yellowstone before it was overrun by tourists and to regale us with an amusing story about life in the retirement home. "There's one person here," she said, "who looks at my all-white hair and calls me 'Mom,' and another who looks at my hair and calls me 'Dad.' Fancy that! But no matter how you look at it, I'm still alive." I kept that thought in mind all the way back to Iowa City, all the while that Kate and I were feeling stressed by the heavy interstate traffic, by the Jeep acting up again, but most of all by the prospect of reentering the day-to-day world of life at home, rather than on the road.

Transitions. I've never been good at making them, probably because I made so many during my childhood, moving from one relative to another, that I yearned for a time when I'd never have to move again, when I could kick up my heels, lean back in my chair, and let the rest of the world go by. But today was much worse, for I knew that the end of this trip would ultimately face me with the question of whether I'd traveled far enough to find a new place in my life, a place where I could really settle down and let the workaday world go by. It never occurred to me that the answer, or a hint of the answer, might come just a few minutes after we left the interstate, heading toward the road to our house, when we suddenly found ourselves driving under a canopy of trees so thick with leaves, luminous in the afternoon sun, that I was momentarily at a loss, carried away by a sight that seemed completely new to my eyes. "Is this where we live? It looks so strange, so different, so shady and leafy." For a moment or two, I kept blurting my surprise. And Kate was blurting too, but then she reminded me of the unleafy worlds we've been living in the past few weeks—alpine, bayside, badland, prairie, and sandhill—all so different from ours that it's strange to see leaves, and so many of them. A new place, at least for a few minutes, and maybe a bit longer. At home—the yard and the gardens so foreign to my eyes that at first I just stood on the terrace staring at them, trying to make sense of the landscape and the layout, until I spotted Rebecca at the back of the lot, her familiar blue tarp spread out beside Kate's perennial border. And then things came into focus again, especially after Laura turned up at the back door and gave me a quick tour of the grounds.

But no sooner had I carried our luggage into the living room than Laura reminded me of the magazine photo session for the winter book that's scheduled for tomorrow morning. Though I'd discussed it a week ago with Sarah, when she called me at Trudy's, I'd forgotten that it would be tomorrow. And then Laura mentioned several other calls from local reporters and radio interviewers wanting to talk about the book, and I remembered the hour-long reading that I have to prepare for Prairie Lights this coming Monday night. Suddenly I felt a slight sense of panic about the days ahead but then an enormous sense of relief that I don't have any classes to teach or anything else to do down on campus. All I wanted to do just then was to show Laura some of the things we picked up along the way, like the stalks of wheat in Montana, the maple syrup in Lake Louise, the carved wooden crow in Vancouver, and the cow's rib in Dubois. And then I wanted to get Pip and Jag at the vet's. And then cook us a simple supper of pasta with a fresh tomato sauce. So I walked in the garden in the cool of the sunset and found what I needed there—tomatoes, peppers, onions, parsley, basil, and a breath of fresh air.

Friday / September 26

The magazine photographer, a young man come all the way from Minneapolis, showed up this morning with such a carful of equipment that in just a few minutes he turned our terrace into a lighted stage set, with the gazebo in the background, the terrace wall in the foreground, and me seated in a niche of the wall, in one of our old-fashioned metal lawn chairs. The winter gardener as philosopher-king. The only problem is that I didn't feel like a gardener, even though I had on my blue work shirt and brown work pants. Nor did I feel like a philosopher, or a king of anything—not even lord of the terrace, which was all I could survey from my niche in the wall. More than anything, I felt like a self-conscious author, sitting for his picture, especially because William, the lean, young photographer, was wearing a large black beret, and Laura was chatting with me while he was setting the scene, in hopes of putting me at ease. And then, just to relax me even more, maybe even loosen me up enough to get a smile or two, Laura started taking snapshots of William taking still shots of me.

A diarist's delight—to be the center of so much attention. The only problem is that William asked me what I do, and all I could think of to tell him just then was that I used to teach writing here at the university. And then I started to tense up again, but as luck would have it he also asked me what kind of writing I taught and the first thing that came to mind was journal writing, and no sooner did I think of journal writing than I remembered the remarkable one that I read last night just before going to bed. A daily journal, called "A Month in Vegetable Heaven," that Laura kept throughout the time we were away. I had no idea she was doing such a thing until late last night when she casually mentioned that she'd left something on the computer for me to read. A tantalizing lure that I couldn't resist, even though I was exhausted from all the stresses and strains of our homecoming. And once I started to read her evocatively detailed journal, I couldn't stop until I'd gotten through the whole thing. At first I was captivated by her rapturous response to the house, the gardens, and the yard:

> To be able to walk out the back door (and to hear that back screen-door slam that is so distinctly evocative of summer and of an expansive outdoors) to harvest dinner . . . is what do I call it? luxury? I feel as if I am living out a novel, matching experience now to what I've read in the carefully crafted pages of a book. Even the harvesting is a sensual extravagance, almost better than eating.

Her enthusiasm was so intoxicating that it made me feel as if I were indeed living in a heaven of sorts. But the further I got into her journal, and the more I thought about it, the more captivated I was just by the fact that she had chosen to keep a careful record of her experience, day in and day out, from the beginning to the end of the month, as if she were a student in the journal writing course that I taught last spring. And no sooner did my thoughts begin to drift in that direction than I wanted to give Laura some suggestions for revising and expanding her journal. Why else would she ask me to read it, if not for my teacherly response? But the more I pondered a detailed response to her work, the more uneasy I became, and not just because I suddenly felt a profound resistance to treading that path again, but also because at last I came to perceive her work as an extraordinary gift, for which I should be as grateful as she had been in writing it. So when I first saw her earlier this morning, and we were chatting on the back porch, I thanked her for the gift, told her how much I had been moved by it, and asked her what she intended to do with it. "I don't know," she said. "I don't want to think about it." And that made me all the more relieved that I hadn't offered her any teacherly suggestions. Especially since my recollection of that moment (and her journal) in the midst of the photo session must have brought a smile to my face, for just when I was thinking about it again William said, "I've got what I need," then folded up his tripod and camera, packed up his gear, and a few minutes later was gone.

Monday / September 29

A day in the office—nine to five. The first time I've spent a whole day at the building since I moved out last May. And what a day it turned out to be, beginning with Kate's gentle nudge at the breakfast table this morning. "Don't you think it's about time to go down to the office? Your new office? That's what you wanted all last spring, and now that you've got it, you can hardly let it sit empty." I could hardly disagree, and besides I could also tell that Kate was looking for some space of her own, especially after a month together on the road. I'd been putting off my return to the building, partly to tend a few things in the garden, also to sort through the mail and answer the e-mail of the past month, but largely because I didn't know what I might find down there or within myself once I returned to the building as a professor emeritus. Still, it seemed like just the place for me to hole up and get ready for this evening's hour-long reading at Prairie Lights. So on this bright fall day, I walked down to the building, just as I did when I was still teaching—a picturesque mile-

and-a-half walk that always gave me time to put my thoughts together before class. But today, without any classes to teach or students to meet or promises to keep, I was thinking about who I might see at the building or what I might do there other than to get ready for this evening and deal with a few unanswered e-mails from the M.F.A. students whose work I'm directing.

What I didn't imagine is that I would find the place so changed the minute I entered the building. Maybe it was the summer redecorating that made the difference. The lighter walls, the brighter halls. Maybe it was the mistake I made of pressing the fifth-floor button in the elevator, which took me to my old office, where someone else's name was on the door. Maybe it was my mailbox stuffed with academic announcements and departmental newsletters, none of which pertained to me or anything I've been doing the past few months. Maybe it was that I didn't run into Dee or any of my longtime colleagues in the nonfiction program, Carol, Hamilton, Paul, or even the younger people, like Patricia and Sara. Maybe it was that I didn't run into anyone who knew me or that I myself recognized. Whatever it was, I felt like a stranger in a foreign land, like an invisible person, like the ghost of my former self.

But the strangest thing of all was that I didn't feel any of the distress I'd written about in the winter book after an anguished dream of wandering the department hallways, looking for someone to talk to when all the offices were shut and no signs of light or life were visible in the gaps between the office doors and the floor. Far from being distraught today, I felt, in fact, an enormous sense of relief. Maybe it was that I didn't want to be bothered in the midst of putting myself together for this evening's reading. Or that I still felt a bit high from our trip out west, as if a part of me were somewhere else. Or that I also had my mind on the upcoming readings in Ames and Des Moines. But one thing's for sure, and that is the genuine delight I felt at not having any courses to teach, which made me wonder why I had ever wanted to keep teaching so much that I launched myself on this diary to cope with the impending loss. The heart has its reasons that reason cannot know.

So it was a hauntingly pleasant day in the building, especially in my new office, where I spent the time choosing and rehearsing pieces from the winter book, filling the room with memories of the year before I retired. And then at the reading this evening, the second floor of the bookstore was crammed with more than 150 people, more than I ever imagined after my solitary day at the office. So many colleagues, students, neighbors, and friends that I could hardly think of myself as invisible. And afterward, when Laura stopped in for a nightcap with Kate and me, it was a pleasure just to savor the strangeness of the day. Before she left, Laura invited me to think about doing some readings in Michigan this spring, also perhaps a few classroom appearances, and I was delighted by the possibility of another road trip, especially now that the service manager at our local Jeep agency assures me that our Grand Cherokee has been fixed once and for all.

Thursday / October 2

Ever since the reading, I've been getting calls and e-mail from colleagues and students, as if to confirm the fact that I'm visible again. And this afternoon, Sara stopped in to visit me at the office. I felt a bit sheepish about not having read her thesis, which had arrived in August just when I was trying to get my head together for the trip out west. And she seemed a bit sheepish about asking me for some advice about one of the new courses that she's teaching. But it looked like we'd both get over our sheepishness soon enough, especially when she reported how some graduate students had spoken of me as being "irreplaceable," and I told her that such talk was "nonsense." Shortly after she left, when I was going to check on the afternoon mail, a shiny young man with eager blue eyes confronted me in the hallway, looked me squarely in the face and said, "You're Professor Klaus, aren't you?" And without even thinking about it, I suddenly heard myself saying, "I used to be," which brought a puzzled look to his face, until I explained that I'd retired last spring. He then told me about his being a new doctoral student last spring in the College of Education, so he didn't realize I'd retired. Still, he wanted to know if I might teach an essay course or a prose style course next year or the year after. "Not a chance," I said. "Definitely not. But there's a new person in the nonfiction program. Her office is right around the corner, and I think she'll be offering exactly the courses you want." So I took him to Sara's office, and he thanked me for the advice. And now as I sit here in the attic, thinking about the day, I wish that I had thanked him for helping me see this journey to an end.

ACKNOWLEDGMENTS

For their thoughtful reactions to the work in progress, I'm grateful to my editor, Deborah Chasman; my agent, Elizabeth Kaplan; my copyeditor, Carlisle Rex-Waller; as well as Connie Brothers, Trudy Dittmar, Patricia Foster, Mary Hussmann, Robert McCown, Dan Roche, and Jan Weismiller.

For her wise reactions to a life in progress, I'm grateful as ever to Kate Franks.